Politics and Society in Urban Africa

Politics and Society in Urban Africa is a unique series providing critical, in-depth analysis of key contemporary issues affecting urban environments across the continent. Featuring a wealth of empirical material and case study detail, and focusing on a diverse range of subject matter – from informal economies to urban governance, infrastructure to gender dynamics – the series is a platform for scholars to present thought-provoking arguments on the nature and direction of African urbanisms.

Other titles in the series:

About the author

Paul Stacey is a postdoctoral researcher at the Department of Social Sciences and Business, Roskilde University, Denmark. He has published on a range of topics including traditional authority, colonial rule, local government reform, processes of marginalization, and the governance of revenues from extractive industries. Ongoing research focuses on agro-pastoralist groups' adaptation strategies in contexts of climate change in rural Kenya, and the political economy of illegally extracted gold in Ghana.

State of Slum

Precarity and Informal Governance
at the Margins in Accra

Paul Stacey

ZED

LONDON • NEW YORK • OXFORD • NEW DELHI • SYDNEY

Zed Books
Bloomsbury Publishing Plc
50 Bedford Square, London, WC1B 3DP, UK
1385 Broadway, New York, NY 10018, USA
29 Earlsfort Terrace, Dublin 2, Ireland

BLOOMSBURY and Zed Books are trademarks
of Bloomsbury Publishing Plc

First published in 2019 by Zed Books Ltd

This paperback edition published by Bloomsbury Academic in 2021

Cover design by Burgess & Beech
Cover image © Nyani Quarmyne / Panos

A catalogue record for this book is available from the British Library.

A catalog record for this book is available from the Library of Congress.

ISBN: HB: 978-1-78699-204-8
PB: 978-1-78699-203-1

Typeset in Plantin MT by seagulls.net
Index by Rohan Bolton

To find out more about our authors and books visit
www.bloomsbury.com and sign up for our newsletters.

To the unsettled everywhere

Contents

List of images

Acknowledgements

The idea for this book originated from Christian Lund as we ate chicken and rice with shito sauce in an Accra hotel in January 2016. This was after another very hot day trudging around Old Fadama talking to all kinds of people and taking in as much as we could. Christian scribbled an outline for the chapters on the back of a napkin, and I nodded enthusiastically in agreement while thinking I will never be able to do that. So, the biggest thanks go to Christian for implanting the idea, and providing constant encouragement along the way (and for paying for the chicken).

Thanks to the Rule and Rupture European Research Council research group, directed by Christian from the Department of Global Development, Institute for Food and Resource Economics (IFRO) University of Copenhagen. Especially in the early stages, the group provided very useful advise and support, so thank you – Penelope Fay Anthias, Rune Bolding Bennike, Jeremy Campbell, Michael Eilenberg, Eric Komlavi Hahonou, Kasper Hoffman, Inge-Merete Hougaard, Veronica Gomez-Temesio, Prathiwi Putri, Mattias Borg Rasmussen, Jesse Ribot, Nandini Sundar, and not least Tirza Julianne van Bruggen. Also at IFRO, I want to thank Iben Nathen for encouragement and support. In Ghana, a big thanks go to Ben Asunki and Sofie Yung Mitschke for their invaluable research assistance and constant good company, and of course all the people in Old Fadama I met and talked to, and who kindly shared their experiences with me. Thanks to the Independent Research Fund Denmark (IRFD), Social Sciences (FSE), for financing the project as an Individual Post Doc grant, and without which the book would not have materialized.

Sections of two chapters have appeared in different forms elsewhere and I want to thank Cambridge University Press for granting permission to reproduce them here: parts of Chapter 3 appear in a journal article, 'Stacey, P. (2018), "Urban development and emerging relations of informal property and authority in Accra", *Africa*, 88,(1): 63–80'. And parts of Chapter 5 appear in a journal article co-written with Christian Lund: 'Stacey, P. and C. Lund (2016), "In a state of slum: governance in an informal urban settlement in Ghana", *Journal of Modern African Studies*, 54(4): 591–615'.

Many thanks to Mike Kirkwood for the unenviable task of improving the language, Colin Dutnall for making the maps, and the public libraries in the Municipality of Copenhagen, for providing a quiet place to write. Thanks to Ken Barlow and Amy Jordan at Zed for help and support, and a big thanks to the two anonymous reviewers for providing substantial, and very useful comments and suggestions for improvements.

And special thanks to Pernille and Alice.

All omissions and errors are my responsibility entirely.

Paul Stacey
Copenhagen, September 2018

Sketch map of study area

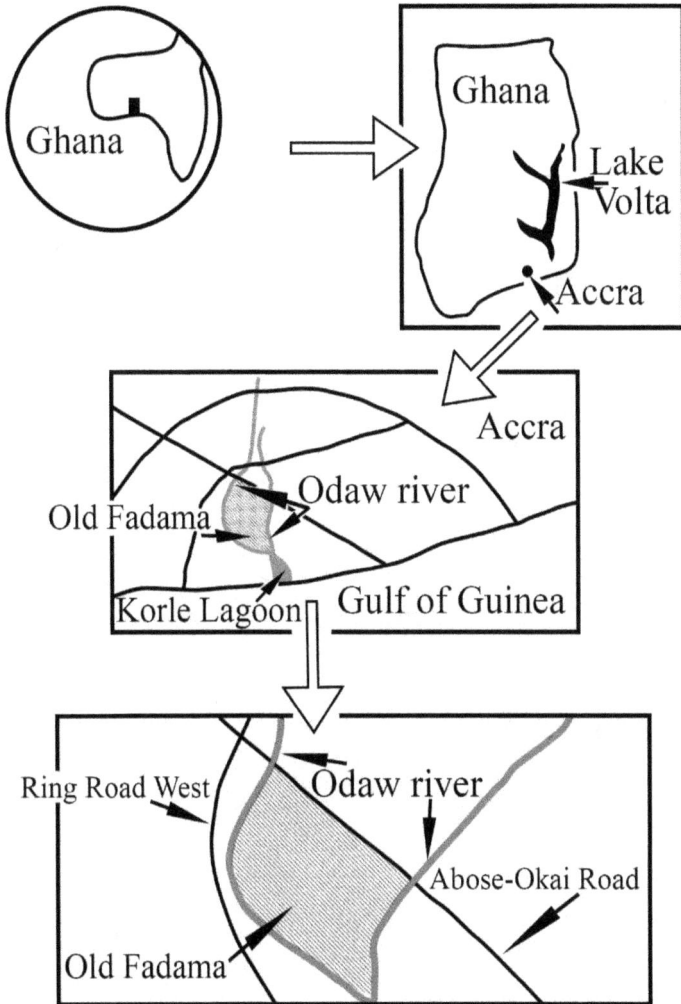

Introduction

In June 2014 a celebration in the large informal settlement of Old Fadama in Accra centred on the opening of a community-driven bakery and an adjoining local NGO that was to offer legal advice to residents. It was a proud moment for Frederick, an Akan-born migrant, local entrepreneur and self-made NGO director who had worked diligently to raise seminal funding for the projects. The new buildings are situated on land that decades ago was grassland and swamp. In the 1960s it was claimed by government but has never been formally developed. Today, after years of sporadic settlement, improvised land filling and building, the area comprises a bustling thirty-hectare site of ad hoc constructions where about 80,000 people live.

Since the settlers were served with an eviction notice in 2002, Old Fadama has come to be known as the largest illegal slum settlement in Ghana. The site is made up of thousands of mostly single-storey, tight-knit, makeshift dwellings, micro-enterprises, kiosks and stalls (Images 1.1, 1.2). These are linked, broadly, by a handful of 'roadways', but mainly by a labyrinth of narrow alleys just wide enough for people to pass abreast. Although the eviction order means that all building activities and residences are technically illegal, physical development of the site has continued more or less unabated over the last thirty years or so, contributing to Old Fadama's emergence as an integral part of the capital city. Yet the site's illegal status meant that the opening of the bakery and NGO was celebrated by some as an act of defiance by Old Fadama against an unaccommodating and unhelpful state. And, for many onlookers, the local projects exemplified a high level of resourcefulness that countered popular depictions of Old Fadama as a dangerous, squalid and uncontrollable place that should be demolished.

Close neighbours of the projects were especially proud of the new bakery, where vocational training is offered for up to fifteen young, susceptible girls. One neighbour of the project talked of few viable opportunities in the area, other than carrying head-loads, that were available to the young, uneducated girls, and that some would probably have ended up working as prostitutes if they had not gained a place in the project. The event brought a brief interval in which the residents of Old Fadama could disregard the nagging issue of their status as squatters and take pride in the demonstration of local development and inventiveness. Among the notables present at the ceremony were the vice-consular representative of the Australian High Commission to Ghana, which partly financed the projects, and representatives from the United Nations Development Programme and Amnesty International. The centrepiece of the occasion was the unveiling of a plaque by a Justice of the Ghana High Court. Some time afterwards I talked to Frederick, who explained his motivation for the projects in the context of his life in Old Fadama:

> You know I have been living here now for twenty-four years. It all started when I lost my father after my secondary school education, and I had to go forward, to proceed, to move, from Kumasi – that's where I'm from. I realized how commercialized Accra was getting, and it looked like it was easy to hook onto something, but it wasn't as juicy [stress free] as I first thought. Unfortunately, you come here and there's a lot of issues. In terms of housing and renting I could not get myself anything. There was no pleasant accommodation because of my financial problems. So, I was advised and I met somebody who was living here and was told if only you contribute to the water bill, go to the public bath house, and live appreciably [amicably and considerately], you can come here and stay with me. So that's how I came to live in this community. It was easy then because the place was not flooded or densely populated and there was casual work that everyone could do. If you are healthy you are qualified [laughs]. I started with unloading lorries and pushing a truck [a hand-drawn, four wheeled cart used all over Accra to transport goods] in the yam market, just like a commoner. When I worked at the market I thought I had to get going on my own thing and move on, because I am not the only child of my father so I cannot depend on whatever he has. So, I tried to have a different mindset, to help people, to bring them together, and to try and solve the problems you now see around you here, and to take myself to another level. I moved on to a polytechnic college and did courses in marketing which got me a job in a bank as a debt collector and I saved money to start my NGO. That was my God-given talent and passion – to help people!
>
> When my father passed [died] I benefited small, small [a little]. That was the driver for me as I got connected to his connections, which was vital because in this place it's overwhelmingly northerners and our tribe is only a minority. From when I set foot

in this place I identified a lot of ills and deficiencies and thought:
How can I turn the misfortunes of this community around? You
know, the AMA [the Accra Metropolitan Authority] has taken such
an entrenched position on this place and I did not want to involve
them because of their negative mindset. So, I was determined
to do whatever, and I wasn't going to ask them for money or
funding, so why then should I get myself involved with them? You
know they [government] have a very poor perception about the
community here, even before they come in. So you have to set an
example! You don't just go there [to government] as they will then
think the people are doing nothing [and begging]. So we go to the
community and that's what we have been doing now for twenty
years. You know we must be globalized and localized so that we
can actually achieve the object of the bigger vision of the
international community! The government? They just think there is
nothing good here, so I want to give them a surprise! (Interview,
12 December 2014)

At another site in Old Fadama, a few hundred metres away from
Frederick's projects, a steady stream of people is traversing three
rickety wooden bridges about fifty metres long over a garbage-
strewn gully that borders the site. At the end of one of the bridges
two youths sit listening to the radio under a parasol, on makeshift
chairs with a plastic bucket inviting coins. We sit with them, avoiding
the morning heat but unwillingly inhaling the lingering stench of
open defecation that is all around, as are thin black polyethene bags
commonly used for faecal matter (Songsore et al. 2014: 15). All who
cross the bridges – apart from schoolchildren, who are exempt –
willingly pay a toll of five or ten pesewas, depending on the length
of time spent 'on the other side'. The bridges join the unprepossessing settlement to an expansive dumping ground for city waste
supplied regularly by trucks on the other side. The sludge in the gully
is pecked at by white herons and streetwise vultures that are covered
with sticky filth. Higher up, the mounds of garbage are nosed over by
white longhorn cows, city goats, and feral dogs and cats. In between
are 'pickers', who come across from the settlement and glean various
leavings for further sale. These are tied into large bagged head-loads
and carried back across the bridge into the city. The bridges serve
as convenient short cuts to homesteads, working places, schools,
transport hubs and markets. A single head-load comes at no extra
cost, while motorbikes, barrows and animals are extra. At the end
of another bridge sits Adam, collecting coins. He is in his fifties and

tells how he built one of the bridges with his brother about fifteen
years ago (Image 3.2). He explains:

> I used to be a yam trader between Ghana and neighbouring
> Burkina Faso, taking advantage of price differences at the time
> and free movement across the border. I came to Old Fadama in
> 2000 to search for family members at my old mother's request,
> who wanted all of us to get back to live in Dagomba [in northern
> Ghana] and take over the family house, which was in danger of
> collapsing. I found my brothers' kids working as scrap dealers
> in Old Fadama. After I got here I saw an opportunity to build
> a bridge over the gully. There was nowhere to cross and it was
> getting flooded. I thought we should do something here because
> there are schoolchildren everywhere on the main roads and at
> any time a car can knock them down. That's why we don't like
> to allow motorbikes on the bridge, because it is for the children.
> I paid some money to a Dagomba chief in Old Fadama who
> allowed me to build. Besides, when anyone used the main road
> at night time they were easily getting robbed and attacked as
> there were no street lights. With our own bridge we could ensure
> there was always someone there. I didn't go to school much and
> stopped in the fourth grade to sell kola nuts. A small boy who
> can trade is respected by Dagomba and is not joked around
> with. It took us over six months to build this thing. We gathered
> scrap wood and bound it together. The first time we made it
> stretch over to the other side we thought the worst was over. But
> the water came and took it all away and we had to start again.
> We learned from that – that any time it rains we can lose the
> bridge. So, we got hold of some big iron girders and welded them
> together to extend over both banks. That was what we wanted!
> Then we built the wood around them. So for the past many years
> I am here for the schoolchildren who I cannot leave. I'm waiting
> for the day the AMA [Accra Metropolitan Authority] come
> and say this place is no more, then I can leave and go home.
> (Interview, 4 August 2015)

The community-driven bakery, the office offering legal advice,
the bridges and countless other micro-level entrepreneurial initiatives are all elements of the local infrastructure, amenities and public
services that are both enjoyed and produced by the residents of Old
Fadama. The people who provide such services demonstrate local-
level agency, governing ability and ambition to take advantage of

opportunities that open up as a result of an absent state and near-total lack of regulation. Individuals like Frederick and Adam arrived in Old Fadama with few resources but have managed to carve out economic and social niches that not only sustain them and their families but contribute to the informal governance of the settlement. Micro-level, self-made and ad hoc entrepreneurial activities contribute to a sense of self, community and organization, and they shape understandings of what is available and what is possible. In brief, such activities help define who people are, what they have, and who is in control.

However, none of the above was envisioned by city planners or government policy-makers, none is formally regulated or managed, and all are considered illegal by city authorities and government. Thus, all are expressions of the interplay between individual initiatives, the demands of ordinary lives, and ability to take advantage of the possibilities that may come one's way living in the illegal settlement. Indeed, they appear as micro-elements in the process of informalization of urban life as recognized across Africa (Simone and Abouhani 2005).

A key feature of Old Fadama, located just three kilometres from Ghana's parliament, is that government and statutory institutions, defined as the judiciary, executive and legislature, are noticeably absent from its everyday governance, as well as much of the decision-making addressing collective problems (Lund 2016). The public imprints of 'public sector', 'state' and 'development' generally associated with modern urban centres and grounded in normative expectations are also missing. Old Fadama sports no such things as pavements and kerbs, tarmacked roads, traffic lights or road signs, pedestrian crossings, parking bays, street names or house numbers (Images 1.1, 1.2). One looks in vain for drainage and gutters, uniform lamp posts, government schools, health clinics, post offices, public buildings or administrative offices; no 'Welcome to ...' nor 'District of ...', no proud emblems or insignia of location. Any trace of an abiding and substantive social contract between the state and local citizenry, or a consistent and progressive force over society that one might term a public sphere, is difficult to discern. Official maps may leave the area blank or provide inaccurate representations of the lay of the land that has been changed by landfill, and printed sources often refer to the site as part of the larger traditional area within which it is situated (Korle Dudor).[1] Alternatively, state officials may refer to this and neighbouring sites by the popular name of 'Sodom and Gomorrah' – used by proponents of the destruction of illegal settlements, but also used by some residents who take pride in or joke about living in an ostensibly notorious neighbourhood.[2] This feeds into popular perceptions of the site as lawless and chaotic but is not borne out by actual crime rates (Oteng-Ababio et al. 2017).

Unsurprisingly, the illegal status of Old Fadama is revealed in long-standing reluctance on the part of state institutions to recognize the area and give it a specific name, signpost it, or call it by what everyone knows it as – 'Old Fadama'. The illegality and size of the site make it a rarity in Accra: it is a place of constant commercial bustle yet offers streetscapes that contrast with much of the city because it is not plastered with billboards of all sizes symbolizing the transnational, global and delocalized character of modern, consumer-oriented urban spaces (Quayson 2014). Instead, its physical, social and local political infrastructure – including water supply, sanitation, the regulating of buildings and construction, access to education, law and order, waste management, much of the electricity system, and a multitude of other services that the 80,000 residents' access – is mostly operated and regulated informally in open view of government, but generally outside of the immediate control of state institutions.

Framing the study: the impromptu city

After several visits to Old Fadama I wanted to find out more about what made it tick and what it could tell about a modern African city. Talking to Adam and Frederick, for example, it became clear that their enterprises were expressions of individual success and successful local development in the heart of an urban centre. They solved common problems not addressed at all by government, and their enterprise impacted on how they perceived themselves as well as helped define the place where they lived and worked. Their actions, and other popular interventions, have inspired the aims of this book: to understand the interplay between the everyday activities of individuals trying to get what they need to solve their own and group problems, and what this means for how they perceive themselves and how others perceive them.

Old Fadama is only one of many large sites of informally governed land in Accra. Indeed, a key characteristic of the rapid physical development the city has experienced in the last decades is the spread of informal constructions. All kinds of edifices and makeshift dwellings that are unregulated and unplanned by statutory authorities are estimated as comprising some 6.1 per cent of all housing in Accra (GSS 2013). The springing up of constructions in urban areas which are not effectively regulated by statute affects all social, political and economic layers of society. It is a phenomenon that penetrates every corner of the city and all types of landholding and land use. Multitudinous and diverse, ad hoc, opportunistic and impromptu creations made mainly from cheap plywood defy clear distinctions between temporary and permanent buildings and the use and misuse of space, and rework understandings of private and public land. The popping up of one sometimes encourages the building of another and yet another next door. Clusters sometimes form and mushroom: from under highways, across disused railway lines, on almost every street corner, at and on roundabouts, upon grass verges, in the car parks of banks, outside supermarkets, clinging onto the outside walls of local government institutions, atop the roofs of hospitals and apartment blocks, within 'unoccupied' private buildings for sale, on abandoned building sites, on near-completed commercial complexes, outside walled and high-end residencies, on overgrown farm plots in peri-urban suburbs. Thus, the city is pebble-dashed with impromptu single dwellings and bunches of home-made houses, market stalls and kiosks clinging together on the margins of city plans. It all means that across Accra inhabitants and occupiers of different slums and informal settlements now comprise 38.4 per cent of the city's population but occupy only 15.7 per cent of the total land (UN-Habitat 2011).

As well as popping up all over the city, the impromptu constructions sometimes disappear as well. Thus, a key feature of the urban land and property complex in Accra is also the omnipresence of slogans in red paint, allegedly the AMA's favourite colour. These are daubed on walls and doors, and hammered up on signboards or glued to doors and windows by the city authority or other claimants. They serve as warnings, naming and shaming exercises, and as a show of might. The slogans endeavour to define legitimate claimants and to expose pretenders. 'DO NOT OCCUPY THIS', 'KEEP OUT! THIS LAND BELONGS TO …'. Words are not minced. Those who pass apparently empty plots of land are urged not to meddle. 'DO NOT TAKE CONTACT WITH ANYONE TRYING TO SELL THIS LAND!' 'THIS LAND DOES NOT BELONG TO THE XXX FAMILY!'. Meanwhile, expired forewarnings in faded paint on kiosks and shacks such as 'HAS TO BE REMOVED BY 27 MAY 2014, BY ORDER AMA' demonstrate government inability to enforce its will, rather than the intended effect of demonstrating power and imposing conformity.

Such messages daubed around the city reflect the never-ending cat-and-mouse contests over a seemingly spontaneous development of urban space between different claimants. All endeavour to access, control and regulate space according to competing logics based on different legal, political, social, customary and individual designs.[3] The extent to which governments accept or assign de facto recognition of informal constructions varies considerably. Recognition may or may not depend on whether buildings infringe individual and communal land rights, local planning and other kinds of building regulation (Hansen and Vaa 2004).

The spread of the informality of urban space, and of widening urban socio-economic inequalities, is regularly attributed to neoliberal polices and the associated retreat of the state from the public sphere that commenced in the early 1980s.[4] In particular, the implementation of a range of Economic Structural Adjustment Policies led to the breaking up and privatization of parastatals, considerable retrenchment, and reduction in the size of the public sector. Public utility provision was privatized and state control of inputs and markets was reduced in a move towards unregulated, market-based liberal economies (Peck and Tickell 2002). Subsequently, the neoliberal agenda has been widely criticized for contributing to a longterm urban planning deficiency in Africa. And it is frequently blamed for a creeping informalization of public service delivery, and for not taking the urban poor, exposed and marginalized into account. In turn, long-term plans for the creation and use of public space lack support because there is an absence of political will concerning the equitable use and distribution of urban land (Carmody and Owusu 2016; Gleeson and Low 2000; Sager 2011).

Against this background, it is tempting to explain the ostensibly negative developmental trajectory of Old Fadama in terms of neoliberal conditioning. Here the *retreat* of the state from the public sphere, and dominance of market- and investor-friendly policies, would explain the imbalance in spatial justice between, on the one hand, Old Fadama, and, on the other, economically successful and politically influential segments of the city. From a Marxist standpoint, meanwhile, the sprawling Old Fadama exemplifies a process of urban accumulation by dispossession through which capital turns the over-availability of very cheap labour into profit and causes struggles over land in urban areas (Bailey 2014/15; Gillespie 2016; Harvey 2003). A contending neoliberal explanation might point instead at the failure of professed progressive and equitable legal frameworks to integrate the urban poor into the broader fabric of the city (Strauss and Liebenberg 2014). Despite the differences, all the above provide plausible explanations for the political and economic conditioning of Old Fadama as well as the mass of unregulated development observable in so many places and forms around Accra.

Yet the unrehearsed growth of Old Fadama cannot be satisfactorily explained, I suggest, by the retreat or reluctance of the state under the influence of neoliberal adjustment, or by processes of accumulation by dispossession. Instead, *State of Slum* highlights the grinding legal predicament and *strength* of the legal decision around eviction as inadvertent drivers of Old Fadama and its position as one of the city's greatest challenges.

A brief outline of land law, government objectives and positions towards Old Fadama

In Accra, as in many other African cities, the successful implementation of land law is hindered by a long history of legal pluralism that contributes to the march of unregulated building, settlement and encroachment all over the city. In brief, one system in Accra comprises configurations of English common law introduced by the British colonial power and which recognize individual ownership under a system of state-recognized formalization and titling. A second system comprises customary and traditional tenure mechanisms, which are based typically in kinship, collective ethnic citizenship and chieftaincy, and where recognition of land claims is socially embedded. The two systems may or may not be in competition with one another but often confound questions of land regulation. The complicated legal system means that settlers on new land may choose to avoid either the formal or traditional systems, or both, and create alternative mechanisms to secure land through processes of settlement.

Formally, customary and traditional authorities control about 80 per cent of all land in Ghana and about 20 per cent is owned by the state. However, the actual process of land distribution, control and administration is highly intricate, and comprises some twenty-three different informal and formal institutional stakeholders with varying degrees of influence. There are often contradictory and confusing areas of jurisdiction with different administrative practices, mechanisms and procedures for applications and appeal (WaterAid 2009; Spichiger and Stacey 2014). Broadly speaking, however, land in Ghana is acquired through membership of a lineage or residence within a community, and through numerous types of transfer, rent, sale, lease, mortgage or pledge. According to the 1992 Constitution it is chiefs, heads of families and other traditional or customary authorities who, as custodians of most of the land, oversee transfers with a fiduciary obligation. And, traditionally, the transfer of land demands the approval of the respective traditional or chieftaincy institutions, called the *skin* in the north of the country and the *stool* in the south. The skin or stool symbolizes the authority of the traditional institution, the territorial span of a given chiefdom and the chief's veneration of the skin or stool ancestors. The skin or stool also symbolizes the inseparability of group identity, land, authority and social relations (Bentsi-Enchill 1964: 30).

In a broader perspective, drivers of unregulated land use and challenges to reforms to improve land issues include population growth, rural–urban migration, a long history of lack of coherent urban planning, mismanagement, distrust of government, and lack of law enforcement (Demissie 2007; Kleemann et al. 2017). The 1999 National Land Policy similarly identified a disabling culture of land disputes and litigation stemming from, amongst other things, the legal pluralist systems, inadequate demarcation of customary land, and a history of state acquisitions without compensation (GRG 2011; Larbi 2011; Spichiger and Stacey 2014). In Ghana urban migration increases by about 1.8 per cent a year and consequently leads to many thousands of people living and working in areas that are on the margins of government control. As exemplified above, what happens on the street level is often one step ahead of government plans, legal disputes, endless contestations over the control of land, and the stream of new provisions, policies and laws that follows in close succession. As in many other sub-Saharan African countries, cities in Ghana have also expanded onto land that not so long ago was either barren or deemed useless. In turn, increasing interest has brought about a collision of different sets of rules that now endeavour to govern land access (Barry and Danso 2014).

Government agencies, departments and ministries have many ambitious and elaborate plans to direct land-based development towards more desirable ends. The latest is laid out in the Land Use and Spatial Planning Act from 2016 (Act 925), running to over 100 pages. This aims to synchronize Ghana's many existing land laws, planning regulations and administrative procedures, and strengthen other ongoing efforts, which include the Land Administration Project 2 (LAP–2). This itself followed LAP–1 (2003–10), and is expected to run for fifteen to twenty-five years and implement policy actions recommended in the Ghana Land Policy of 1999. Ghana is thereby currently pursuing a comprehensive programme of land reform which carries further challenges in terms of how to tackle informal and illegal settlements. Guiding the reforms is the 1992 Constitution, which provides for the right of privacy, non-interference with the privacy of one's home, and right to freedom from arbitrary deprivation of property, and which states that these rights *'shall not be regarded as excluding others ... inherent in a democracy and intended to secure the freedom and dignity of man'*.

The right to adequate housing, meanwhile, is enshrined in international treaties which aim to protect human rights and which Ghana is a party to. Still, there is no legal protection against forced eviction, housing rights are not covered in the Constitution, and most economic, social and cultural rights are directive principles not justiciable in courts. The judgment in the 2002 case against the AMA bought by Old Fadama residents in the High Court of Justice confirmed the settlers' lack of legal protection:

> The defendants are under no obligation to resettle or relocate or compensate plaintiffs in any way before evicting them from their illegal occupations ... The mere eviction of plaintiffs who are trespassers, from the land they have trespassed onto, does not in any way amount to an infringement on their rights as human beings. (Amnesty International 2011)

Clearly, the ruling that settlement is illegal places the sovereignty of state-recognized property rights as paramount. Yet it has proved impossible to execute and, as we shall see, is 'dissolved' in everyday relations between the settlement and formal institutions of authority. In practice, this means that, together with the constant message that they live on land illegally, for years the inhabitants of Old Fadama have been exposed to a stream of inconsistent formal utterances and media commentaries.

Globally, the solution to ambivalence and insecurity related to land and the growth of informal settlements has been the drive towards the formalization and registration of land titles, based on a legalistic approach to poverty reduction and social stability (De Soto 2000). Faith placed in the formalization of titles also builds on assumptions that titles optimize land use, provide an efficient base for taxing land occupancy, and act as positive incentives for land investments. Yet there is no automatic link between the issuing of land titles and attainment of the goals of poverty reduction,

social stability and increased certainty, and titling itself can cause
new contestations about rights of ownership (Lund 2008). Indeed,
central to the imbroglio of Old Fadama is not title as such – as one
clear feature of the settlers is that they generally do not claim ownership of the land and fully acknowledge the land they live on is not
theirs.[5] Rather, it is a question of getting the settlers to comply with
existing titles.

Ghana agencies, departments and ministries also pursue the
National and Regional Spatial Development Framework (2015–
2035). This extends beyond regulation for land usage to address
tensions and contradictions among sectoral policies' concerning, for
example '*conflicts between economic development, environmental and
social cohesion policies*' (GRG 2015). Previously, law recognized
Metropolitan Authorities as the leading urban planning authority,
with the power to grant, enforce and retract building permission
(WaterAid 2009). However, Act 925 established a new institution,
the Land Use and Spatial Planning Authority, which shall '*ensure
attainment of a balanced distribution of urban population and a spatially
integrated hierarchy of human settlements to support the socio-economic
development of the country*'. To fulfil these and other objectives, the
new authority has to make and implement a Local Plan. Chapter 72
of the Act states, for example, that:

(1) A local plan shall have as its key object, the judicious
use of land for attaining a sound, natural and built
environment and an improved living standard.

(2) A local plan is required for each specific physical
development.

(3) A local plan shall be drawn up and adopted before *(a)* the
approval of a development scheme in respect of the layout
of land for more than twenty individual plots each of
which is not less than one hundred and ten square metres;
and *(b)* major redevelopment schemes in urban areas.

(4) A local planning authority shall prepare a local plan,
where that authority intends in respect of an urban or
urbanizing area to establish legally binding regulations
for *(a)* the land coverage for a construction on a plot in
the zone; *(b)* the type of structure on the land; *(c)* the
form and height of buildings; *(d)* tree preservation; *(e)*
the preservation of buildings with a cultural heritage
and historical structures; and *(f)* any landscaping or tree
planting requirements.

In urban contexts at the heart of these agendas is the aim to reel in and control the spread of informal economic activity and related land occupation and congestion. These aims are themselves grounded in a deep-seated normative perspective that all which is informal is ineffective, bad and wasteful and has to be improved with (more) planning, regulation and better and stricter formal laws that will improve urban life for all (Koster and Nuijten 2016). But at the same time, local and national governments are under pressure from a broad spectrum of local, national and global stakeholders to improve the supply of low-end housing and upgrade sites of business and settlement that are informally accessed and controlled, and mainly outside the reach of statutory designs. In 2011, this line resulted in a UN-Habitat report (with the participation of a range of government agencies, departments, ministries and civil society groups) which concluded that '*The issue of housing finance for low-income housing to prevent and upgrade slums should be addressed in a comprehensive manner to include both demand and supply sides*' (UN-Habitat 2011). Recognizing divergences between needs, government actions and plans, the report found that the AMA had an '*unclear policy on slums without a strategic approach to addressing the different types of slums*' and that this, '*coupled with the low collaboration with slum communities does not foster good development relationship with communities*' (ibid.).

Clearly, then, there are mismatches between the unarranged realities on the ground in Accra as experienced by the needy, the noble aims of governmental-level urban planning, and what different levels of government actually do. The corollary is that land access and distribution in Accra are not moving from less to more coherent forms of transfer, control and increased compliance with regulations. Rather, they are '*increasingly being unveiled as a complex mix of rule violations and compliances*' (Boamah and Walker 2016). Regardless of the eviction order, plans, regulations and formal state law, in Old Fadama the extent to which government institutions allow or recognize buildings, settlement and residency is a constant source of debate, gossip and everyday conversation, and influences decisions about building and investment. So, clearly, the indecisive stance of successive governments has caused near-havoc in terms of local notions about 'what rights do we actually have here?' Although the official view is that all building is illegal and wholly unacceptable, different actions of state actors, and the fact that the place continues to thrive, feed into the general sense of 'nobody really knows what is going on here', and 'if it goes it goes', and 'some governments are better than others'. As we shall see, new buildings are sometimes knocked down while others that appear much more intrusive in terms of land rights, planning and regulation are left alone. The fate of this and other sites of informal and unregulated buildings can also depend on the resources available to the enforcers of law, as well as the influence of squatters. But both 'sides' contribute to different local understandings of what is allowed and not allowed, who decides what, and who can do what.

Subsequently, although statutory institutions have decided the legal state of affairs, successive governments have been wholly unable to control the consequences of the legal conditions that have been defined. In practice, and in different times, statutory authorities may turn a blind eye to the thousands of illegal constructions, quietly or begrudgingly accept settlement, extract levies, sporadically bulldoze with perfunctory prior notice, channel resources through informal networks, or woo the population with promises of improvements, typically prior to election times. The range of interactions and encounters between 'government' and 'Old Fadama' produces uncertainty and unpredictability that neither can really control. City authorities come around annually and collect levies from businesses in Old Fadama and issue certificates of payment for metropolitan coffers. Yet payment does not validate or bestow formal recognition on settled existence, and shopkeepers do not doubt that their business could still be destroyed at any time – as does happen periodically with clearance operations in peripheral areas. Further, there is a widespread perception, as emphasized in Frederick's narrative, that 'government' is a main cause of the decrepit condition of Old Fadama because of the entrenched position following the judicial decision to evict. Thus, it is common that residents do not expect or look to formal institutions of government for improvements or help. But at the same time, state officials may support micro-level projects as 'patrons', or as 'concerned individuals', thus distancing themselves from the formal political position regarding the site and accruing political and social capital (Paller 2014, 2015). The contrast between state officials endorsing what goes on, and local and national government not solving serious everyday challenges, feeds into the sense of inconsistency.

Thereby, Old Fadama proliferates in a grey zone where multiple claims and contests over land and settlement reflect individual prowess, 'can do' ability and opportunism, and skills at bargaining and negotiating with opponents in processes outside the reach of formal state law.[6] On the one hand, Old Fadama is a lively and significant economic hub close to the geographical and political centre of the city; it creates employment for tens of thousands of people as a marketplace, transport centre, and site of countless small businesses. And as a home to tens of thousands of voters, it is also an important site for politicians seeking to rally support in national elections. Yet by other measures and in an everyday capacity it is outside the political and developmental reach of the state and city authorities in Accra. And in terms of modern, normative visions of what a city should be like and should suggest as a political ideal, Old Fadama is resolutely on its margins (Hoffman 2017: xxi). This is evident from the physical absence of statutory institutions; serious local ecological and environmental conditions that remain unaddressed; dilapidated slum housing; and massive infrastructural neglect. Thus, it is both important *and* marginal to formal state institutions, and to the city at large. The conundrum plays out in contradictory positions taken by different statutory institutions and state actors towards the site. Attempts to regulate building and economic activity are undermined by a simultaneous marginalization of the population by depriving the site of social amenities and a basic level of public services. Meanwhile, patronage networks between the site and different levels of government may provide ad hoc resource flows that 'drip feed' the settlement and well-placed local actors. Yet, in turn, city government also constantly hassles people to move away and not settle, and the lack of systematic government support effectively strangles the site, and shuts off regular flows of funding.

Thus, one significant feature that defines Old Fadama and is implicit in everything that is done by the people who live and work there is the awareness that *yes, we are not supposed to be here, but for the time being it seems we are allowed to be.* This is also evident in the often contradictory positions of statutory institutions and actors, and, for example, from the vignette about Frederick, in which a High Court judge openly validates the new community-based project while an eviction order is pending. On the one hand, there is a near-unanimous understanding that such actions are good and positive. Yet on the other, they exemplify the workings of informal governance and participation of high-placed state officials that undo 'state' efforts to regulate and implement formal plans. They also make it difficult to differentiate between public officials performing as private individuals and vice versa. Either way, the resources they control and popular interpretations of their role feed into the legitimacy of local developmental projects that appropriate space and power for the stakeholders behind them. Together with the differing stances of domestic statutory institutions, the opening ceremony reveals further the central role that the institutions of foreign nation-states, in this case the Australian High Commission to Ghana, can play in local initiatives that defy the will of city authorities seeking to halt settlement and construction.

Although the illegal status has remained constant, successive governments have had changing relations with the settlement. Still, from the perspective of successive governments, Old Fadama has always been disobedient, a burden, an eyesore, and a difficult place to rule and categorize administratively. The legalistic positioning not only means that governments cannot recognize settlement. It also makes it difficult to formalize productive relations with the actual 'governors' of Old Fadama, who themselves are only loosely organized, changing, and aspiring to represent an 'illegal' polity.

Since the return to democratic rule in 1992 governmental power has swung between the two largest political parties in Ghana, the NPP (New Patriotic Party) and the NDC (National Democratic Congress). The NPP government of John Kufuour (2001–09) adopted an overall confrontational stance towards Old Fadama and pushed for the enforcement of the eviction order. Similarly, the Accra municipal authority at the time argued that the settlement undermined environmental clean-up efforts. For years, the AMA and the main national newspapers, including the *Daily Graphic*, characterized the site negatively (Grant 2009). But Old Fadama, situated in the constituency of Odododiodioo, has been an NDC stronghold since 2004, and residents' fears of imminent eviction were lessened further as the NDC won the presidential elections, with John Dramani Mahama as president from July 2012 to January 2017. Currently, the constituency remains under NDC control, under the NPP government of Nana Akufo-Addo (2017–). Despite NDC support in the area, the AMA under Alfred Okoe Vanderpuije, who was mayor from 2009 to 2016, initially pushed for the 'squatters' to be evicted without redress to housing alternatives – a hostile position reinforced by different demolitions around the city. Therefore, since the eviction order in 2002, public gestures from city authorities and parliamentarians have swung considerably, and have included both demands for the enforcement of the eviction order and promises by political parties to upgrade the site in return for electoral support. There are also plans for selective population relocation and sporadic upgrading. The most recent ideas emanate from the international NGO Peoples Dialogue, which proposes government support for low-cost housing financed through micro-loans to residents.

Although historically the AMA has pushed for total clearance of the site, in recent years this has shifted to plans for moving only the neighbouring large agricultural market of Agbogbloshie, which draws many thousands of migrant labourers to the area (Chapter 4). Currently, however, there is little evidence of any of these plans materializing, and widespread local opposition has been mounted to the moving of the market. Similarly, it remains to be seen how the grand ambitions of laws and reforms including the LAP–2 and the Land Use and Spatial Planning Act will play out in the capital. What is clearer is that while statutory institutions aim to convince all urban dwellers that 'the state' is in charge, the realities of life in Old Fadama often demonstrate otherwise.

Old Fadama: a political context of precariousness and uncertainty

The above has manufactured a deep-seated sense of unknowability that fits well with dimensions of the concept of precarity as used increasingly in the global North and inspired by the work of Guy Standing (Standing 2011). Here, a new socio-economic group with class characteristics, the 'precariat', has emerged. This is driven by experiences of a combination of precarious living and working conditions, and proletariat status, with long-term working conditions of intermittency, unpaid labour and unpredictable conditions of (under)employment (ibid.).

There are many features of the precariat observable in Old Fadama. A difference, however, is that for the many long-term residents of Old Fadama, living and working conditions have probably not deteriorated much in recent years. Nor have they experienced a downward transition from waged labour to insecure precarious contracts, as is otherwise recognized as taking place in many sectors in the global North. In brief, the conditions of 'permanent temporariness' and precarity are inherent features of their urban lives. In Old Fadama everyone I talked to confirmed that the economic foundation of their livelihoods is unpredictable (and always has been) and that they have little influence over the immediate political context that defines their living conditions and which are similarly impossible to predict. Despite relatively high living costs, there has, for many, never been such a thing as a regular and knowable amount of 'income', and even after many, many years in Accra, a safe and comfortable place in which to live remains elusive.

As we shall see, the legal entanglement enables new social and political spaces to appear that can increase levels of vulnerability as well as open up new avenues of positive opportunity. The need for protection and safety, and the experience of human rights being undermined, were issues that arose regularly in talking to residents. Thus, the roots of precarity and inconclusiveness in Old Fadama are not purely economic but conditioned by the political, legal and sociological context. To exemplify briefly, numerous market traders I talked to spoke of chronically uncertain income-generating conditions which were key features of their urban life, as well as concrete experiences of 'government' undermining all they worked for. On the one hand, all this provided reminders of their 'inferior' citizenship status, yet on the other it made it imperative that they develop their own sense of belonging and values (Chapter 4). Many others commented on 'just getting along' while 'not really knowing what was going to happen to Old Fadama', and worrying about 'how long it will all last' at the same time as developing local relations of recognition that were meaningful and useful and which reduced the uncertainty of living in the settlement. Thus, residents shared a nagging sense of precariousness. This stemmed from the legal status of affairs and meant they could not enjoy a sense of permanence and familiarity with their immediate surroundings.

A different sense of inconclusiveness was expressed by many state officials I talked to, who did not have sure answers to questions such as 'So what are the plans for Old Fadama?' Local government officials' range of answers spanned from plans for 'upgrading the area', 'a partial relocation of residents', 'normalization', 'a mass clean-up', a need for 'more control', to 'nothing is going to happen there', and 'we have to wait and see'. The different answers were not necessarily contradictory but certainly pointed to a lack of a substantive plan and communication strategy, and they revealed different interests and positions at play across levels of government. Diverse stories about developments, agendas and plans inevitably filter down to the street level and, together with the legal entanglement, provide fertile grounds for gossip, rumour and stress.

For the metropolitan authority, narratives of 'uncertainty' and keeping the population in the dark about the fate of the settlement are both enabling, transformative and constraining. For example, even though government is unable to execute the judicial decision, it hangs metaphorically over the settlement like an albatross and sustains a strong image that it is the 'government' who is in charge.[7] Yet the issue of illegal settlement also creates a condition whereby the AMA does not have to fully justify its actions to residents. This provides political space for 'government' to sometimes act with impunity and deny responsibility for its actions, and afterwards appear as a protector of rights and of those who deserve them. For example, after the AMA bulldozed hundreds of shelters in an adjacent illegal settlement (Chapter 3), one resident who lost many possessions recalled an AMA official telling of how 'they had to do it', and of 'not having a choice'. Another resident spoke of the AMA saying 'it's not our fault' (that you are losing your possessions), and 'you have bought this on yourself', and 'you should not be here', and 'nothing good will come from living there', etc. These messages justify a minimum level of consultation between 'government' and 'settlers', increase worries, and recreate the image of the AMA as in charge. Simultaneously, pressing questions of where people should move to or what they should do are not answered in terms of what government 'should' or 'ought' to do. Rather, they are answered in terms of 'we are doing all we can', 'look at what we are trying to do', and 'look at what we have to contend with'. So, the judicial issue gives rise to different situations of ambivalence, produced by statutory institutions, and creates an environment where people are left in the dark. This reaffirms ideas that government is the sovereign power.

Hence, on the one side, the legal conditioning allows the AMA to digress from acting fairly or as accountable representatives of the city's inhabitants. Instead, shows of occasional raw power increase the sense of precariousness. Yet, on the other, local understandings of 'government' as powerful (but also unproductive and intolerant), and that it is sometimes necessary for the 'state' to use force against 'offenders' and take back control, are produced (Peck and Tickell 2002). But in other instances, the uncertainty of slum life translates into the AMA working with informal organizations of governance based in Old Fadama to undertake tasks it cannot or will not do itself – for example the collection of refuse and regulation of building (Chapter 5). This fosters stories of 'cooperation' and 'progress' between 'government' and the settlement, but which again are confounded as the most pressing developmental and infrastructural challenges go unheeded.

So, in an everyday sense, Old Fadama eludes legal definition because mundane understandings of who is in change, what is allowed and not allowed, and who has a right to what, often change and are subject to debate. Encounters with inconclusiveness and agency, and the contrasting lived situations of ordinary people, are what motivates this book to explore further what people experience and how it impacts on their socio-political organization in a vibrant, urban area where government seldom governs. The inhabitants of Old Fadama have experienced decades of legal limbo and have carved out their own niches of organization and different practices regarding land access and informal governance to offset the sense of impermanence and uncertainty. At the same time, opportunities are unevenly available to settlers, and this impacts on their sense of belonging and what their citizenship status actually means. This makes Old Fadama a kaleidoscope of experiences concerning what people have and how they define themselves and others, and where diverse power relations play out, compete, and shape multiple constraints and provide opportunities. For some, Old Fadama is a dangerous place; for others, a source of agency, power, status and influence. For the very poor and marginalized it can be a trap of want and poverty; yet for runaways it can be an escape, a maker as well as a breaker of ambitions, and for others still it is a rabbit warren of opportunity. Needless to say, such diversity defies the common impression of slums in developing countries as 'holding centres' for superfluous global labour pools (Davis 2006).

State of Slum explores Old Fadama as a site of agency and power. It follows how different lives are carved out, how opportunities are won and lost, how possibilities arise for the rewriting of one's past and reimagining of one's future, and how for others Old Fadama provides reminders of the forces of marginalization they hoped to get away from when they migrated to the capital. For some, this means living out their lives in the temporal gaps between moving on, moving around, or moving back whence they came, if they can. For others, the combination of indeterminacy and vibrancy provides new-found opportunities that allow new lives to be carved out. The gaps between the laws, formal plans, lived realities and general uncertainty of Old Fadama make it an interesting place in which to study the everyday lives of ordinary people and the workings of urban governance. The aim is to draw attention to important differences between the ways ordinary people actually organize and conjure their lives under the often very difficult conditions in which they live in a modern city in Africa, and the overarching logic of the formal systems of governance they are supposed to abide by.

Theoretical framework

Slums, informal settlements and everyday urban life experienced by millions of people in developing countries have drawn research interest across all the social sciences in recent years, against a background of hectic urbanization. Almost three-quarters of Africa's urban populations currently live *informally*, where housing, shelter and businesses, etc., are not titled or regulated by statutory authorities. Still, the conditions of housing vary considerably, although the terms slum and informal settlement are often used interchangeably (Owusu et al. 2008). For clarity, this book uses the UN-Habitat (2011) definition of 'slum' as meaning households that lack one or more of the following: durable housing, sufficient living space, easy access to safe water in sufficient amounts at an affordable price, access to adequate sanitation, and security of tenure preventing forced evictions. And the book uses the UN definition of informal settlement as a housing area which occupants 'have no legal claim to, or occupy illegally'. Thus, the difference between slum and informal settlement lies in the legal dimensions, as slum areas need not be illegal or informal (UN 1997).

Of particular relevance to this study are others that attempt to understand cities in the global South in their own right and from emic perspectives of lived lives and from what actually is, rather than from theoretical and conceptual standpoints and expectations developed in the context of the global North. They include the works of Chernoff (2003), De Boeck and Plissart (2014), Simone (2004), Grant (2009), Myers (2011), Saglio-Yatzimirsky (2013) and Hoffman (2017). Despite differences in empirical focus, all reject Eurocentric conceptualizations of urban phenomena which remain pervasive in development thinking, and many tend to focus on ordinary people and the shaping of livelihoods, deals, norms, everyday negotiations and situations, social encounters, and experiences of urban processes from below. Thus, these works establish knowledge that much of the fabric of African urban life is in fact 'invisible' to urban planners and convincingly defies conventional urban development thinking (Simone 2004; Hoffman 2017). Consequently, *State of Slum* aims to take up opportunities missed by conventional approaches to urban life and see '*African cities as important loci of global processes or generators of urban stories worth telling and worth learning from*' (Myers 2011: 6). This is done by exploring everyday struggles, the reimagining of lives by ordinary people, and the shifting conditions of relatively ordered rule, and by approaching Old Fadama as a social arena of agency and power (Ansell and Torfing 2016: 10–15).

I pay attention to everyday, mundane activities, micro-opportunities, and random chances that arise from the suspension of formal governance and which create new socio-political spaces for informal governance to emerge. By informal governance, I mean

the loose, non-institutionalized organization of non-state actors that
sometimes provides residents with the resources and services they
need. The focus on relationships between everyday encounters and
the ad hoc shaping of local power relations contrasts with a view of
societal agency as developing from processes of deliberate decision-
making (Obrist et al. 2013). It is not that informal governance in
Old Fadama is unplanned, or unpolitical, but the synergies that
sometimes gel from ordinary peoples' everyday encounters and negotiations do not emerge from, or within, a community-wide system
of management. This view is in line with critical governance studies
that question the orthodoxy of governance as akin to government
and power relations around the central state, or where political and
social transformation is assigned to government-driven governance
(Walters 2004). Rather, governance in Old Fadama is approached
as a process involving combinations of statutory powers, understood
as the judicial, legislative and executive branches of formal government, and non-statutory powers (i.e. different institutions, actors and
organizations that yield influence but do not partake in processes of
formal state law-making). In different ways, both try to regularize
social actions and behaviour, and they experience varying degrees of
success as their efforts are accepted or rejected (Moore 1973).

It has long been recognized that an overt focus on the formal
economic domain renders invisible much of what is most significant to the mundane economic activities of ordinary people. This is
because a vast amount of economic activity is unregulated, under the
radar, and takes place in the informal sector (Hart 1973). This book
extends Hart's understanding to the sphere of local politics, governance and everyday life, asserting that a focus on statutory institutions
alone will not provide adequate insight into *actual* governance and
power relations. This is not to romanticize the 'informal' or to say
that non-statutory governance is an emancipatory project of popular
rule. For many, life in places like Old Fadama remains nasty, brutish
and short, despite the myriad local efforts at improvement and
informal regulation (Stacey and Lund 2016).

Broadly, there are two dominant, often overlapping views of the
organization and functioning of informal settlements worthy of
discussion, and which focus on 'what should be' and 'what is missing'.
The first is a conceptualization based on state-centrist theory, while
the second foregrounds dysfunctionality and contention.

The state-centrist approach typically highlights the incapacity
of state institutions and dysfunctional developments in outlying
areas as evidence of antagonistic relations between the periphery

and the centre. State formation is thereby equated with the development of central government: power is projected from a central entity and geographically circumscribed (for example, Evans et al. 1983; Herbst 2000). But, as more recently highlighted, this view imposes a Eurocentric understanding of the African state as intrinsically weak and is based on ideal trajectories (Freund 2007; Locatelli and Nugent 2009). State-centrist understandings also position formal and informal institutions as mutually exclusive and contentious: state institutions are assigned positive traits of rationality and formality, and society is framed as the state's ineffective or disorganized counterpart (for example, Chazan 1983; De Soto 2000). In this optic, the power to regulate society is assigned to statutory institutions, and government becomes a synonym for governance. Further, Western standards of functionality are applied to African settings, as is common in developmental discourses. Here, 'development' means the 'rest of the world' mimicking the developmental trajectory of the 'Western world'. Moreover, the transfer and export of superior technology and improved systems of management and regulation from the North to the South are understood as key to economic and political success. Slums and informal settlements are automatically reduced to less worthy and ineffective sites of social, economic and political organization. And space that is not formally regulated or is outside the 'rule of law' is framed teleologically as 'waste' and 'ineffective', and in need of movement towards 'better' and more optimal conditions after a sequence achieved in the West.

Invariably this projected view depoliticizes and negates the structural conditions that create slums, and waste and ineffective space. And state-centrist and legalist approaches shoulder government with the task of solving society's challenges by shaping the city through law and policies. Still, the position assumes a false dichotomy between ostensibly effective government institutions and their supposedly disorderly opposites. As recognized by Simone (2004), this misses the inventiveness of ordinary people who carve out their own life trajectories, and, importantly, the reasons why they should choose to do so. One could add that the inventiveness and social situations of people living at the margins are nevertheless influenced by images and imaginings of the 'state' as the most powerful actor (Greenhouse 2012).

The legalist approach to development supposes the existence of a capable set of state institutions that are willing to undertake improvements, and the automatic willingness of people to step into line. The corollary is that any heterogeneity of formal or informal institutions, and lack of incentives for people to not follow the law, are glossed over. In brief, state-centrist approaches point our attention to formal political systems, institutions and political decision-making processes that are assumed to be based on rational thinking and 'what is best', while the existence of a coherent state is always taken as a given. Strikingly, despite the widespread critique of state-centrist thinking and developmental discourse more generally, and their resounding failures to address the social and political realities which people actually inhabit, it remains a cornerstone of much development thinking, planning, and policy.

Against the state-centrist perspective, the point of departure for this book is a focus on subaltern dynamics and local political agency, with particular attention to actual social realities. This view recognizes that governance is not produced by the state alone but established through people's everyday lives as shaped by engagements and entanglements between heterogeneous statutory and non-statutory actors and institutions (see Fourchard 2011; Locatelli and Nugent 2009; Roy 2005; Stacey and Lund 2016). The focus on social process means that less attention is given to the mechanics of formal governance: the holding of regular elections, the administration of the welfare state, the paying of taxes, and the bureaucracy of government institutions. In this way, matters of grassroots activities are in focus without invoking the agency of national governments (Pierre 1999).

The second dominant view often emanating from state-centrist depictions is of informal settlements and slum areas as powerless and weak in resources, underproductive, and occupied by the losers of globalization. The understanding of inherent weakness supports interpretations of informal domains in terms of socio-political and economic homogeneity, or as predominantly detached from processes of globalization (Mohanty 2006; Shabane et al. 2011); as lacking agency or chaotic (Kaplan 1994; Davis 2006); and as areas prone to violence because of the conjoining of poverty, lack of rule of law, and cumulative social pressures (Barry et al. 2007; Beall et al. 2011; Lombard and Rakodi 2016; De Soto 2000; De Souza 2001). Such studies may juxtapose the formal and efficient city against its informal and chaotic counterpart. For example, by highlighting urban spatial divides between, on the one hand, wealthy, gated communities, and walled and privatized residential areas under constant surveillance, and on the other shabby sprawls of unregulated settlements, filth and urban 'microstates' (Harvey 2008). These positions support a view that there is something wrong and out of kilter with

African cities, and that growth and prosperity emerge from formality and chaos and filth from informality. As exemplified later, in Old Fadama grassroots activities are often unsystematic and disjointed, but the place is not particularly chaotic or conflict-ridden, and is not ungoverned or ungovernable. Rather, the informal settlement is shown as a producer of political and social power and as a potential creator of new opportunities and an escape from poverty, rather than as an arena prone to decay and as a depositary of the poor.

For liberal developmental economists, the key to unlocking the massive potential of informal settlements (and aligning them with Western developmental trajectories) is to formalize titles to land. Here, documentation, state recognition of land claims and the rule of law reduce informality and conjecture, provide access to credit, stimulate growth, and reduce poverty (De Soto 2000). However, the frequently drawn connection between the promotion of law and poverty reduction has been widely criticized for simplifying complex social realities, assuming linear transitions between informality and formality, and establishing causal links between recognition, stability and growth (Otto 2009). The dominant standpoints often fail to provide satisfactory understandings of the tribulations of ordinary people. And the multiple forces that influence 'what they actually do', and shape the organization of the places where they actually live, can easily be missed.

Besides arguments that the persistence of the informal sector is based in weak state institutions, a general informalization of urban political and economic life is often attributed to the diminishing of urban planning and regulation, and socio-economic and political fragmentation following Economic Structural Adjustment in the global South. This has widened gaps between ordinary people's everyday lives, on the one hand, and government plans and policies on the other (Watson 2009). The dominant role assigned to the neoliberal agenda (although the term is often loosely defined) is also frequently used to explain why state institutions are sometimes automatically assumed to be absent in informal settlements (see, for example, Fernandes and Varley 1998).[8] The focus in *State of Slum* on the legal imperative, however, means that the governance of Old Fadama is not explained in terms of fuzzy neoliberal processes, which include spatial inequalities and class struggles driven by unleashed market forces, and the privatization and suppression of common land (Harvey 2007; Pinson and Morel Journel 2016). This brings us to framing Old Fadama as a case study and the conceptual and theoretical contributions.

Old Fadama as a case study

There are many empirical features of Old Fadama which make it an interesting place in which to undertake social science research, and there are many conceptual dimensions to it as a case study. The primary focus here, however, is that, on a general level, Old Fadama exemplifies what can happen when a significant judicial decision concerning a large, densely populated urban settlement is upheld for a long period of time but not implemented, and the impact this has on the socio-political organization of the people living there. In short, *State of Slum* argues that context-specific forms of citizenship, property and authority form at the margins of the state in Old Fadama, which are not orchestrated by government but emerge from micro-level power struggles, negotiations and contests.

Initially, I was drawn to the place as a bustling urban site in the heart of an African capital city and where a large number of rural–urban migrants go about their business in open defiance of the law. Immediately, this gave rise to queries such as, 'What does this mean for the rule of law, for urban plans and policy, and particularly, for the people that live there?' *State of Slum* is thereby a concrete case of the social and political development of an urban area that proliferates despite a judicial decision against it. The fact that the mere existence of Old Fadama defies formal state law and forces all levels of government to adjust to it gives it elements of an 'extreme' or 'deviant' case that provides rich information about the situations studied (Flyvbjerg 2004). Hence it is also a case study of how people settle, live and organize in an area under constant conditions of unknowability and pressure from all levels of governments not to live there. Its continuation as a settlement tells of urban development as a process that is socially and politically productive yet also increasingly legally disruptive. Of particular interest, therefore, are relationships between, on the one hand, the everyday activities and organization of the settlement's residents, and on the other the legal entanglement, and the workings and non-workings of formal state law. This dynamic I find produces micro-opportunities as people manage to take advantage of the near-absence of statutory institutions and carve out social and political resources and space for themselves. And also, the political conditioning of the site produces potentially devastating living conditions as people fall between the cracks of different and changing systems of rules and emerging norms, which the already vulnerable are least able to improve upon.

Thus, empirically, *State of Slum* concerns unique sets of specific events which make and deny rights and which are forged by the particular social and political conditions of the broader context. As explained below, in a conceptual sense *State of Slum* is an exploration of changing forms of property, citizenship and informal governance that are interrelated and emerge on the margins of formal state law. But the social and political conditions and representations that shape such things are not unique to Old Fadama, so it is not assigned any intrinsic level of complexity, nor should it be understood as a bubble of extremes. Similarly, it is not approached from the perspective of post-colonial urban studies' focus on exceptionalism and particularism, or as exemplifying 'planetary urbanism', where 'the city is everywhere and nowhere' (Storper and Scott 2016). Moreover, it is not deemed particularly unique in terms of its socio-political relations, linkages, assemblages or power configurations. Again, there are numerous other urban sites in Accra and elsewhere in developing countries that are similar in the sense that urban migrants squat and defy formal property rights, develop informal access to a wealth of everyday services, challenge and change the objectives of formal government systems, and establish informal systems of governance with state and non-state actors. Accordingly, informality and processes of informalization, as well as the power relations they produce, are key features of urbanization all over the global South which Old Fadama shares. And despite widespread political, normative and developmental expectations, there is no clear linear transition taking place in Old Fadama from informal to formal societal organization. Similarly, there is no clear-cut movement in Old Fadama towards impersonal forms of representation and participation, as normative prescriptions of political development otherwise suggest (Roy 2005; Storper and Scott 2016).

Old Fadama has attracted research attention as an element in Ghana's recent social and political history. And its development has run parallel to the master narrative, promoted by the international community, of the country experiencing a successful transition to liberal democracy that began in earnest after 1992 (Afenah 2012; Grant 2006, 2009). On a West African regional level Ghana continues to be held up as a shining example of how African democracy *can* work, how successive and peaceful transitions of power between governments *have* taken place, and more recently, how economic growth now means the country has middle-income status. Thus, one important part of the 'story' of Old Fadama is that it has persisted and proliferated in the wake of national political stability, hailed democratization and economic growth. So, it is not that Old Fadama has been left behind in terms of economic and political development. On the contrary, *State of Slum* endeavours to show how it has shaped political development in the capital by informalizing governance. At the same time, its pressing developmental, infrastructural and governmental challenges have not been adequately addressed by statutory institutions.

What can Old Fadama tell us about relations between processes of formalization and informalization? First, that the processes are fragmented and simultaneously complementary and contentious. To exemplify, the upholding of the eviction order over many years shows that the judicial decision is not diminished by the informalization of governance. On the contrary, the conditioning of Old Fadama as an 'illegal' settlement provides meaning and legitimacy to the judicial ruling. It is also an expression of strong political and general support for a separation of the executive and judicial branches of government. The upholding of the judicial ruling similarly aims to affirm a norm that society should be organized after principles of formal state law, that there should not be political interference in judicial rulings, and that formal property rights should be respected. The corollary is that the settlers are defined as illegal squatters and denied formal political representation. In this perspective the case of Old Fadama is in broad agreement with actor-based approaches that trace changing and often conflictual social and socio-political relationships developing at the interface of formal and informal institutions and stakeholders (Long 2001).

The micro-opportunities that emerge from the absence of formal institutions in Old Fadama reflect structural disjointedness and discontinuities. These develop as the aims of statutory stakeholders to bring Old Fadama to heel are thwarted and overrun by the creativity and ambitions of actors at the local level. The latter often succeed in appropriating and defining space, and provide evidence of local actors not only 'navigating' between formal and informal procedures, but defining the rules of the game in the emerging social and political arenas (Koster and Nuijten 2016). In an everyday sense, therefore, the inability of statutory institutions to control Old Fadama sometimes translates into 'government' having to dance to the drums of Old Fadama. This tells of structural disjointedness as well as improvised processes of informalization and formalization which compete with as well as derive value and significance from each other.

The book draws inspiration and insights from other studies of Old Fadama, which has been analysed from numerous perspectives within many disciplines. It has been explained in terms of processes of exclusion and class-based dispossession as state institutions rally against an 'informal proletariat' (Gillespie 2016). And it has been understood as a site of informal mechanisms that provide legitimacy for formal political institutions, and where access to land is dependent on the positioning of actors in patronage networks (Paller 2014, 2015). It has also been shown that negative discourses of 'informality' and 'squatters' in Old Fadama make questions of development intractable and isolate the site from Ghanaian society at large (Afenah 2012; Obeng-Odoom 2011). Research has also focused on the area's serious environmental, health and ecological problems, which pose threats not only to the immediate vicinity but to many other parts of Accra as well, and which contribute to negative depictions (Songsore et al. 2014).

A broader range of social science studies of informal settlements in the global South also emphasize environmental, ecological, cultural and geographical dimensions. These include urban and rural connections (Lynch 2005; Trefon 2011); informal economies (Hart 1973; Bryceson and Potts 2006); urbanization as a feature of globalization (Appadurai 2000; Grant 2006); youth culture and mobility (Langevang 2008); governmentality; heterotopias (Carmody and Owusu 2016); questions of and crisis in urban development (Pieterse 2008); and livelihoods.

Conceptual and theoretical contributions

The contribution of *State of Slum* lies in the discussion of specific events and particular situations, and their decontextualization to abstract ideas and general patterns (Lund 2014). From a normative perspective, judicial rulings concerning eviction are key to upholding law and order, reducing land-based contestations and discouraging illegal settlement.[9] The general argument of this book, however, is that judicial decisions concerning densely populated areas also have serious political consequences when they are *not* implemented. Hence, *State of Slum* is an effort to understand some of the social and political forces that a 'suspension' of an important judicial decision creates and limits. One argument is that the non-execution of such judicial decisions accentuates challenges of governance because social and political space opens at the grassroots level with multiple and fragmented claims, rules and norms. The non-implementation of the eviction order thus drives the emergence of fluid, informal systems of governance and provides space for 'alter-native' notions of rights and belonging to develop – specifically, informal relations of property and local understandings of citizen-ship. These derive from the ineffectiveness of formal institutions of property and formal citizenship rights, and develop as ordinary people endeavour to secure the things they need and define who they are in order to secure them. This has inspired the investigation of Old Fadama to use the analytical concepts of property, citizenship and authority. Thus, on a general level, the aim is to contribute to knowledge of informal governance and human organization in urban areas outside the everyday reach of statutory powers. The focus on non-statutory forms of governance and human organization shows that life strategies in modern urban Africa often have very little directly to do with formal institutional designs, although they are very much conditioned by them, and often negatively. Conversely, the actions of statutory authority often have little to do with formal plans and law and are often influenced by a range of alternative and informal logics that have developed on the margins.

Conceptually, 'citizenship', 'rights subjects' and 'relations of property' emerge as residents try to improve their lives, gain support from those around them, and take advantage of micro-opportunities and potentialities that arise from the absence of formalized rules. The forms that citizenship, property and authority take are often fleeting and unpredictable because they are shaped by the unknow-ability and impermanence of the broader context and the refusal of statutory institutions to recognize settlement. Thereby, the analytical contribution of *State of Slum* lies in it showing how the forms that local rights and authority take are shaped by the broader context they play out in. In this optic, the book endeavours to exemplify a trajectory that local state formation can take in a modern African city where a large, densely occupied area is effectively cut off from statutory powers following a judicial ruling. Empirically, the aim is to exemplify that to fully understand socio-political change and governance in African cities it is necessary to look beyond formal decision-making and planning processes to arenas where decisions are suspended or pending. The everyday life of residents and their experiences of the legal situation thereby provide the raw material for the theoretical and conceptual contribution.

The loose system of governance in Old Fadama is thus shaped by processes of both formalization and informalization. As the example of the opening of Frederick's community centre alludes to, informal activities can have formal elements as well. It is therefore useful to approach formalization and informalization as social processes and the 'formal' and 'informal' in terms of a continuum rather than as distinct sectors, domains, or as each other's opposites (Koster and Nuijten 2016). Moreover, there is nothing inherently antagonistic or complementary per se between formal and informal institutions, and relationships can range between degrees of convergence and divergence (Helmke and Levitsky 2004). Exploring the movements and relations between formality and informality contributes to understandings of the role that statutory institutions play in the organization and governance of informal settlements, which recently was described as under-researched (Brown 2015). All dimensions of political and economic life can have important dimensions of informality where the formal rules may be confirmed, circumvented or broken. Processes of informality can similarly develop and be subject to their own logics of norms, behaviour and customs with their own elements of formality, in the sense of rule-following and sanction. In brief, informalization is not an inherent character trait of social, economic and political organization on the margins, nor is formalization necessarily a key feature of government decision-making.

Governance

Governance is a slippery term used across numerous disciplines.[10] In this book, it is used to capture the everyday processes through which individuals and loose groups gain and lose rights and access to resources, and shape authority in Old Fadama (Hagmann and Péclard 2010; Pieterse 2008; Myers 2011). This approach intends to challenge the more conventional concepts and narrow definition pertaining specifically to the actions of statutory institutions and formal levels of government. Instead, here it encompasses a range of other processes, actions and decision-making undertaken by non-statutory actors and groups of individuals at the grassroots level. These include networks, neighbourhoods, communities and other informal organizations. In keeping with this broader reference, the book uses the term to convey, in a political sense, the process of the '*forming of collective will out of a diversity of interests*', and, in the context of polity-making, to unravel the process of '*rules shaping and regulating the actions of social and political actors*' (Ansell and Torfing 2016: 3).

Governance of the site appears as a paradox. On the one hand, locally produced norms and powerful local actors sporadically enjoy the power to govern and control resources but have no legal backing to exercise authority. On the other hand, institutions of government with the formal authority to rule often lack the power to do so, but still influence the informalization of governance by upholding the judicial ruling and tacitly recognizing settlement and the powers that are in control there. In the middle, so to speak, are ordinary people who try and get by, navigating if they can between different systems and sets of rules, and making their own where possible. In other words, in the state of slum, there is a divergence between locally powerful socio-political and cultural networks and norms that shape individuals' ability to benefit from resources such as land, and formal rights to the resource and formal citizenship rights, which are less significant (Ribot and Peluso 2003: 155). Sometimes, the delivery of resources and individuals' recognition of those that provide them produce public authority. This is defined as the ability to exert a non-covert, impersonal power over a demarcated space with popular legitimacy that does not rely solely on coercive force (Lund 2006). Loose systems of governance emerge from efforts to improve everyday life but have varying degrees of success. Governance thus comprises of changing social and socio-political relationships and manoeuvrings at the micro level, and is not a unified system imposed from 'above' (Migdal et al. 1994; Stacey 2015). And the different forces that shape social and political organization and rights in Old Fadama make it important to draw distinctions between the often conflated concepts of government, governance and state institutions. This is because it is often not government that is doing the governing or bestowing and removing rights, and local powers and social configurations that may enjoy the ability to define and defend rights are not 'state', in the normative sense of the concept.[11]

Stigma of not belonging

There is a fluid sense of belonging in Old Fadama that changes as people move in and settle down, sometimes stay for years, or experience hostility and move away. Affinity to the place can develop as rights are acknowledged by others and as people try in different ways to overcome the apprehension, vulnerability and temporariness that all share. This can contribute to a sense of community, although the diverse interests and backgrounds of settlers and differences in their everyday experiences, levels of resources, life situations and luck can also mean that common points of reference are limited. Despite spending many years in the settlement, and perhaps enjoying success and having many friends and family living there, people may still deny their attachment owing to stigma about living in 'that place'.

As emphasized by a leading member of the native Ga community, there is moreover a sense of shame and even disgust attached to children who are born in Old Fadama. This is because, according to him, being born there reveals that '*you do not really belong anywhere and do not have anywhere to go*'. Also, for opponents of Old Fadama, to be born there means you have to carry the humiliation of not belonging 'anywhere', of being born in a filthy place on land that belongs to others who do not want you there, and where there is no history, tradition or pride, and where those who live there have no cultural worth. These viewpoints reflect the high cultural significance in Ghana of having a home town, of having community or family land, of belonging to a place with history, of having ancestors from that place, and having the status of being a *native* of a specific place. The stigma of being born in Old Fadama is replicated after death as the deceased are transported back to home towns for a decent burial. Popularly, Old Fadama is therefore not a place where anyone wishes to be buried.

Accordingly, stigma attached to being born and raised in old Fadama accentuates the standing of ethnic groups native to Accra who proclaim and celebrate such things, in contrast to settlers, who do not enjoy such privileges. On similar lines, a district nurse told of how runaway pregnant females can give birth (or abort) in Old Fadama with the advantage of anonymity because '*nobody would ask where they came from*'. A group of Ga also laughed as they told of how discarded children born in Old Fadama can earn the nickname of '*throwaways*', or '*born-here-thrown-away*', a whispered term that carries the multiple indignity of defining the subject as parentless, unwanted and not having a home town to return to. I was unable to confirm these claims, but they nevertheless affirmed stigma and negative depictions of the area and its people.

Konkomba migrants who moved to Old Fadama many years ago spoke of hearing regularly that they do not belong in the city because they choose to settle on land against the will of the owners. And for migrants from historically marginalized ethnic groups such as the Konkomba, such utterances play into unsettled contentions about their rights as citizens. It is not that Konkomba migrants have lost their rights as Ghanaian citizens and do not belong in the city, but common mentioning of them by opponents in negative terms often highlights that their staying and living in Old Fadama against the will of government is evidence that they 'do not belong anywhere'. The contrasts of belonging and not belonging and processes of exclusion and inclusion in Old Fadama exemplify urban mobility to peripheral areas as producing 'estuarial zones', where people live for many years but often sense alienation from the rest of the city (Landau 2014).

Authority and social contracts

Although living conditions in Old Fadama accurately fit the UN-Habitat understanding of a slum in terms of high population density and poor living conditions, etc., the term automatically conjures up negative if not derogatory impressions, and so deserves discussion and justification (Gilbert 2007, 2009). The title *State of Slum* is borrowed from a journal article co-written with Christian Lund, 'In a state of slum …' (Stacey and Lund 2016), that forms part of Chapter 5. Primarily, the intention of using a take on this title is to theoretically pursue it and confront dominant thinking about states and slums in the global South. So, the title has the theoretical ambition of wrenching the analysis of 'state' from its common associations with a powerful, central government and statutory institutions to local politics and dynamics. Also, the title intends for the concept of slum to be moved from the normative 'margins' of the 'state' to the 'centre' of analysis. With this, the concept of 'state' denotes a confluence of loose socio-political forces that contribute to governance. These include government and statutory actors and institutions (the executive, legislative and judicial branches of government) as well as non-statutory forces, defined as such because they are not part of the process of formal state law. Although formal levels of government are logistically the most powerful forces, their ability to exert their will over Old Fadama is exercised only occasionally and is often limited. As the analysis aims to bear out, the terms 'state' and 'slum' are not used as emotive or static categories.

Residents' identification with the Ghanaian state – public officials, bureaucrats, police, local government institutions – is generally negative, save at election times, when Old Fadama, as part of the Odododiodioo constituency, is wooed with promises of development and improvements in exchange for votes. The long history of governments not doing what they said they would do and the dire need for infrastructure, social services and all kinds of amenities has shaped understandings of 'government' as an unreliable and distrusted power, and many residents expect very little from it, regardless of its party political composition. Thus, there is little evidence of an enabling and constant social contract between the 'state' and 'citizenry'. Still, it is common that different resident groups and individuals make demands on politicians and other state actors. But both residents and governments appear to have turned their backs on each other in terms of the everyday, systematic functioning of the site. Simultaneously, the local grounding of 'state' and the ability to have rights that are substantiated locally are clearly more important. Generally, 'central government' is predominantly experienced by residents of Old Fadama as a belligerent and unhelpful external force that does not recognize the worth of the place or its people. However, the heterogeneity of the population also means residents have different experiences and expectations of different levels of government, from the sub-district offices of local government to national government. Nevertheless, one hears many versions of 'government does not help us'. There is a widespread sense that government departments, agencies and ministries do not provide basic needs, services and amenities. This social contract is therefore shaped by the mutually exclusive standpoints of statutory institutions not wanting people to settle and stay, and the settlers not wanting, or being able, to move. On a basic level this means that government has limited ability to enforce collectively binding decisions on residents without 'inside' help or resorting to coercion and raw power.

Within the settlement other social contracts form which are more intimate and personalized than those between the state and society at large. They form as people negotiate deals or are levered to comply with informal rules made by others. The social contracts impact on local rights to resources and can be based on combinations of coercion, cajoling and compliance. A key dynamic of governance in Old Fadama is thereby the changing ability of different statutory and non-statutory actors, institutions and organizations to establish and maintain rights, and gain the recognition of the settlement's inhabitants.

This means that some of the non-state organizations of governance in Old Fadama undertake similar tasks and functions to the formal 'state' and statutory institutions. One of the most visible is OFADA (Old Fadama Development Association), explored in Chapter 5. OFADA endeavours to do many things normally associated with levels of formal government. This includes trying to provide the settlement with security, regulating building and construction, establishing law and order, building infrastructure, and managing refuse. Its activities are often unsuccessful, its powers of conviction over residents are limited and sometimes opposed, and it does not have the resources it needs to undertake such a broad range of tasks. However, there is also evidence that OFADA sometimes executes functions more effectively than government, undertakes tasks for city authorities, and enjoys local acceptance. Countless other loosely organized actors provide services such as education and health, and endeavour to regulate access to land (Chapter 3). The ability and capacity of non-statutory actors to function like government provides evidence of diverse social contracts in the making. These are driven both by the practical needs of Old Fadama's population, who look to others for help and support, and more resourceful actors with the ambitions and ability to develop the area and increase their own socio-political standing. The diversity of non-state actors means they have very different abilities to organize and provide, but all contribute to Old Fadama as a centre of agency with loose systems of informal governance and power, and changing social contracts.

Although stigma can be attached to those born and bred in Old Fadama, the legal position and the uncertainty it produces also contribute to a shared sense of belonging and understandings of citizenship. And despite the heterogeneity of Old Fadama inhabitants, there are significant experiences all can relate to. For example, almost all inhabitants originate in the north of the country, and importantly, successive governments do not want any of them to live in the place they have settled in. Moreover, many long-term residents have attended or at least been supportive of demonstrations against eviction around the time of the court action. And on a day-to-day level all residents have had to learn to live with the risk that one day their shelters, houses and businesses could be lost to government bulldozers. Disruptive events such as the bulldozing of dwellings in areas close to waterways and everyday experiences of crime mean that people depend on each other for support and are often more than mere cohabitants of the same urban space. Furthermore, practically all residents face the same challenges of lacking basic services and amenities which, in their view, is due to the entrenched position of governments. Besides a sentiment of statutory institutions as generally alien to the needs of residents, there is therefore a long-term view, often based on painful first-hand experiences, that Old Fadama will always be marginalized (Appadurai 1996; Bourdieu 1977; Tanabe 2008).

Such sentiments are evident in everyday utterances about urban life at the grass roots that stress an ethos of 'doing it yourself', 'getting things done', 'if you don't do it, no one else will', of 'no help is coming', and that Old Fadama has to 'fend for itself'. Consequently, authority isn't exercised by government as an extension of formal state law but emerges through everyday negotiations of claims by ordinary people on the services and resources they need. In turn, authority develops through the capabilities of other actors to provide for those needs while demanding, expecting and asking for obligations in return. The upholding of the judicial decision and combinations of unwillingness, inability and indecision on the part of formal government thereby provide myriad opportunities and potentialities for 'alternative' authorities to emerge. They provide services and endorse a variety of rights covering land, building, settlement, infrastructure and security, to name only the most basic needs. The institutions that deliver such services exercise authority and the claimants that enjoy them are entitled as 'rights subjects' (Stacey and Lund 2016). The emerging authorities are informal, personalized, pragmatic and non-bureaucratic.

The role of chiefs in Old Fadama exemplifies one form of emerging authority and an informal social contract. There are numerous 'chiefs' that endeavour to solve domestic disputes and reduce crime in the area; in return, residents who benefit from their services will recognize the chiefs' authority and pay customary homage. In this way, the recipients of the rights and services legitimize the authority or governance capacity of the actor or institution in question. The exchange creates a dynamic between residents' claims to different resources and rights, and the governing capacities of stakeholders able and willing to deliver the goods.

The pursuit of rights is often not considered by the actors themselves as a decisively political act. But all the same, it can have important local social, cultural, economic and political consequences. For example, when Old Fadama residents acknowledge that a local chief is in charge of allocating land in a part of the settlement, they also recognize and buy into the idea of his status as a traditional authority, even though there are no chiefs in Old Fadama that are formally recognized by government. And when people access land from chiefs that are not recognized by government, the authority of chiefs *who are* recognized by government is undermined. This is the case of non-recognized Dagomba chiefs controlling and distributing land in Old Fadama while state-recognized Ga chiefs lose the power to do the same. Furthermore, routine actions such as renting a room from a local 'big man', working in a market and paying dues to the 'market manager', or volunteering to partake in communal clean-ups, all reflect how individuals enter into and consolidate informal relations of power and social contracts which defy the will of local and national government to halt settlement.

Thus, the forms that citizenship, property and authority take are context dependent and social processes, and their practical worth is related to the extent that 'rights' are enjoyed and recognized (Lund 2016). In brief, the shaping of social contracts in Old Fadama is informal with a very low level of institutionalization and

reflects *work in progress* that may or may not proceed to a consolida-
tion of recognized local rights of property and citizenship by local,
public authority. Exploring these social dynamics provides useful
insights into the ongoing fabrication of modern urban areas through
mundane activities, which theoretically aims to contribute to understandings of state formation in urban Africa which is not prearranged
by statutory branches of government.

The wider context: urbanization and government dilemmas

By the end of the twentieth century there were more people living
in Ghana's cities than in rural areas (GSS 2013). The overall
annual growth rate of African urbanization is around 3.5 per cent
and is expected to lead to about 84 million more people living in
the continent's capitals by 2050, and increase total urban populations to about 1.23 billion.[12] The combined effect of economic
migration, a deficit of urban planning, and expensive accommodation is that many newcomers to capital cities are destined to find
shelter in informal settlements or slum areas. This is because most
urban migrants originate from impoverished rural areas and can
afford only the cheapest urban accommodation. Moreover, social
and extended family networks, remittance streams, informal safety
nets and information about casual labour opportunities are all pull
factors to low-end shelter (Cohen 2006: 24; UN-Habitat 2011:1).
Despite the attraction, however, living and working conditions
for rural–urban migrants can remain uncertain for decades. Plots
that are occupied and built upon seldom belong formally to those
who live on the land, and formal documentation is often ignored,
meaning that rural–urban migration has accompanied the proliferation of numerous sprawling slums and informal settlements in urban
sub-Saharan Africa.

Confronted by the sheer scale of the political, social and economic
challenges posed by either large-scale eviction or relocation (at Joe
Slovo in Cape Town, for example, or Mathare and Kibera in Nairobi),
reluctant governments often have to unwillingly accept long-term
occupation of urban land. Informal settlements support the livelihoods of millions of people, but often the reach and authority of
statutory institutions is limited or even non-existent. The proliferation of urban settlements outside government planning and
regulation demonstrates that processes of informality and mobility

are significant features of contemporary African development. Despite the illegality of many sites, African governments are under constant pressure not only to tolerate but to upgrade conditions by introducing utility and service provision along with necessary infrastructure, as in the case of Africa's largest slum, Kibera in Kenya (Mitra et al. 2017).

It is likely that pressure from multiple sources on governments to recognize and develop informal and illegal settlements will increase in coming years. Yet at the same time, governments' ability to solve the seemingly never-ending, myriad, complex challenges of urbanization and establish decent living standards will be increasingly limited. Across developing countries access to and use of social media for civil society mobilization are increasing and levels of education are higher than in previous generations. There is a heightened awareness of human rights and ability to organize, a surge of NGOs focusing on civil society and urban issues, and growing attention to public health standards in urban areas. Nationally, democratization, local government reform, the holding of multiparty elections, and various land reform plans all place pressure on governments to ease off informal settlements.

The global ambitions of the hyped Millennium Development Goals as well as the ongoing Sustainable Development Goals (SDGs) place further pressure on governments to alleviate the living conditions of the poorest urban inhabitants (Chapter 6). The fulfilment of global developmental ambitions such as the SDGs can mean that governments may be forced to abandon large-scale evictions as a policy option and to shift political rhetoric to the relocation or upgrading of illegal sites of residence. This change is evident in Ghana, where momentum for the clearance of Old Fadama began to slacken after pledges and pro-poor statements made by African governments (including Ghana) at global events. These included the International Covenant on Economic, Social and Cultural Rights (ICESCR) in 2003, where forced eviction was highlighted as illegal, the 2004 World Urban Forum in Barcelona, and the 2006 World Urban Forum in Vancouver. Still, in January 2004 the Ghanaian Minister of Tourism and Modernization of the Capital City emphasized that Old Fadama would be gone by September of that year (Songsore et al. 2014: 84). One of the most recent global events aimed at improving life for the most marginalized urban inhabitants and addressing the combination of ecological and economic crisis of cities was the United Nations Conference on Housing and Sustainable Urban Development, held in October 2016 in Quito,

Ecuador (Schindler 2017). As pressure mounts from global agendas, there are also numerous other international agreements that obligate Ghana not to undertake forced evictions and to commit to protecting basic rights. These include:

- The International Covenant on Economic, Social, and Cultural Rights
- The Convention on the Rights of the Child
- The Convention on the Elimination of All Forms of Discrimination against Women
- The International Convention on the Elimination of All Forms of Racial Discrimination
- The African Charter on Human and People's Rights
- The African Charter on the Rights and Welfare of the Child
- The Protocol to the African Charter on Human and People's Rights on the Rights of Women in Africa.
  (Amnesty International 2011)

Although a toning down and assuaging of eviction rhetoric is evident over the last decade with hints of upgrading, the legal imbroglios of Old Fadama remain. Successive Ghanaian governments are all too aware that any recognition of Old Fadama risks encouraging other squatters to settle on land that is not theirs. And simultaneously, and somewhat ironically, the global drive to reduce the number of people living in slums has been used by developing-country governments (including Ghana's) to justify their demolition and evict settlers (Huchzermeyer 2011).

The cumulative effects of local, national and global burdens and generally increased awareness of human rights are that Ghanaian governments have struggled to secure a balance between, on the one hand, the fulfilment of diverse pro-poor socio-political and economic developmental agendas, and, on the other, the formulation and affirmation of a coherent set of land laws that protect property rights, and discourage unlawful settlement. In these perspectives the examination of informal governance in Old Fadama may be considered as *representative* of similar processes occurring in other urban African countries where government's ability to govern is restricted. Hopefully, the themes of the book consequently resonate beyond its immediate empirical setting and can add to our understanding of what we consider 'ordinary' cities (Robinson 2006), and of African cities transformed by globalization, or emergent as 'globalized cities' (Grant 2006). In a broader context, therefore, I suggest that the growth of informal settlements in Africa should be seen not only as exemplifying urban crisis but as exemplifying an informalization of governance that runs parallel to formalization processes. As discussed below, the two processes can be both complementary and in competition with one another. This shows African governments trying to strike a balance between different and often contradictory developmental, political and democratic objectives. The corollary is often ill-conceived 'quick fixes' that belie the immense challenges of altering the forces that produce illegal and informal settlements.

Method considerations

The investigation was exploratory, inductive and processual, with the observation of everyday events and recording of local people's experiences extrapolated to gain understandings of broader societal processes. As such, the book is based on micro cases and situations that for the most part were immediately observable and constituted common knowledge for local people, who are both the observers of and participants in the actions and events (Lund 2014). The data collection was inspired by an interest in wanting to understand everyday struggles, rudimentary activities, and how people generally tackle living in the informal settlement. Therefore, features of everyday life are the main focus while decision-making processes of formal levels of government are secondary. Still, I did not plan to focus on how legal conditioning shapes urban governance. This only came about after numerous visits to the site that established a realization that the settlement's legal status actually had significant influences over a whole range of activities.

The book is the product of research undertaken between 2014 and 2017, based predominantly on qualitative data collected by the author and research assistants in Old Fadama and Accra over numerous visits. The main data collection methods were semi-structured interviews with informants chosen semi-randomly and from snowballing, participant observation, and focus groups interviews. Over fifty semi-structured interviews were carried out with a range of stakeholders, notably with residents of Old Fadama, community leaders, traditional authorities, local entrepreneurs, representatives from NGOs, local business owners, public officials from local government, and parliamentarians.[13] Data collection from residents focused on their experiences of getting by and gaining access to shelter, employment, education, security and land,

and how encounters and situations around such things structured daily lives, shaped socio-political relationships, and configured informal governance and local rights. Interview topics and focus group discussions covered numerous relevant topics. They included understandings of belonging, relations between city authorities and the settlement, personal histories of settlement, everyday concerns and reflections about making a living, efforts to reduce uncertainty, social norms, understandings of recognition and power, physical and material features of life and development, and avenues of informal representation. Moreover, the focus group interviews and discussions with different groups of residents covered topics such as the pros and cons of living in Old Fadama compared to northern home towns; the best way to find a good place to stay and places to work; understandings of the most influential people in the community; and what it means to be a member of a community.

To gain knowledge about informal governance, data collection also focused on local initiatives that solved community problems as well as group norms and expectations of compliance, obligation, security and law and order. Besides the specific data collection methods, Old Fadama was visited on a daily basis and hundreds of hours were spent hanging out in different places and talking to different people. Participant observation and semi-structured interviews proved valuable for revealing respondents' subjective viewpoints and opinions, and the countless visits enabled trust to be established and necessary adjustments to be made as research progressed. However, it was at times difficult to triangulate the data and to substantiate individual testimonies of specific events. And it was often impossible to verify whether things actually occurred as they had been described. This inability to corroborate sources and stories often meant that data could only be used to ascertain subjective views and could not be used as factual data. To exemplify briefly, one group of residents complained that many plots of land in the settlement had been sold at high prices by a particular chief, but it was not possible to verify the claim. Still, the uncorroborated data were useful as they revealed tensions between different groups over land control. Another challenge, rather like that of trying to pinpoint multiple moving targets, was to find out what has happened and what is happening, while the situations themselves and people's understandings of them are changing and in the making. Therefore, I have endeavoured to present different and relevant perspectives grounded in the ethnographic present, although there is still a risk that things may have played out differently to how they are presented here.

With explorative and ethnographic data collection it is often the case that gaining access to interlocuters and the successful gathering of data are often due to good fortune – in striking up conversation; being able to track down people of interest; establishing trust and rapport; meeting respondents interested in sharing stories; or simply being in the right place at the right time for chance meetings with influential individuals. Still, the data collection was spread over a range of informants with the aim of reaching as many different types of people from all social layers and positions of power. So, even though the number of informants was limited, it was possible to distinguish patterns. Through triangulation and iteration, a satisfactory degree of saturation was therefore reached to the point where the information retrieved from different people and situations started to become predictable (Lund 2014). Overall, the data collection from the site as well as secondary sources enabled the examination of different dimensions of the settlement in local, national and global perspectives. Particularly, the field work allowed individual representations and experiences at the micro level to be situated in the broader institutional and structural features in which they were entangled.

To ensure internal validity and quality in relating gathered data to the formulation of conceptual and theoretical propositions, it was important to question the credibility of the book's constructed narrative at every stage. In practice, this meant a constant dialogue between my own interpretations of the data and ongoing assessments of whether these were accurate representations of the realities under scrutiny (Bryman 2008; Sarantakos 1994). A further concern was the realization that research *locations* could influence the quality and type of the data collected, the ways in which questions were posed and answered, and inadvertently lead to an overemphasis on the roles of 'researcher' and 'interlocutor'. For example, meetings in government buildings often yielded coy and formal answers because informants assumed the role of 'professional government official sitting behind a desk'. Information gathered from the same respondent in Old Fadama, by contrast, often had a more chatty and spontaneous character, as the unwitting role of 'government official with sleeves rolled up in touch with the locals' was assumed by the informant. As data collection progressed, the frustrations of arranging meetings and interviews with senior political figures meant the focus turned more to exploring the micro-level experiences of ordinary people. In turn, this has meant that more attention is given to the interests and positions of and differences between 'ordinary people' than those of formal political actors, institutions and levels of government. One consequence is that the heterogeneity of state institutions and different positions of specific state actors are not detailed.

The above experiences confirmed that it is often neither possible nor helpful to completely detach oneself from the object of a social science investigation. And fieldwork provided constant reminders that, as I was trying to understand manifestations of authority and power in Old Fadama, so my presence and continual questioning were influencing how this 'evidence' was performed, expressed, interpreted and experienced by others. Predictably, the biggest challenges of data collection arose because of my own individual characteristics that could not be changed or concealed – such as being resourceful, male, British and a white outsider seeking to 'understand' Africans who were much poorer. The power inequalities between me and almost all others made it impossible to melt into the background. And the very obvious physical depravity of Old Fadama made it difficult not to adopt a vision of the place as exceptional, postcolonial particularism. It was therefore difficult not to continually make mental lists of all the surrounding developmental failures and normative deficits, from lack of basic sanitation, to finding a quiet place to talk, to breathing clean air. The challenge here was to gain an understanding of the Old Fadama environment and disregard a personal, robotic cultural urge to make comparisons between the things I took for granted in my home environment when these were wanting in Old Fadama.

The unprepossessing aspects of Old Fadama ensure its low status ranking among many residents of Accra. This came out clearly in conversations with well-to-do Ghanaians such as professionals, politicians and academics, as well as members of the affluent, 'blingy' middle class in Accra's vibrant night life. When sharing plans related to writing about and studying Old Fadama, I was frequently met with looks and words that said plainly: 'What the hell are you hanging out there for?' or 'There's nothing in that place for people like you!'. Sometimes, public officials appeared bothered I was writing about 'that place'. Their views appeared to reflect either a genuine sense of embarrassment that a foreigner should want to pry into and write about such a place, or well-meaning attempts to direct me to towards a worthier and more productive object of study. Either way, the views exemplified how 'Old Fadama' experiences stigma. My 'high' status, however, also made it easier to manoeuvre between stakeholders in different positions of power and gain the confidence of a wider range of individuals than would otherwise have been possible.

I have endeavoured to reproduce and replicate recorded voices as accurately as possible in written form, without changing the meaning and spirit of what was said by the informants. However, although almost all interviews were undertaken in English, it was often necessary when writing up to reconstruct and reformulate sentences, as well as to compress narratives, and sometimes to omit or add words for clarity. The object is to ease reading and improve understanding and grammar, but this has meant that some of the quotations are not verbatim reproductions. To protect identities many of the names have been changed and anonymized.

Outline of the book

The book is structured around individual reflections and experiences of different residents in Old Fadama. The situations that these ordinary people find themselves in and their experiences provide a grounded basis for the analytical concepts of property and citizenship, emerging authority and local logics of informal governance, and the broader social, economic and political imperatives (Thorsen 2017). The chapters aim to provide empirically rich extracts that capture the successes and failures of six protagonists who comprise a diverse group of long-term residents. A few have managed to escape the forces of poverty that drove them to the city in the first place and have established successful careers from the micro-opportunities that have come their way. The protagonists have all experienced random elements, lucky breaks as well as near-crippling bad luck, and there are no clear-cut drivers of their various successes and failures. They include two women and four men, and generally the men are more successful than the women. Although all experience long-term, precarious life situations, the relative success of men compared to women is not a coincidence but, in some ways, reflects important patterns of cultural and socio-political gendered power relations evident all over Ghana.

Frederick is a male, ethnic Akan, and fifty-five years old. He is married, with three children aged five to seventeen, has a BA and is saving to study for an MA in business or politics. Appearing in the first vignette, he is a small-scale entrepreneur and the director of a one-man NGO. He raises money for various local development projects and also aspires to formal politics. He has experienced success in attracting foreign donors. His main concern is to develop Old Fadama from below and bypass government that 'always gets in the way'.

George is male, forty years old and ethnic Bassare, divorced with two young children. He runs a highly successful chemist shop in Old Fadama, where he has lived and worked for over twenty years. He aspires to be a parliamentarian in a northern Ghana constituency. He is involved in local politics in Old Fadama and the emerging local government organization, OFADA.

Adam is male, in his early fifties, and ethnic Dagomba. As we saw from the second vignette at the start of this chapter, Adam initiated the building of a toll bridge constructed with the aid of his brother to connect Old Fadama with a refuse site frequented by traders in discarded goods. Although he is content, the chronic insecurities he experiences day in, day out mean he regularly thinks about moving back to his home town.

Jemima is female, thirty-eight years old, married with three young children, and ethnic Konkomba. She has a primary-school-level education and has spent her working life as a yam marketer in adjacent Agbogbloshie, together with many family members. She works ten hours a day, six days a week. She describes the yam trade as '*a hard business that is almost never going well; there are many doing it and we all expect it to be hard*'.

Adjua is female, twenty-six years old, single, and ethnic Dagomba. She is an untrained schoolteacher and first started work in Old Fadama as a porter in the vegetable market, bearing heavy head loads. She progressed to employment in a local NGO office providing a savings scheme for young girls, and now looks after up to 100 children in an NGO-run day care centre. There are no 'wages' but in return for the work she receives an allowance that just covers the cost of her one-room lodging. She has a secondary-school education and has lived in Old Fadama for about seven years. Adjua would like to return home but can't because her family is involved in a long-standing and sometimes bloody chieftaincy dispute.

Yaw is male, ethnic Gonja, uneducated, and fifty years old. He is married, with four children under the age of fifteen. Throughout his life he has been a small-time criminal and at times led gangs of bag snatchers and pickpockets. He has lived in the area for almost thirty years but lost 'everything' in a bulldozing operation by city authorities in the summer of 2015. He now sleeps with his family on wasteland in a makeshift cardboard and plywood shelter that has to be dismantled every morning for fear of it being destroyed yet again by police.

Frederick and George are examples of near-nobodies from very modest backgrounds who have become successful middle-class businessmen aspiring to formal politics. Their income sources are much more certain, their livelihoods and homesteads are more established, their socio-economic networks are stronger and their income more regular and business-oriented than the others. But all the protagonists live under the veil of not knowing the political fate of the place they call home, and even the relatively successful often live and work every day for meagre or no income. What stands out from all the protagonists' experiences is therefore that an important dimension of life strategies and life trajectories in Old Fadama is the diversity of exposure to social, economic and political vulnerability. In all, this points to a range of life trajectories in the state of slum which at first glance appear uniform. For Adjua and Yaw, by contrast, life is often harder than when they first arrived in the settlement many years ago, and they ask themselves regularly whether they should move back 'up north'. They represent individuals who experience misfortune in their attempts to navigate changing living situations beyond their control and a general inability to secure meaningful rights from the multiple systems of rules they are surrounded by and invest in. For Adjua and Yaw particularly, the searching out and taking up of opportunistic and insecure labour is an integral part of urban life. As such, they are representative of a substantial part of the working-age population of Old Fadama who have never experienced, and probably never will benefit from fixed wages and agreed working hours, and have experienced near-decades of unending, precarious accommodation conditions. In the 'middle' are Jemima and Adam, who in some ways are relatively settled yet at the same time similarly experience first-hand the nagging, continual uncertainty that comes from living and working in an urban setting where the government does not want them to.

Despite their differences there are also commonalities, as most of the protagonists (except Frederick) have experiences of the conflicts in the northern regions of the country that in different ways either influenced their move to Old Fadama or their reasons for staying. Moreover, all share experiences of the Konkomba yam market, where Jemima continues to work, and where all found their first means of income after arriving in the city. Also, all are examples of individuals who, one way or another, have decided to stay put in the Old Fadama area, even if this was not a first choice and is not a decision they are fully in control of. Some are loosely connected in other ways too: Adjua is a neighbour of George and knows him as the owner of the pharmacy she frequents and as a member of OFADA. Both George and Frederick have worked actively for years for the informal institutions of local government in Old Fadama, OFADA. And all know Adam and have regularly used his bridge. Meanwhile, Frederick is well aware of the crime and insecurity associated with the area where Yaw lives and operates (and which Adjua avoids) and has been a keen supporter of demolishing that particular area.

The following chapters build on the protagonists' experiences and are analysed using the concepts of citizenship, property and authority, and as dimensions of informal governance. The empirical chapters also contain text boxes that supplement the main text with background data, facts, statistics and additional material.

The next chapter, 'Origins and destinations', provides a broad historical background on the north of Ghana and presents drivers of rural–urban migration. A further objective is to provide background features of Old Fadama, with a brief history of settlement and a tour of some geographical and institutional features.

Chapter 2, 'Seeking shelter', substantiates the broad depiction of political and economic development with individual experiences of migration, seeking shelter, and settling into Old Fadama. It examines social and cultural tensions in home towns as a driver for urban migration and discusses how the reproduction of negative perceptions about home justify staying in Old Fadama. Finally, it shows how divergence in migrants' resource levels influences their citizenship status in Old Fadama, their access to viable shelter, and the informal relations of property they develop.

Chapter 3, 'Gaining and losing land, and soft property', details the making of informal property by looking at the process behind the large land-based developments taking place in Old Fadama. The focus is on how groups of stakeholders manage to access land for developing a school and a hotel that improve local conditions and shape the urban landscape. The chapter also exemplifies cases of government clawing back land from informal settlers which complete the picture of the toing and froing of contests over land between statutory and non-statutory stakeholders.

Old Fadama is situated next to a sprawling agricultural market that draws in traders from all over the country. Chapter 4, 'Shifting yam, and marketplace citizenship', therefore provides a socio-political exploration of the market and forms of citizenship that are produced there. Particularly, we explore the challenges of working in the temporary site of the Konkomba yam market positioned adjacent to Old Fadama from the perspective of yam traders, and show how the perennial inconclusiveness about the issue of relocating the market feeds into historical understandings of regional divides and different forms of citizenship between the north and the south.

Chapter 5, 'Solving problems, and emerging authority', explores the emergence of OFADA as a loose organization of local government in Old Fadama. This organization endeavours to provide a range of basic public services to residents in response to serious developmental challenges, including security, law and order, regulation of construction, and waste management. When OFADA is successful, it shapes the rights of residents and social contracts with the community that underpin local ideas of law. As it endeavours to solve pressing issues, self-governance develops at the same time as the role of statutory institutions oscillates between tacit acceptance, denial of important challenges, and opposition.

The concluding chapter seeks to ground and draw together the main arguments. It reflects on how Old Fadama helps us to think about contemporary urban governance in Africa and draws perspectives regarding the fulfilment of Sustainable Development Goal 11, concerning urban development.

1
Origins and destinations

This chapter outlines the political-historical structuring of developmental divides between the north and south of the country that started with British colonial policy from around 1900. This is relevant because for over a century migration from the north to the south of Ghana has driven urbanization and with it the growth of Old Fadama over the last forty or so years. Thus, the aim is to provide an understanding of the political and historical forces that continue today, contribute to driving rural–urban migration, and which are 'imported' to Old Fadama together with social and cultural norms of home towns in the north of the country. A second objective is to sketch in the background and socio-political and cultural features of Old Fadama. This includes a brief history of the settlement and geographical and institutional characteristics.

A brief history of north–south divides

As in much of West Africa at the start of the twentieth century, colonial expansion in the country known today as Ghana resulted in an unequal distribution of power, wealth and development that favoured southern and especially coastal zones at the expense of inland and northern areas (Ayee et al. 2011). From around 1900 the north and south of Ghana pursued contrasting social, economic and political trajectories that persist today. Southern regions experienced considerably higher levels of investment and development, with the economy grounded in the production, extraction and export of primary produce – mainly cocoa. Up to the present the pattern of 'southern bias' has generally continued, with productive regions the main beneficiary of agricultural investment policies that pursue cash crop and export-oriented production in return for political support as a 'winner-picking' intervention (Diao et al. 2014). Subsequently, the political economy of the south has historically been extraverted, with widespread commodification, market-led growth, limited regulation over goods aimed at increasing exports, and the objective of expanding agricultural markets to the rest of the world (Kay 1972: xvi).

In contrast, the north of the country was established as a protectorate under British rule. As the term suggests, the aim was to control
the pace of economic, social and political development, as well as
to shield the region from the various forces of modernity that were
encouraged explicitly in the south. To these ends the colonial administration designed a set of rules different to those in the south. For
example, restrictive land laws were designed to discourage capital
investment and commercialization. So, in the north the idea was not
to modernize the territory, but to keep things as they were, hold back
on investment and restrict commodification. Controlling the pace of
development in the protectorate aimed at fulfilling a key objective,
which was to channel the north's human resources to the south and
coastal areas, and to establish the 'north' as a labour reserve.

The pursuit of contrasting regional developmental paths in the
colonial period exemplified a dualistic political-economic model.
This was intended to *'dissipate any tendency which might have existed
towards an assimilation of the north into the southern dominated Gold
Coast'* (Staniland 1975: 41). The model ensured a steady flow of
migrants that were necessary for labour-intensive southern plan-
tations, farms and mines, and it transformed northern subsistence
farmers into a migrant force of waged, unskilled labour. The social,
economic and political experiences of the north of Ghana under
colonial administration were reminiscent of other British, as well as
French, West African countries. Governments responded to combinations of agricultural stagnation, disinvestment and developmental
neglect commonly experienced in the northern realms of their colo-
nies by encouraging outmigration and channelling investments and
resources to southern zones. In a Ghanaian context the dualistic
model has been explained as a policy of pacification, deliberate
underdevelopment and explicit isolationism (Brukum 1998; Dickson
1968; Sutton 1989; Plange 1984; Staniland 1975). Underdevelopment
produced characterizations of the north of Ghana and its populace
as backward, resource poor and undeserving, which in turn justified
the concentration of resources and energies in the progressive and
vibrant south. Between 1916 and 1920, for example, labour from the
protectorate constituted 19 per cent of the total labour force of mine
workers in the south, while in the early 1950s some 200,000 northerners moved southwards to work on Gold Coast cocoa farms. A
decade later, the 1960 census recorded a net north–south migration
of over 82,000 (Iliffe 1995: 219; Ladouceur 1979: 22).

The political-economic differences between the north and south of
the country became important features of the national debate with the

formation of political parties in the early 1950s. Politics in the north was infused with references to ethnic and traditional citizenship, and elites demanded that any national government should continue to protect the 'unique' and conservative interests of the north. As such, the 'conservative' north was juxtaposed against the south, and framed by many emerging political leaders as morally inferior and underdeveloped. Consequently, leading political ideas defined the 'north' as having nothing in common with the south (Ladouceur 1979: 101). Still, southern destinations and workplaces remained hugely attractive to migrants seeking to gain an education and to experience social and political change – even if efforts to instil a Ghanaian national sentiment in the 1950s and 1960s were challenged by regionally based interests and deep-seated grievances based on the contrasting colonial experiences of social, political and economic change.

In the decades following independence in 1957 Ghana experienced considerable political upheaval as well as cyclic economic malaise.[1] The long-term political consequence was that it was not until the inauguration of a new Constitution – decades later, in 1992 – that democratic rule returned. From the mid-1980s onwards Ghana embarked on a widespread programme of structural reform programmes demanded by donors and international financial institutions. As was the case in many other sub-Saharan African countries, the general objectives were to liberalize the economy, break up inefficient state institutions, and increase productivity and stability – although the long-terms effects of structural adjustment programmes, and their success in fulfilling their stated objectives, remain unclear (Konadu-Agyemang 2000).

From the late 1980s Ghana also embarked on an ambitious programme of non-partisan local government reform with the demarcation of many new districts and administrative boundaries, together with financial mechanisms that distributed public funds to district assemblies. In 1983 new regions were established in the north and gave the country its present-day political administrative boundaries (Bening 1999). Structurally, however, Ghana's Constitution still provides scope for strong and far-reaching executive power exercised at the centre, which keeps local elites in check and often less responsive to the everyday demands of ordinary citizens (Ayee 2013; Shepherd and Gyimah-Boadi 2004: 9).

The 1992 Constitution requires political parties to have a national base and there are therefore no obvious party-political lines of division between the north and south today. Political mobilization along ethnic or regional lines is also hindered because there are over 100 ethnic groups in Ghana, while national politics is dominated by the two largest parties (the New Patriotic Party and the National Democratic Congress), with some twenty-eight other political parties registered. Subsequently, since Ghana's return to democratic rule in 1992, successive governments are considered in research contexts as ethnically neutral, although public discourse and popular media frequently portray political parties and national political figures in terms of regional or even ethnic sympathies.[2] Political rivalry along regional or ethnic lines is also limited because of the country's diversity in terms of socio-economic, political and cultural categories, and identification in terms of autochthony, gender, age, religion or education. As we shall see in subsequent chapters, the playing out of everyday politics in Old Fadama often presents a microcosm of some of these broader national political and social features of mobilization. For example, it is common to hear that certain ethnic groups only support certain political parties; that groups and leaders 'native' to Accra may perceive 'northerners' as not belonging in the city and urge them to 'go back where they come from'; that government is only interested in the 'south' and is not concerned with the plight of 'northerners'.

Contemporary northern Ghana: poverty levels, inequalities and economic growth

Ghana now enjoys the status of a middle-income country after average economic growth of more than 7 per cent since 2005. But disparities between the north and the south are still observable from a wide range of socio-economic indicators, including health and income levels, the degree of seasonal labour, life expectancy, education, access to drinking water, sanitation, electricity, and the provision of all-weather roads.[3] In almost all rural areas of the north water is scarce and of poor quality, and households are invariably dependent on unreliable standpipes or streams and rivers. Meanwhile, a mere 9.2 per cent of rural households have access to secure sanitation (GSS 2013).

In the Northern Region levels of rural household poverty, defined as the inability to meet all food and non-food needs, have fallen only slightly in recent years owing to the lion's share of economic growth benefiting a burgeoning urban middle class. Nationally, however, levels of extreme poverty since 2006 have nearly halved, and levels of poverty more than halved from 1992 to 2016. This has fulfilled the first Millennium Development Goal, and now just under a quarter of the entire population is considered as living in poverty, less than half the 1992 level. Nevertheless, rural poverty remains over three times higher than urban poverty, and disparities between rural and urban areas continue to widen because rates of urban poverty are falling faster than rural rates. At the same time, child poverty is actually increasing. Meanwhile, consumption by Ghana's wealthiest has increased in recent years at a greater rate than the corresponding level of the poorest, while economic differences between regions have increased at the same time as disparities within regions have widened (Cooke et al. 2016: 1–2).

The geographical developmental disparities in Ghana mean that urban migration continues to the extent that all three northern regions in Ghana experience a net outmigration, which in 2000 amounted to over half a million people (Kwankye et al. 2009: 11). So, despite successes in significantly reducing poverty, outmigration exemplifies prevailing and widening economic inequalities both within and between regions. Altogether, economic development has meant that urban and especially north-to-south migration continues to be an important consideration for many northerners to escape poverty and improve life chances, and as a result nearly 20 per cent of those born in northern Ghana now live in the south of the country (Van der Geest 2011).

The widening economic disparities are evident in relationships between Ghana's human development index and per capita income growth.[4] The economic growth in recent years has not brought widespread improvements in human development across the population and there is very little trickle-down. The dynamics of recent economic growth and shifts in inequality have continued since the discovery of the offshore Jubilee oil field in Ghana's waters in 2007. Moreover, the discovery of oil and gas has meant that Ghana's economy remains dependent on the world prices of a handful of raw materials and commodities for a majority share of its foreign currency. As a continuation from the colonial period, for example, it is still heavily dependent on the export of cocoa, which typically raises about 25 per cent of GDP. And although there has been significant economic growth since 2000, it has not yielded improvements in health and education (Oxfam 2016: 10).[5]

There is a broad political recognition of the need to invest in agriculture as a means both to lift impoverished rural areas, stave off an increasing reliance on the import of basic foods, and curb rural–urban migration. Still, there are few indications that the historical neglect of public investment in agriculture in the north of the country has halted (ibid.). And agriculture in the north is still dominated by small family farms of less than two hectares practising bush fallow with limited mechanization and limited investment. Ultimately, political efforts to support the sector do not balance out the structural challenges of seasonality, market vagaries, credit access difficulties, and other input constraints (ibid.: 55). There are also numerous environmental climatic challenges that are expected to worsen in coming years (Darko and Atazona 2013).

Annual population growth rates in the north are considered high, at over 2.7 per cent, but the three northern regions together comprise only about a sixth of the total population, with a density of settlement that is only about a third of the national average. There are thus fewer political constituencies than in the high-density urban areas of the south; for some critics, this explains the absence of political incentive for substantial agricultural improvements in the north.[6] In recent decades northern economies have advanced considerably across a range of indicators, such as the level and quality of infrastructure (roads, telecommunications, water and electricity) and growth in the service sectors, agribusiness, and numbers of medium-sized companies, although this is predominantly concentrated in urban areas and, particularly, the Northern Region capital of Tamale. For many households, the income from farming alone barely covers basic household expenses and school fees, and they must turn to other income sources such as petty trading. The combination of historic marginalization and climatic and geographical challenges in the north makes it unlikely that uneven levels of regional development will balance out any time soon.

There is a fundamental investment bias towards the south that also draws in migrants from far-flung rural villages. The bias is based on superior economic, social and physical infrastructure, favourable geography and business environment, availability of specialized labour, levels of human resources, services, transport, education, market characteristics, and institutional path dependency, to name but a few. These forces drive people from the north to the south and do not appear to be diminishing. To exemplify how Greater Accra holds much greater incentives, promise and interest, the area attracted approximately 83 per cent of different FDI projects, 4,278 projects, between 1994 and 2015, while the Northern Region attracted a meagre 0.95 per cent, or forty-nine different projects (Obeng 2016: 8).

Cultural and ethnic contentions

The history of economic and political developmental differences between the north and south of the country have been a key driver of rural–urban migration and especially migration to the capital. Other drivers of rural–urban migration in Ghana, however, include social, cultural and ethnic contentions, which often overlap with economic and political dimensions. All over Ghana different groups can experience marginalization, and it is not unusual for mundane contentions to sometimes flare up because stakeholders interpret the situation in ethnic terms. It is particularly the north of the country, including parts of the Northern Region, that have experienced the most widespread and disruptive episodes of ethnic-based violence in recent decades. In different parts of the north there are long-standing disputes over landownership and property rights, identity and citizenship status, which accentuate the significance of ethnic identity and sometimes overlap with clashes about the appointment to positions of traditional authority and chieftaincy.

This was the case following a new 1979 Constitution when pressure for political reform meant the land claims of the largest ethnic groups in the north of the country were supported by government at the expense of the claims of numerous minorities. As a result, parts of northern Ghana experienced a series of ethnic conflicts in the mid-1980s that rippled on over twenty separate episodes from 1985 to 1995.[7] This series of conflicts was marked by the protagonists of the numerous ethnic contests often being described (and describing each other) as superior and inferior, or as stratified or ranked communities, with chief-based, centralized, majority groups fighting against acephalous, minority settler groups.[8] This is the case in contentions between the Dagomba and Konkomba – the former claiming native, higher status over the latter, categorized as a settler group with inferior rights – that flared up sporadically during the colonial period and most seriously in February 1994. Thus, the country experienced structural tensions between, on one side, an 'old' colonial order based on ethnically defined rights to land and higher and lower forms of citizenship grounded in ostensibly traditional power structures, and, on the other, 'new' forms of political authority and representation based on universal national citizenship and ballot-box logic.

Although ethnic violence is not an everyday occurrence, situations can flare up and lead to intimidation, insecurity and anxiety on the basis of one's ethnic identity. This has meant that historically, ethnic identity has been a driver of migration to Accra (Awumbila et al. 2014). The characterizations in terms of 'ethnic' conflict, however, can belie the centrality of land and struggles for political power in such contests (Peters 2004).

Besides rivalry between different ethnic groups, Ghana also experiences a number of internal ethnic group disputes which predominantly centre on competing versions of tradition and customary procedures for the appointment of chiefs. The most significant is between two clans of the Dagomba ethnic group, the Abudu and Andani, and centres on a seemingly unresolvable disagreement over the selection of and appointment to the powerful position of Dagomba paramount chief (Ya-Na). This dispute has erupted in violence on several occasions, notably in 1969, when the traditional dispute became intertwined with national political elections, ethnic voting and factionalism (Staniland 1975). Serious violence also broke out in 2002, when the incumbent Dagomba paramount chief and numerous others were killed in the traditional capital of Yendi (Tonah 2012). Both intra- and inter-ethnic contestations are related to the central role of chieftaincy and traditional institutions. At stake are not only issues of culture but control over land and the occupation of power positions in society.

Communities continue to make their voices heard by powerful state institutions by developing images and symbols that draw on custom and tradition, while historically state institutions have either accommodated or dismissed the different claims. The downside has been that, since the colonial period, some groups' versions of tradition have been erased from history while others have gained opportunities and privileges (Stacey 2014). Thus, *'tradition became a bottomless well of uncertain practice from which endless arguments could be drawn to justify whatever was thought desirable in current practice'*.[9] The 1992 Constitution endeavoured to erase the politicization of tradition by banning chiefs from party politics, guaranteeing the institution of chieftaincy, and forbidding party-political interference in matters associated with customary and chiefly appointments. The separation of chieftaincy affairs and party politics is now an inherent feature of Ghanaian political culture, but at the same time it is very common for political actors to face accusations of interfering in ostensibly traditional affairs, and for traditional actors to face accusations of meddling in party-political affairs.

This section has offered a broad depiction of Ghana's historical, political and economic trajectory, with a focus on developmental disparities between the north and the south and ethnic contentions.

Now we consider the expression of this trajectory in background features of Old Fadama.

Old Fadama: a brief history of contentions and drivers

Settlement in the area known today as Old Fadama is traceable to Hausa and other migrants who established peri-urban villages around Accra from the late nineteenth century (Acquah 1958). Ga settlements date back farther, and the Ga settlement at Agbogbloshie was recognized as a 'native town' by the British colonial administration prior to 1920 following the development of trade between Ga merchants and Europeans (Amoako 2016: 7). Of significance for contemporary contests over land are three political-historical dimensions, all involving competing customary and government interests, and exemplifying entanglements between colonial and traditional systems of law (Grant 2006).

The first dimension was configured in the colonial period when the traditional claims and customary rituals of the Ga ethnic group, for whom the land and lagoon are sacred, confronted a colonial administration seeking to expand urban infrastructure and planning into the area, where by 1920 commercial interests were also looking to lease the lagoon and build a harbour (Grant 2009: 118). In the 1950s a similar political struggle ensued when government planned low-income housing for the Ga in Agbogbloshie and for northern migrants. The housing project was part of a broader plan to accommodate a growing urban population. At this time, however, the serious environmental degradation experienced in later years had not become apparent and the lagoon continued to support numerous fishing-based communities.

The second dimension also involved the Ga ethnic group but took the land-related contest into the period of independence, when Ghana's first government under Kwame Nkrumah expropriated and gained direct control over a large area named 'Accra-Fadama for Korle Lagoon Development'. Accordingly, the land mass was earmarked for manufacturing and light industry in 1961. The land was acquired by government in the public interest, which meant that all other land rights, including customary claims, were annulled. Nonetheless, the area known today as Old Fadama was left largely undeveloped and its relative vacancy and centrality meant it gradually became an attractive site for rural–urban migrants seeking somewhere to settle. Gradually, the expansion of the site by dredging and landfill changed the profile of the landscape and made existing maps inaccurate (ibid.: 120).

The third dimension of land contests in the area was driven by inward migration of people escaping the ethnic conflicts in the north. Further waves of migration swelled the population of Old Fadama and brought high-density housing, informal building and a steady deterioration of the environment. During this process, the socio-cultural significance of the land for the Ga appears to have been ignored by governments and migrants alike. At the same time, Ga influence over Old Fadama lands has waned under the pressure of competition from the range of actors who have carved out niches over land access and distribution. The relatively recent, strong influx of migrants explains present-day, popular narratives that the place now dominated by northern ethnic groups was practically uninhabited some forty years ago and comprised mainly bush, swamp and flood plain.

Members of various ethnic groups, most of whom were Dagomba, fled from northern Ghana to Old Fadama to escape the conflict erupting in the Northern Region and to seek better economic opportunities in the capital. Since, sporadic urban decongestion purges in other parts of the city have driven people to the site. In turn, the increase in population of Old Fadama and neighbouring Agbogbloshie has meant the whole area has become a very significant site of informal economic activities and opportunities. To this end, many street traders and hawkers made the area their 'temporary' home following decongestion and street-cleaning exercises under-taken by city authorities in 1991, when diplomats and governments were in Accra for the Non-Aligned Movement Conference (ibid.: 121). And in 1993, during further ethnic confrontations in the north, the government gave traders temporary permission to establish a yam market in Old Fadama. This meant that the area, already attractive as a refuge, became a hub of agricultural trade linking urban-based Konkomba traders with brethren in the northern yam-producing areas (Chapter 4). More broadly, push factors to Old Fadama have included the historical forces of rural–urban migration as well as the national dearth of rural employment opportunities, cycles of economic contraction, and the withdrawal of state support for agricultural inputs as a consequence of structural adjustment programmes from the late 1980s.

As outlined in the introduction, the growth of Old Fadama has accompanied the common but often ill-defined 'neoliberal' develop-ment of urban space experienced all over sub-Saharan Africa. In this perspective the expansion and persistence of Old Fadama are due to the combination of numerous push and pull factors that include an ever-shrinking volume of affordable housing, the retraction of the state as a provider of social housing, an increased privatization of public space, investor preference for high-end property, a property market lacking effective regulation, the dearth of substantial and realistic long-term urban planning, maladministration and ambiguity of landownership, and pressure on governments to ease off on plans of eradication. The persistence, attraction and growth of Old Fadama as a site of residence is therefore indicative of similar processes found in many other sub-Saharan African countries, where home ownership and affordable renting are out of the reach of most families (Grant 2009: 67). More generally, urbanization in Ghana is also driven by increasing commercialization and commodification of agriculture, an expansion of cash crops, and agricultural fatigue experienced in many rural areas (Amanor 2001; Songsore 2009). Together with the different push and pull factors, the growth of Old Fadama has also been influenced by the contradictory and hesitant stance of different governments, which have either downplayed the 'the issue of Old Fadama', tried and failed with inadequate solutions, and passed the responsibility on to successors.

So gradually, as one public official put it, '*the tumour has grown*'. The settlement has taken root with de facto extension by different governments and tacit permission for or acceptance of people residing and operating businesses there temporarily. Each government 'pass' means Old Fadama continues as a magnet for new and returning rural–urban migrants, and its developmental challenges are notched up. Now, a plethora of services including food stalls, accommodation, technical facilities and transport offices link the area with Accra as well as with inter-regional agricultural trade. This was another step towards Old Fadama becoming a significant first stop for all kinds of hopeful urban migrants seeking cheap accommodation and casual labour in the capital, or returning to the capital to take up seasonal, casual labour within the agricultural cycle.

The position of numerous Ga traditional authorities and customary figures from the seven key priesthoods of the Ga state is that successive governments since 1961 have breached their side of the expropriation agreement of the early 1960s. They emphasize that all governments have failed to provide the promised local development and to preserve the natural ecology of the Korle Lagoon, acknowledged as a sacred site. Ga traditional and spiritual figureheads frequently voice strong opposition to the settlement (interview, Ga priest, 9 July 2014).

Old Fadama: general living conditions

As an informal settlement Old Fadama stands out because of its size, homogeneity in terms of physical containment, history of contentions with governments, and its clearly visible, myriad developmental challenges. It comprises mostly single-storey buildings, shacks, dwellings and kiosks. The combination of small rooms, the ever-present blanket of heat, its population density, outside working conditions and the constant movement of people make it broadly 'horizontal' (Hoffman 2017). The mass of badly built constructions with poor ventilation and lighting means that people are also inclined to spend long periods of the day outside, and this makes the site buoyant for everyday social encounters and it is often busy. Old Fadama is thus very much a face-to-face, or sometimes an in-your-face, kind of place, and it's a challenging task for many residents to find peace and quiet. A combination of shacks that have been patched up countless times, one-storey dwellings and kiosks that have predominantly been put together by those who live and work there, and warped lengths of panelling and shoddy breeze-block walling give it a sense of 'homemade-ness'. This means that Old Fadama comprises both 'places' that are defined and definable, as well as mere 'spaces' which are less so (De Boeck and Plissart 2014).

In the national capital of Accra, it is estimated that nearly 40 per cent of the population, or over 1.6 million people, live in slum conditions where a lack of adequate sanitation is one of the most serious concerns (UN-Habitat 2011). The population density of the city as a whole is about 250 persons per hectare and in slum areas averages about 600. Accra has 78 urban slum settlements that vary considerably in size. Of these, 34 are categorized as having either 'insecure' or 'no' access to land tenure (ibid.: 3). Of all these sites, Old Fadama is by far the largest with insecure tenure, and without formal recognition by statutory authorities of rights of residency or occupation. Of all the informal settlements with 'insecure' tenures, however, Old Fadama also stands out because of the long-standing eviction order against it. As in other sites classed as 'illegal', this means that the flow of public service provision is 'low' (Paller 2012). With a population density of over 2,500 people per hectare, Old Fadama is probably the most crowded place in the city, if not the country, and is about ten times more densely populated than Manhattan, even though in Old Fadama the majority of people live in single rooms and few structures are higher than two storeys (Farouk and Owusu 2012: 55).

1.1 Old Fadama street view
Source: author

1.2 View of Old Fadama over clogged waterway
Source: author

In the Hausa language, 'Fàdáma' means marshy agricultural ground, and the site's physical geography contributes to the mounting and multidimensional developmental pressures. It comprises a 31-hectare, roughly triangular site that is hemmed in by a major trunk road, the Abose-Okai Road to the north, and the Odaw river and Korle Lagoon waterways that flank the other sides. Settlers manage to expand the site by filling in and diverting waterways, building on banks, and levelling off flood plains with crude mixtures of sawdust and assorted city waste. The landfill provides a spongy and often unstable foundation, causing many constructions to collapse or subside, and acting to discourage the erection of multi-storey buildings. According to city authorities, the unregulated practices of encroachment, landfilling and building by settlers have greatly increased the risk of flooding not only in Old Fadama but farther upstream in central areas of Accra, because the flow of water, waste and effluent from the city out into the Gulf of Guinea is obstructed (Image 1.2).[10]

In aerial pictures the most obvious change in land use since 2000 is the diminishing of forest and bush cover which used to cover the south-east side of the settlement but has now disappeared completely.[11] What remained was an unfertile wasteland, which up to 2010 became a new site for house building, but by 2015 appeared to have reverted to wasteland again, possibly because houses and other forms of shelter had been destroyed by rising water levels after storms and heavy rains. The site has experienced small fluctuations of distances between 'border' areas marked by the last row of housing, gullies that mark waterways, and where wasteland turns to scrub and mud. The relative shrinking and ballooning of Old Fadama over a cycle of several years is reminiscent of atrial fibrillation. Occasional heavy flooding can effectively shrink the size of the settlement by forcing the abandonment of patches of shelters, and sporadic demolition exercises undertaken by city authorities along perimeter areas similarly suck in its diameter, increase distances to permanent waterways, and encourage a retreat of perimeter housing. However, flooding recedes and demolition gives way to a gradual renewal of building and creeping encroachment. And the site balloons anew with a narrowing of distances between constructions and waterways and an increased risk of flooding yet again (Image 1.3).

The environmental context

Old Fadama suffers from serious pollution and environmental degradation and constant blame is heaped on the settlement for destroying the natural ecology of the lagoon area, the environmental and ecological degradation of the area, and damage in particular to the drainage system of the Odaw river. However, the widespread damage does not emanate solely from Old Fadama, but stems as well from numerous other high-density informal settlements in the

1.3 The Odaw river with Old Fadama
Source: author

northern reaches of the Korle Lagoon. Pollution is moreover attributable to countless unregulated small- and medium-sized oil and
chemical industries located all along adjoining waterways (Image
1.3). These discharge waste at will, including *'motor oil, diesel fuel,
petrol, paint, solvents, dry cell and vehicle batteries, metallic and/or oily
sludge or solvents and asbestos materials'* (Songsore et al. 2014: 65). In
the early 1990s the adjacent site of Agbogbloshie emerged as a centre
for scrapping, dismantling and reusing domestic and imported
household appliances, e-waste and computers, and since then has
attracted global media attention as an expanding, if also toxic, high-
tech junkyard.[12] The site has developed to such an extent it has been
described as *'the highest toxic threat to human life'* on the planet in a
2013 study of 3,000 sites in 49 countries.[13]

The eviction notice served in 2002 by the Accra Metropolitan
Authority followed approval of an internationally funded, large-
scale environmental clean-up campaign named the Korle Lagoon
Restoration Project (Grant 2009: 120). Since the early 1990s
numerous other interventions have aimed to improve the environmental status of the Korle Lagoon area, including investments in
hardware and software for waste management and plans for a drastic
reduction in the flows of waste effluent directly into waterways.
There have also been awareness campaigns, drainage improvement
systems, sanitation upgrades, and landscape beautification plans. To

date, however, all have failed to provide substantial and long-lasting solutions (Songsore et al. 2014: 3). Indeed, the casual observer of Old Fadama and the Korle Lagoon area would be hard pushed to find evidence of any government or investment successes in terms of basic pollution control or environmental management. The various efforts to restore the lagoon have been impeded by numerous factors, including contractual disputes, mismanagement, litigation, politicization, and the encroachment of building onto lagoon banks. The waste management challenges experienced at Old Fadama are part of a much wider problem experienced in Greater Accra. Only 15 per cent of the population are connected to a sewer system, and for years on the other side of the estuary to Old Fadama (and up to November 2016 at least) up to 750 tons of untreated faecal sludge were poured directly onto the beach and into the sea every day at Korle Gonno (disparagingly known as Lavender Hill owing to the stench) in the absence of effective sewage treatment facilities (Diener et al. 2014).[14]

Demography

The rate of increase in Old Fadama's population is uncertain because of limited demographic censuses in an area officially unrecognized as a residential area of the city. In 2009 a census of Old Fadama was carried out that coincided with large-scale demonstrations against eviction, an increased organizational capacity of residents, the formation of local NGOs, and international support gained from global movements taking up the cause of Millennium Development Goals. The census numbered the population at just over 79,000, which was much higher than government envisaged (Housing the Masses 2010; Farouk and Owusu 2012). Some 99 per cent were Ghanaian and 73 per cent from one of Ghana's northern regions, comprising Northern Region (66 per cent), Upper West (3 per cent) and Upper East (4 per cent). About two-thirds were Muslim.

There were almost equal numbers of males and females, with 38 per cent below the age of 18, 76 per cent aged 35 or under, and just 1 per cent above 55 years of age, making a large working-age percentage of the population. Ethnically, the largest group was Dagomba (49 per cent), followed by Akan (15 per cent) and Konkomba (12 per cent). Some sixteen other Ghanaian ethnic groups constituted the remaining quarter, while nearly 90 per cent considered Old Fadama their permanent home, and just 1 per cent of residents were non-Ghanaian (Housing the Masses 2010). Regarding the drivers of settlement, a majority (95 per cent) had moved there primarily for business purposes or in search of work, while a small percentage had migrated because of conflict (2 per cent). For some 83 per cent, Old Fadama was their first destination after arriving in Accra. Out of the population of under eighteens, about 65 per cent had not attended any form of schooling (ibid.).

Conclusion

The broad characteristics of Ghana's historical development explain why generations of people have moved from the north to the south of the country. Despite significant social, economic and political advances, many northern-born individuals feel a deep sense of unfulfilled ambition, and yearn to explore their potential in a national capital that lures them with the promise of opportunities, excitement and independence. It is therefore understandable that capital cities are favoured over a rural life often characterized by labour-intensive agricultural graft and the meagre income accrued from family farms. But, at the same time, Old Fadama is certainly not an easy place in which to live and, for many, the ambitions that drove the decision to migrate remain unfulfilled for years that often stretch into lifetimes. In many ways, these forces make Old Fadama an 'estuarial zone' that is peripheral to the rest of the city and statutory institutions, and where alternative logics of exclusion and inclusion develop (Landau 2014). In the next chapter we focus on individual cases of migration and experiences of ethnic contention as explanations of migration to Accra, and follow different outcomes in the lives of those who sought to settle within Old Fadama.

Health and environmental burdens
(Songsore 2014 et al)

Old Fadama is part of the much larger Korle-Lagoon complex, which covers other squatter settlements and market areas as well. All are characterized by poor housing, inadequate potable water supply, lack of sanitation facilities, overcrowding, insect manifestation, and the predominance of infectious and communicable diseases including HIV/AIDS. As an area of countless unregulated small-scale industrial enterprises, and poorly regulated large industrial sites, the waterways of the complex are extensively polluted. In Old Fadama there is no systematic pest control, collection of waste, or management of the blocked and polluted drainage systems. This creates *'ideal conditions for mosquitos, flies, cockroaches, rodents, and other vermin to breed'* (Songsore 2014 et al: 8). Old Fadama provides ample evidence of *'people cooking very close to choked gutters and dumping sites [and] people defecating around food vending and cooking areas and also food prepared with unwashed and rotten vegetables'*, making the settlement endemic for *'cholera, typhoid, and diarrhoea'*. Subsequently, a high proportion of diseases recorded in the Accra Metropolitan Health Area are attributable to the poor environment. In 2008, malaria cases comprised 43.2% of all recorded diseases, ARI (Acute Respiratory Insufficiency) 10,3%, hypertension 5.9%, diarrhoea 4.4%, and skin diseases 3.5%, with between from 67 and 100% of all recorded diseases in the Korle Lagoon complex ascribed to the environment (Songsore 2014 et al). Serious air pollution has many sources, including almost constant traffic congestion comprised of often very poorly maintained lorries, buses, taxis, and motorbikes, the burning of tyres and electric cables on waste ground to recover copper, the spread of dust from timber merchants, and fumes and gases from welding, blacksmiths, and vulcanizing workshops. Across 12 water sample sites in the complex the following 'highs' were recorded.

	High	WHO level	Sites at or above WHO level (n=12)
Temp.	39°	> 35	8
pH	12.76	6-9	2
Colour	900	200	6
Turbidity[i]	188	75	5
Conductivity[ii]	72,200	1,500	11
Alkalinity[iii]	28,500	400	7
TDS[iv]	42,252	1000	12
TSS[v]	644	50	8

i   NTU Nephelometric Turbidity Units
ii µS/cm
iii mg $CaCO_3$ per litre
iv Total Dissolved Solids, mg/l
v   Total Suspended Solids, mg/l

In 10 out of the 12 water test sites, the concentration of lead (Pb)
exceeded maximum WHO limits. In 3 out of the 12 sites the level
of arsenic was exceeded. Levels of mercury were exceeded at 5
sites and all except 2 had *'heavy loads of coliform and Ecoli'*. Of
8 sites tested, 7 failed to meet the recommended WHO level of
5 mg/l of DO (dissolved oxygen). Adapted from Songsore et al
2014:73

2
Seeking shelter and freedom

Old Fadama is full of individual destinies of rural–urban migrants who share the common feature that none are actually from Old Fadama. The priority for all who arrive is therefore to search out viable shelter or land wherever they can find it. The journey to Old Fadama is also about escaping from a range of unfavourable social conditions at home and deciding things for yourself. This chapter consequently focuses on individual experiences of moving to Old Fadama because of ethnic tensions and restrictive social customs at home, and the pursuit of opportunities and experiences of new-found freedoms. It explores how migrants' ideas and perceptions of northern home towns justify their remaining in the challenging urban setting of Old Fadama. Related, it is shown that the process of 'settling in' is rarely finalized, confirmed or considered finished for the migrants. This is because there is a constant striving for stability and a certain future that is persistently offset by events in home towns as well as the unknowability, flux and tensions of the new, urban surrounding context. The process of establishing oneself in the community to reduce the uncertainty that comes from living in a place illegally means that people do not settle here as squatters in the same way that they squat in vacant public buildings and *neglected* spaces, and where the goal is to inhabit ruins and make use of the 'already built' (Hoffman 2017). Rather, individual investments in shelter, and the sweat equity involved in carving out both social and physical space in the densely populated Old Fadama, provide emergent possibilities to reinvent oneself while redefining the surrounding physical space.

Conceptually, seeking shelter and settling in exemplify how citizenship and property do not derive from legal status but emerge from the social contexts people find themselves in and their ability to negotiate, adjust and improve on their status as they move from the rural to the urban environment. Similarly, informal property relations and local citizenship status are established not through specific institutionalization processes of politico-legal authorities but through ad hoc social engagements and encounters between ordinary people. In a broader perspective, the chapter shows how the new urban environment impacts on the unfolding lives and social organization of migrants, and how migrants' lives shape the urban environment they become a part of (ibid.).

Escaping social pressures and ethnic contentions

Many of the people living and working around Old Fadama spoke of social and cultural institutions in home towns as a primary influence behind their migration, rather than specific economic motivations (Kwankye et al. 2009: 4). Young people especially in northern Ghana can experience a range of constricting social and cultural norms based on age and gender. These include compulsory obedience towards elders and senior family members, the restriction of movement, the inability to pursue ambitions and, particularly for females, control over who they are friends with. It is commonplace amongst poor households that older children are expected to care for siblings, and females often miss out on primary-school education. This is because of family demands for their (often unpaid) labour, either in the home, on farms, in family businesses or as petty traders. Labour demands on children in rural areas often combine with long distances to schools and a dearth of transport (Porter et al. 2011: 407).[1] Thus, children can experience a sense of entrapment as they have little influence or choice over family decisions relating to the numerous demands placed on their labour, which come to define their marginalized position within homesteads.[2] Such restraining conditions inevitably influence the movement of young people away from homesteads to cities. In 2000, for example, some 18,000 Ghanaian children between the ages of five and seventeen were registered as working in Accra, although the real figure is undoubtedly much higher. Just under half of those registered, moreover, had migrated to Accra from other parts of the country independently and were unaccompanied by adults (Awumbila and Ardayfio-Schandorf 2008: 171).

As presented in the last chapter, escape from ethnic conflict is a driver of rural–urban migration in Ghana and a common explanation given especially by older migrants who moved to Old Fadama in the late 1980s and early 1990s.[3] One such seemingly irresolvable dispute erupts from time to time in the town of Bimbilla, the traditional capital in the state of Nanun.[4] On the surface it concerns a deep-seated disagreement over the selection of the Bimbilla Naa, or paramount chief of Nanun. The vexed issues include which families, institutions and actors should have the right to decide the matter, and which stakeholders should be able to decide if the 'correct traditions' have been followed. In recent years the dispute has been traceable to 1999 and arguments about who was to succeed as paramount chief after the death of the Bimbilla Naa, Naa Abarika II. A stand-off culminated in June 2014 with the killing of a leading chief in the traditional area, Naa Dasana Andani. Since then, ethnic violence and killings in and around Bimbilla have been sporadic but common events and typically result in a heightened security presence, the imposition of curfews and increased tensions between different communities.

In February 2017 the dispute erupted again when an estimated twelve people were killed in gunfights. As is typically the case with ethnic conflicts, in Bimbilla everyday disagreements as well as relatively banal criminal acts risk being interpreted in ethnic terms, with the danger of igniting communal fighting between rival youth groups. For ordinary people it is the fear of violence as well as violence itself that disrupts the flow of life and brings everyday activities to a stop: markets are not frequented, schools are closed, transport options are limited, shops do not open, streets are quiet, soldiers roam the area, and people stay inside, scared to go outside or tend to their farms. For many in Bimbilla, the dispute is both annoying and frightening. For some people, their close affinity to one of the contesting lineages has made Old Fadama a necessary refuge, although the move is not made by choice. This is the case for Adjua, who in the following explains her predicament of not wanting to stay in Accra, but not wanting to return home to Bimbilla, either.

> In Bimbilla the trouble kicks off now and then, usually followed by bloodshed. When it happened in 2014 there were senior members of my family and brothers there. So, if I return I can easily get dragged into it. This wasn't the original reason for moving to Accra, but it has meant I am kind of stuck here now. In 2012 I went back to Bimbilla to see if I could further my education but I couldn't get the money together and it was also getting hot [there was trouble brewing] so I went back to Accra. Being in Bimbilla you cannot get work or earn money for one day in a whole month. In addition, there is no peace. Therefore, I cannot stay in Bimbilla for now. Sometimes you may be in your house, and you do not know what is happening in the town, and then you suddenly hear that people are dying. Then when you come out you will see and hear gunshots all over. So, when you're in this kind of town you may lose your life. You can be in the

wrong place and when it happens and you run, you can get hurt or you may die. One of my friend's fathers died in the conflict. Then later, the same thing happened to some of the boys I went to school with. They were shot. Three of my friends have lost their fathers in the Bimbilla conflict, and my grandmother's house was burned down. She was there in her room. They admitted her to hospital for a week before she was discharged but she passed away two months later. Had it not been for the fire she would still be alive. They also shot an uncle of mine. Every year, every June [the anniversary of the killing of the paramount chief], is when they start fighting.

She continues:

I am more concerned for my young brothers, so I encourage them to be sent to the next village. They are still young, only twenty-one and twenty, so for them, whenever they are in town and it's happening, they have to run home and lock themselves in. If they don't have the means to get home early something can happen to them. They will be targeted because of the family. So, it's all waiting to be retaliated. What will happen is that they will also kill someone from another family so that the other family will feel the same pain. So, for now Bimbilla is not something that will resolve itself. Maybe this is what God wants but you know northerners! So, it's a difficult choice. In Old Fadama too you can have a good cause to run! But here is somehow better than Bimbilla. (Interview, 18 July 2015)

Adjua's account shows how her formal citizenship status is of very little practical use in the unstable local environment of Bimbilla: the formal political system she has access to as a Ghanaian has proved wholly unable to solve the long-standing traditional dispute, while her 'status' as a member of royal family does not translate into any protection of civic rights and actually puts her in danger.

Freedom, 'rightlessness' and agency

Young female head-porters are everywhere in Accra and in terms of citizenship are certainly those that experience the weakest and most ineffective 'rights' because they are predominantly unguarded, poor and resource weak. The issue of young people moving to Accra on their own was a topic of conversation with a group of six young female *kayayei* (head-porters) introduced by Adjua.[5] They were gathered in the office of the NGO where Adjua used to work without pay. They came in weekly to pay small amounts into their savings books, receive advice, and meet and catch up with other head-porters. Although the amount saved by the girls was minuscule, the scheme instilled an awareness of the need to look after money. All of this group were quite timid and appeared immature, and all said they had had very little schooling. This was confirmed when all replied that they could not write and could only read street signs, although it was also clear they were competent at text messaging. None was sure about their age but all were numerate, which was an absolute essential life skill. I imagined the tallest girl to be the oldest and about fourteen years old, although she looked much older.[6] Their appearance together in dusty second-hand clothes and headscarves, clinging to grimy and basic mobile phones, revealed their vocation as head-porters scouring for work. They had a twelve-hour working day that stretched from first light to dusk; on a good day they could earn up to twenty cedis (ca. \$5: 1 cedi = 25 cents), but on a bad day nothing. Still, all were adamant that they enjoyed their everyday life in Accra, despite the hardship.

A main reason given for staying in Old Fadama was because it contrasted with life in their far-flung rural home villages, where there was an expectation and demand that they should obey unquestioningly the wishes of older male members in their household, as well as the random demands of older people around the village. They nodded in unison, saying that at home they felt not only bored and disillusioned with rural life, but downtrodden and restricted as well. Moving to the city on their own was an escape and an emancipatory project. With some contributions from the others, the oldest explained that they had all worked a couple of seasons in the yam market and that it was normal for them and their peers to travel unaccompanied. They could move freely between the north and the south, but seldom did so because of the expense:

> We are all from the north, but different parts. For me, it can
> take two whole days to get home from here. In my home village,
> wherever I go, there is always someone older telling me what to
> do. There are my older brothers, my father, and my fathers' wives
> at home.[7] Then there are the housemasters and bigger boys at
> school, and the older women in the market. They all tell me what
> to do, where to go, who to be with and not be with, what to wear,
> when to do this and not to do that. Who needs all that? Living

in Old Fadama there is much less of all that. Yes, it is hard and you are on your own, and you have to be careful how you behave. You can get in trouble [get pregnant], get robbed, and beaten. You need money. You really need money. But there's more than that here, and there is much more here that is up to you. We can't do what we want, but it's more up to you to do the right thing, without having everyone else telling you what to do. That's the difference between here and our homes. That's why I am here. (Interview, 3 August 2015)

The importance of deciding for oneself was reaffirmed when I asked whether any one of them would like to go home, and if they would if they could afford the fare (I was considering giving all of them the bus fare home). But at this, several laughed and replied they would like to visit home but would almost definitely return to Accra as soon as possible. The young girls' views on the matter arose from a combination of experiences of unfavourable and sometimes deteriorating social relations at home, a longing for something else and better, and developing understandings that if 'something' was going to happen for the better, it would happen in the new urban environment. Hence, the understanding was of infinitely more and better opportunities available in the city than at home, and of trying to stay in the city and decide for oneself for as long as possible, almost regardless of how bad things got. Related, the principal aim of these young girls was not to earn a lot of money and fulfil dreams of richness, for they had all learnt very quickly that such an outcome was highly unlikely and it was stupid to expect it. Rather, embarking on a new life in Old Fadama, even for a few months, was about getting away and maximizing an individual ability to do what you want. A group of young boys working in the yam market as labourers had a similar outlook. On the one hand they understandably wanted to earn as much money as they could, but on the other they were well aware that this was unlikely. For them, staying in Accra was an end in itself, almost a rite of passage to adulthood. And to do this one needed money, but earning was not the only driver for their presence in Accra. It was the pursuit of freedom – a desire to make basic lifestyle changes, to choose things for oneself, to (re)define oneself, including what one did and with whom.

Independence, individuality and the pursuit of adventure were the goals that made hardship, mundane work and risky living conditions worthwhile for the young male and female migrants. Their motivations and dreams of independence were more realizable than the pursuit of wealth and provided explanations for why young migrants often spend years sharing expensive, cramped and decrepit accommodation. The freedom that went with moving to the city contrasted with what they didn't experience at home. This made the arduous work worth doing and the hard living conditions worth putting up with; as a young man remarked, '*Hard work makes you tough and look good.*' Hence, urban living provided new opportunities to remake who one was and provided a 'kick'. Inevitably, the lifestyle decisions of the young head-porters and labourers did not always arise under conditions of their own choosing. Still, some money could be earned and was often quickly spent on a few treats and essentials. For young females this could mean a new cheap phone, brightly coloured and tight clothes, and new hair, while for older males it was an expensive-looking phone and baggy jeans. In turn, a show of relative ostentatiousness established respect amongst peers and a social footing.

The manager of the local NGO with an office in Old Fadama which initiated the savings scheme for young head-porters near the bottom of the consumer ladder inadvertently pointed this out, saying that many girls had no savings to their name even after many years working long hours. This affirmed the idea that settling in and staying in Old Fadama were not purely a money-making exercise but a social undertaking, and not solely about finding a new livelihood strategy to specifically overcome poverty or lessen economic vulnerability (Oberhauser and Yeboah 2011; Awumbila and Ardayfio-Schandorf 2008).

Still, the pursuit of freedom often had a high price in terms of vulnerability, harassment and exploitation, commonly experienced by young head-porter girls (Yeboah and Appiah-Yeboah 2009). Unaccompanied young migrants to Old Fadama are in effect 'rightless', and it is only through their ability to establish themselves amongst peers and competitors and through social encounters that their 'rights' to belong, to be there, to earn and live and so on have any real value. A key source of harassment and annoyance for young head-porters, as well as all other street traders, and a negator of the local rights that young migrants work hard to establish, is the AMA itself, and particularly AMA revenue collectors, who patrol market areas daily. From a normative perspective it would seem ironic that a threat to the most exposed and vulnerable migrants comes from public officials of state institutions which ostensibly are there to uphold citizens' formal rights.

Perceptions of government

The young head-porters spoke of difficult daily encounters with the AMA, whose staff can frequently be seen scouting and prying around market areas in their orange vests, and who demand an on-the-spot 50-pesewa ($0.12) fee every day from all head-porters in exchange for a ticket, regardless of their age.

In an informal market area close to Old Fadama, we see a bigger version of this cat-and-mouse contest play out between established traders and the AMA. The area is jam-packed and the traffic is at a near-standstill, and pedestrians try to weave through hawkers who wave all kinds of things in their faces. Young head-porters negotiate their way through the crowd with heavy loads. And in the middle of it all are sedentary, haggling traders. They are pitched on the pavement with their wares displayed in front of them and appear oblivious to the build-up around them. Everything from vegetables, fruit, tinned food, notebooks and pens to shoes, second-hand clothes, hardware and telephones accessories is on sale. Suddenly, the bubbling congestion changes to unease. The traders and hawkers scramble to gather their things together and all run in the same direction. The AMA! AMA! AMA! are coming! After a quick initial shout from someone farther up the road all get the message. Women with children under one arm and all they can carry under the other and on their head sprint in unison with the head-porters and hawkers away from a near-charging force of a score of orange vests that descend on the market. In support are a handful of police waving their batons. A tug-of-war ensues as the city authorities go about confiscating the property of the unlicensed traders. Goods spill across the pavement and road and traders grab back and gather what they can before fleeing. The orange vests throw the lion's share onto a flat-bed truck that follows, leaving a trail of jumbled wares and bits and pieces. Different traders curse, shout and cry that they have lost everything and that they didn't get a receipt for all that was taken. Less than an hour later, however, things are more or less as they were before with the gridlocked traffic, and scores of traders, hawkers and head-porters making the pavements and roads near-inaccessible.

The youngest and most vulnerable head-porters (aged ten or eleven) explained how they dread meeting the AMA and despise having to exchange the few coins they earn for a worthless paper ticket. The youngest (who are often the smallest as well) systematically earn the least, get the worst jobs, are least able to bargain and negotiate reasonable prices, and often end up rowing with customers who refuse to pay an amount agreed to beforehand. When stopped on the street by the AMA, it is therefore not uncommon that they are unable to pay the 50 pesewas demanded, simply because they have not earned anything yet. Non-payment normally leads to a combination of bullying and the humiliation of having a single flip-flop confiscated by the AMA, which forces victims to continue working around the city barefoot. The confiscated flip-flop can be returned if the fee is paid, but this demands that girls find the relevant collector, which can be difficult as both porters and collectors do not stay in the same place. One girl explained that if you don't get your flip-flop back the same day you can forget it. In effect, this amounts to a full day's work to replace a pair of flip-flops, which typically cost between 5 and 10 cedi ($1.25–$2.50). The AMA denies that young girls are exploited or that the collection of fees from them amounts to a recognition of hazardous labour undertaken by children under eighteen, which is illegal in Ghana.[8] The AMA skirts around this issue by claiming there are numerous bogus revenue collectors operating in the city, and they are not the ones who collect fees and hassle young girls – a claim that is dismissed outright by all others. City authorities consequently represent controlling and potentially predatory and exploitive forces, which young head-porters may understandably seek to distance themselves from, just as they do from older male figures in home towns, and new, imposing figures they meet in their new environment of Old Fadama. Accordingly, rights and status are carved out through everyday encounters, as new arrivals have to navigate between and adjust to often competing systems of rules and norms stemming from home towns, city authorities and new powers within the informal settlement.

To stay or to go?

So, there are numerous downsides to the new-found freedoms. On the one hand, young migrants experience a meaningful break from rural homesteads where, as one head-porter explained, *'nothing ever happens'*. And Old Fadama allows the moulding of new friendships, the sharing of living space, and the exploration of new horizons. And the young head-porters shared the perspective of a young male working as a scrap metal collector who remarked happily that, yes, he was poor, and often slept under the open sky, but *'I am enjoying my life here. Things happen here, while most of my family are trying to earn a living from very, very, very petty trading back in the north'*.

On the other hand, there are endless disappointments and unpredictability attached to earning money, the inability to save, the insecurities and fears about personal safety, the risk of losing belongings, and the substitution of controlling factors in the city as well as within Old Fadama for controlling elders at home. There are also the grinding social and economic obligations that a return to one's home town after a long stay in the capital entails, which is often a factor when deciding whether it is worth going home or not.

Migrant optimism about remaining in the city thus shapes the production of perceptions about home, and feeds into the common understanding that 'returning home' is akin to some kind of defeat, while staying in the city reflects feisty determination and defining your own course in life. Of course, returning to home towns empty-handed has always been a daunting challenge for migrants, a reminder that home towns are inclined to measure the success of migration in economic terms. This partly explains perhaps why many of the people I spoke to were in one sense proud of their rural home towns yet often problematized life there. Framing home towns negatively helped justify to themselves and to each other their remaining in the city, almost regardless of how bad things actually get, and in the city they were somebody.

The constant pull of the city also means that community leaders in Old Fadama have to accept the futility of 'sending young girls back home' – something that many elders and politicians nevertheless sometimes endeavour to do. Effectively, they are admitting an inability to sustain the dominant social role of males in Ghanaian society as guardians and patriarchs, and the important cultural norm of 'older men knowing what is best for young girls', whereby it is men of high status who bestow 'rights' on younger generations. Clearly, the social organization of head-porters along lines of gender (female) and age (youngsters) suggests agency and opposition to these dominant norms. In effect, their refusal to 'go home' is an assertion of their hard-fought right to decide for themselves to stay in the city. As such, 'sending home' negates both the will and the agency of young migrants and their own ambitions and ability to define their own lives. Old Fadama thus reflects a playing out of much broader generational and societal power divides, the persistence of an ingrained gender and age grid that defines young and resource-weak females as irresponsible and incapable, and the ability of the young to carve out their own futures, endeavouring to organize and improve as best they can their own living and working experience together with peers and like-minded individuals. And while they continually negotiate and endeavour to come to terms with the changing pros and cons of living in the city as compared to returning home, young migrants produce their own norms and 'rights' of belonging that are socially recognized within and between peer groups. As such, what we see are micro-processes of effective citizenship being produced that are influenced by realizations that formal rights do not mean much in the new urban environment and that a main source of insecurity is in fact city authorities themselves. The following now explores how social recognition around gaining access to shelter in Old Fadama influences the making of local property rights.

George

George was one of the many thousands of northerners who moved to Old Fadama in 1994, aiming to escape the ethnic fighting and pursue an education in the capital. At the time the fighting erupted he was about twenty years old and attending Yendi Secondary School, in the capital of the Dagomba traditional area. With relatives in Old Fadama and 'nowhere else to go', he promptly left school for the capital. His first shelter in Old Fadama was a half-open wooden shed used to store yams, in which he ended up living for about six years. Next door was the yam market, where he worked during the day, loading and unloading lorries, at the same time as pursuing senior high-school education. Later, he completed an eighteen-month course as a pharmacy assistant, the break needed to start his own business. Reflecting on moving into Old Fadama, he commented:

> To live in the slum is not easy at all. The shelter I lived in was
> not a *shelter*. It was cold and you got wet. It was not safe and not
> '*yours*', and I could not have any things there. If you are *home* you
> can make it as good and nice as possible. But I couldn't do that
> in that place. I don't think *you* would ever think of living like that
> in this community! It's a difficult decision for anyone to take in
> order to succeed in life. But if you go back to your village there
> will not be anything for you to do. If I had stayed in my village,
> I wouldn't have been who I am today. To live here is very difficult
> but it's useful too. You *really* have to suffer before you can get
> anything! But in the north, there are no businesses to build upon
> and that's why they all still run down here. I was moving yams
> from trucks to start with and it was not easy. You get all types of
> problems, with dust in your eyes and an aching body, but that's

the only way to survive. So, to live in a community like this, you
have to be strong. If you're from a good home you will never live
here! I just came here straight with a bag and still hear every year
we are going to get evicted. So, what should I do if they clear the
place? Should that mean I go back again? What should I do there?

Thus, George also juxtaposes the economic and business opportunities available in the north as compared to the south. He continues:

You know the money I used for this? I couldn't ever use that
money to get anything like this anywhere else in the city, because
the price was very low here. The shop belongs to me. I bought
the place and built it, and the money it cost, you know, you can't
even rent a place for one month in the town! I initially started
a shop not far from here. After the trouble up north, we [nine
siblings and I] all drifted down here. My first pharmacy business
collapsed financially and I had to start again. I moved back north
and started farming ... oh, farming! I earned a little, came back
and bought a lot of drugs in Accra, and looked for land here to
establish a chemist – that was 2008, when I started this place. I
bought the land with no papers from a guy. I knew him but when
word spread I wanted a place to buy, someone put me on to him.
He immediately sold it and left the area. I paid everything in cash
in one go. The deal here, though, is like, if the community can see
you respect yourself, then they will respect you. It worked for me
because the guy knew I was credible, so when he sold the place
to me I didn't face any problems, I just established my business.
But if you're a rascal you will be dealt with like one! (Interview,
7 July 2015)

He asserts that success in Old Fadama is due to good fortune and
doing your own thing without interference, and that this has enabled
his transition from the toil of loading and unloading yam lorries to
owning a pharmacy. Hence, he has managed to take advantage of
the surrounding contingencies and temporariness of the settlement
to succeed and establish his standing in the community. Here it is
possible to pursue ventures that would not be feasible in other parts
of the city. In one of the main alleys into Old Fadama, wide enough
for a small truck, George now has a well-kept shop that stands out
from the surrounding rickety wooden shacks and impromptu stalls
that line the sides of the alley. It is made of concrete and is bigger
than many other premises. It has a tin roof, tinted glass and doors,

and a raised tiled pavement area that is swept clean. Inside, a television on the wall provides background noise and distraction. There are ceiling fans, a tiled floor, and shelves well stocked with all kinds of medicine. For George, a very hard-pressed initial existence has now eased, although his relative economic success is still stalked by the spectre of demolition, even after twenty-five years in Old Fadama. In the absence of formal documentation, his hold over the plot of land is based on social, economic and local political capital. Neighbours who initially acknowledged that the seller had the 'right' to sell also recognized the 'right' of George to purchase the plot. He clearly had to buy his way in, but support was also gained locally because there was a need for a pharmacy. In this way George claims that he has a 'right' to the land because of his efforts in the community and the nature of the business he operates. This extends to helping others directly. As he emphasizes,

> I can have five people sleeping here in this shop and I won't ask anything from anybody, or I can rent it out and then every month I will get my money from them. In this place we can put up our own lights and nobody can stop us. We can do whatever we want. If you only want to spend 5 cedi [$1.25] then fine, you will get your cheap food. And if you have no money, then at the end of the day nobody will push you with a bill to come and pay by this and this time. If you know the right people, in this place nobody will even collect anything off you for a whole year! There is no one who comes to my shop every month to collect his money, so I am only earning and not paying. Now take my old place, which I am renting out. The guy who lives there also works for me, so if he pays the rent or not I don't have a problem with it. I can even say the past six months I haven't collected anything from him because he works for me and I know his situation very well. I don't need to force him to pay because he has children and the money that he would be paying monthly goes to school and feeding fees for his children. I realized that this man was suffering, so I looked the other way and told him to pay when things get better. (Interview, 7 July 2015)

Here we see how expressions of generosity, credibility and honesty are used to gain local backing and recognition. At the same time, the ability to 'to do whatever we want' reflects an understanding that the relative low costs in Old Fadama provide ripe business conditions that are not available 'outside' or in home towns. Endeavouring to do 'whatever you want' is also a strategy aimed at combating the ever-present fear of not knowing the fate of where one lives and works. For George, one way to overcome the unknowability is to shape a social niche in the community and establish a reputation for helping others.[9] Hence, he projects himself as generous. In a practical sense, helping out means that he also expects others to support his claim to the land. Conversely, the nature of his business and his economic success also mean that the local community expects him to help them out. Both dynamics were obvious from not only talking to George but spending many hours in his shop and observing customers receiving medicaments for free or on the cheap. Accordingly, a local constituency of informal property rights based on loose obligations of reciprocity takes shape, lessens uncertainty, and provides 'shelter' for both George and his local customer base.

George's claims of contributing help change his status within the community from a 'squatter' who faces eviction, as government sees him, to that of a worthy local citizen with rights recognized by those around him and as an active member of the community. Consequently, he actively tries to reduce the ambivalence of Old Fadama by framing himself as 'benign'. His experiences of accumulating money, getting an education, setting up a successful business after economic failure, and now being able to provide free shelter for others outlines a livelihood trajectory of seizing micro-opportunities. Still, his reliance on social recognition to achieve these things is evident in the following. George comments:

> I must be honest with you. This community has really helped me and has really bought up a lot of people. [I]f you look at our ministers or MPs of yesterday or today, a lot of them lived here, and if you look at our police officers of high, high rank, many came from here but they would never disclose it today. And as I'm seated here in my own shop, I'm also an aspirant MP in my home town up north and contesting a position, and I'm also at university thanks to this place so gradually I'm building up. All fingers are never equal! Some people are born into privileged families and others have to work 100 times harder. I came from a farming family. But look at the leaders that started here. Look at the MP now in the north. He was a little guy who started by unloading yams, being discreet doing this and that and today he's an MP! He was a close friend. (Interview, 7 July 2015)

Here, George emphasizes the opportunities offered by Old Fadama as a springboard to bigger things, and importantly, urban migration means that one is 'freed' from the social and cultural constraints which people experience in home towns. Yet it's apparent that to gain prestige outside of Old Fadama it is normal that individuals downplay roots in the settlement. This suggests that individuals are wary that ambitions of social mobility can fail if they highlight such a background and are fearful of exclusion by others in high positions of power. Thus, success and status gained from Old Fadama do not immediately translate into actors capitalizing on rags-to-riches stories. Rather, 'leaving' demands a new subjectivity to be made that reproduces dominant understandings of status based around economic wealth, political prowess, class and respectable upbringing. Similarly, there is a sense of injustice on the part of those 'left behind', and the successful find it necessary to join the chorus stigmatizing the settlement. Thus, 'to make it' demands not only a great deal of luck and resources, but the ability to rewrite one's past and 'escape' both physically and sociologically from the imprint of Old Fadama. In this way the negative imprint of Old Fadama is reproduced both by settlers who strive to escape from it, and by escapees who deny links to it and dismiss its potential. In George's case, success has come from the ability and good fortune to tap into and supply a service that is much in demand. In what follows we sketch the sharply contrasting experiences of Adjua concerning access to shelter, making a living, and pursuing independence.

Adjua

Adjua has numerous relatives living in Accra, including two uncles, an aunt, two brothers and a sister. She sees them all at least monthly and several also live in Old Fadama. But despite her family network Adjua has been unable to find paid work that she can manage, or get the financial help she needs to pursue an education as a teacher. Since moving to Old Fadama she has also been wholly unable to find safe and affordable long-term accommodation. Accordingly, her trajectory is the opposite of George's because she experiences weak local support and recognition. She rents a small room a stone's throw away from George's shop and they know each other through Adjua's visits to the pharmacy. She explains her first experiences of living and working in Old Fadama:

The first time I arrived in Accra, I was about twenty and sold boiled eggs for about three months. My uncle gave me the money to start up and I went around with my sister who was selling bananas. From here I worked as a *kayayoo* at an electrical shop, carrying loads on my head from the store to the bus station and customers' cars. I did that for about eighteen months but there was little money and the loads were very heavy. No shit, I often carried fridges around the city! The work made me ill, with pains in my head, neck, back and legs. I got between 2 and 5 cedi [$0.50 and $1] per journey depending on the distance, but there were long periods with no journeys. The money frequently went on painkillers. In one week, I could get about 20 or 30 cedi [$5–$7.50] of which 5 [$1.25] went to the rent. (Interview, 18 July 2015)

Like many others, on arrival in Accra from the north Adjua found shelter in Old Fadama through home-town connections. Accommodation comprised a single room of about fifteen square metres that twenty-five girls shared (Image 2.1). All worked as day labourers and head-porters around the city and Adjua joined them the day after she arrived. She showed me the room. There was no space for furniture and only a large, woven plastic mat to sleep on that barely covered the floor. There was not enough space for all to sleep at the same time, so it was necessary to agree on a rota for sleeping times. The tin roof was deafening in thunderstorms. It leaked, and rainwater ran down the walls and seeped up through the cracked concrete floor. The *kayayei* kept their belongings (typically a few essentials like a change of clothes and toiletries) in coloured plastic buckets with lids on that were hung on string and hooks along the walls while the bare essentials of money and telephone were slept with. Another much-guarded possession of any *kayayei* is the large aluminium bowl used to carry goods in, which is costly.

In their dwelling, the bracket for the padlock on the single door had been broken countless times and the door was now permanently ajar. So, the young girls took it in turns to stay in the room to ward off petty thieves. As a further precaution against theft, belongings were left with friends and family living in safer places. Still, Adjua reasoned that having few possessions was an advantage because it was easy to get up and out quickly in the event of thieves, violence, fire, flooding or demolition, which are the main threats. Shelter conditions for the vulnerable were thus insecure not only in a physical sense: the temporariness and unknowability of these living conditions mean that upheaval can occur very fast,

2.1 Living space for over twenty head porters
Source: author

at any time, for a number of reasons, and with game-changing consequences. She explained further that no one *really* sleeps in such a place at night. You just lie down exhausted and rest in a *kind* of sleep, trying to escape the disturbances from within and from neighbours through thin plywood walls, from the noise of people coming and going, from music, from telephones, from chatting and shouting, from motorbikes, and, at daybreak, from mosques calling the faithful to prayer.[10] Hence, during the heat of the day head-porters can be seen all over the city in cool shadows where they catch naps: on the backs of lorries, on shop forecourts, balancing precariously on narrow benches, and wherever and whenever they happen to be slouching around between jobs. If someone was away from the room for several days at a time there was always a chance their place would be given to someone else by the landlord. Rent was collected weekly and those who couldn't pay would sleep outside until they could, or until they moved on. The tenants do not enjoy the security of a private sphere and their living space is more public than private. Much of their daily life is spent looking or waiting for work, simply finding a place for peace and quiet, or staying outside because of the heat inside the room. As Adjua puts it, 'you can never hide', which sums up the difficulties involved in constituting oneself as a local citizen.

She continues:

I had to stop the portering because of pain and joined my sister selling food. It was still hard with the carrying of beans, maize and firewood, but it was easier than before and I was given the food and earned more – about 7 cedi [$1.75] a day. From here I worked for an NGO looking after the *kayayei*. They needed someone who could count, read, and write, and it helped that the manager was from the same area up north as me. They promised to pay me every month and I needed the money to return to school, but after six months' work I had received nothing. This meant I worked there for free and had to get my sister and uncle to give me money for my basic needs. In turn, I was supposed to pay my younger brother's school fees but couldn't, so he owed when he completed secondary school but I managed to pay the debt so he got his certificate. When the NGO still didn't pay me, I left and started working at a nursery school they also run, and where they look after the children of head-porters. The idea is that I get training as a teacher and at the end of the month I will get an allowance. I can eat there as well but I haven't had any allowance yet. It's now been nearly a year. I moved out of the room where you met me last time. Now I'm living in my own room that costs 35 Ghana cedi a week. Luckily, I don't have any issues with the landlady as she is together with the manager of the nursery so she can't drive me away. But when the need arises and I can't pay she will, and I will be parking my things outside as someone will be parking theirs inside! (Interview, 18 July 2015)

Adjua's difficulties and disappointments stem from the combination of working but not earning, not having money to afford reasonable accommodation or pursue studies, and generally not accumulating social capital to progress. She is tied to the unpaid job because it enables her to stay in the room, but this is only because the landlady is in a relationship with her boss at the nursery. And farther afield, worry about violence in her home town forces her to stick things out. This means she is dependent on the will of others that keeps her locked in poor living and working conditions. At the nursery, she looks after, often single-handed, up to 100 children aged between two and five in a large single room with sparse, old-fashioned wooden school furniture, limited ventilation and light, and few supported activities. Still, Adjua is adamant that working in the nursery is much easier and better than being a head-porter,

Staying put in the countryside

While many migrate to cities, some remain in their hometowns to challenge restrictive norms, or for various reasons are either unwilling or unable to move. This was the case of Aisha, the long-time girlfriend of one my research assistants, Ben, who had weighed up the lure and challenges of Accra against the potential for personal development at home, and chose to stay in her hometown. Aisha's story demonstrates a hard, but successful opposition to conservative norms in pursuit of personal ambitions, though the contest with her cultural and social environment has never let up. Aisha and Ben had been together for about four years in their hometown, the small district capital of Kpandai in East Gonja, Northern Region. However, Ben has never been popular with Aisha's family for numerous reasons: he is ethnic Nawuri, young, and a non-church-goer from a Christian family. Ben's maternal uncle, who raised him, is a devout Pentecostal priest while his mother, besides being a practising Christian, is the chairperson of the district Witch Hunters Association, which undertakes to protect the sacred lands of Nawuri from evil spirits with ceremonies and animal offerings. Aisha, meanwhile, is ethnic Dagomba, and from a relatively devout Muslim family. Problems started when Aisha, despite dating Ben, was obligated and pressured by her father to marry a much older man. A family quarrel rapidly developed and Aisha was thrown out of the family house and threatened by elder male family members. Ben and Aisha ran away together to different towns and once took refuge in the Accra hotel I was staying in. She feared for her safety and was distraught that her family had abandoned her, but was adamant she did not want to stay in Accra. Arguments continued for over a year, but Ben and Aisha managed to work out a plan where she could stay in Kpandai and her family would not feel they had lost face. With a little extra money Ben saved, she started a small beauty salon offering braiding and nail extensions. Luckily it proved successful enough to finance the building of a brick house, which, as Aisha points out, is for her only to live in! Her successes in business and newfound economic independence gave her the confidence to move back to Kpandai and expand the shop; and in turn her father grew to accept that, while he now had little control over his daughter, this didn't mean she was untrustworthy or irresponsible.

and she is happy finally to have her own room after years sharing with over twenty others. Yet it too leaks when it rains, and water seeps up through the floor, making it dangerous to use the electric light or fan. Her room is part of a badly built wooden structure that includes five other rented rooms where break-ins are common. Adjua's room also backs on to a perimeter area of the settlement that the AMA clawed back in the summer of 2015 by demolishing a long line of neighbouring structures (Chapter 3). At that time, her shack escaped the bulldozer by about three metres and this has left her room exposed and vulnerable. As we speak she points to a group of male youth playing dominoes and smoking pot just across from the doorway to her room. She says they are the ones who are always stealing things in the area, but there is nothing she or the landlady can do. Hence, her trajectory and those of other young and vulnerable head-porters exemplify that those with few resources and possessions often also have few meaningful and effective rights: to privacy, shelter, education, social security, a fair wage or reasonable working conditions, etc.

Conclusion

Rural–urban migration is often explained in terms of single and distinct causes such as constraining socio-economic conditions and ethnic tensions in home towns, as well as improved earning opportunities and prospects of education in cities (Awumbila et al. 2014: 17). For Harvey urbanization continues as a class phenomenon driven by uneven distribution and control of surpluses (Harvey 2008: 24). This chapter contributes to the structural and singular explanations by exemplifying some of the many personal dilemmas and considerations that migrants face in their decision-making about either 'staying' or 'going' and success in settling in. Further, it exemplifies how different life trajectories develop as migrants settle into Old Fadama. The cases featured here show that considerations of moving back or staying are often never finalized and pose nagging issues that migrants have to contend with regularly. They drive individual efforts to stay in Old Fadama (almost no matter what), and demonstrate how migrants are very often not in full control of vital issues that constantly influence and steer their everyday living conditions. A feature of the ongoing reflections about moving and staying is thus that they are often not clear cut. Deliberations do not offer easy, definitive or certain answers but sometimes allow sense to be made of an inexact and sometimes dangerous urban existence. Knowledge about the different places is subjective, changeable and open to interpretation. Still, such deliberations allow specific ideas to be formulated about the conditions of where people are now, and what the place they left is now like.

For the vulnerable, the process of settling into Old Fadama is thus determined not only by tangible and concrete push and pull factors, but also by changing social norms, experiences and perceptions of ethnic contentions, household traits at home, and personal anxieties. These can combine and influence choices about staying in Accra and go beyond purely economic motivations and rational decision-making based on certain knowledge about different locations. It is in these contexts that local rights to belong, to be included and to exclude others are produced. Meanwhile, opinions about adverse conditions in home towns make available the justification for living in squalid conditions in Old Fadama with few effective rights for a long time after the initial move. Experiences of navigating between and within different social sets of rules, and the ability to help define a place for oneself within them, can help deliver the conviction to young migrants that urban life can and will eventually deliver opportunities to them that will never be available in home towns. In short, migrants do not withdraw attention from, or abjure, their origins.

From these perspectives, it is therefore helpful to approach migration as a process that produces and changes social contexts where rights are established. Further, migration is not only about socioeconomic change, but also self-reflection about origins and destinations that produces knowledge and provides individuals with the determination to overcome vulnerability and adversity. We have also seen how the production of 'self' relates to the perennial uneasiness of the surrounding environment and extent of social recognition. Beyond the ability to earn, save and spend, urban survival for newcomers therefore depends on demonstrating to others their ability to be reflective, resilient, autonomous and versatile. For some, the mere act of 'staying in the city' is a criterion of success in itself.

The changing experiences and situations of different individuals in the state of slum produce a range of context-specific relations of identity and landholding status. At one end of the scale are the young, unaccompanied, female head-porters who live for long periods in insecure accommodation at the mercy of unaccountable landlords. They are mere tenants, subject to a range of more powerful interests in land, and have to endure very unequal relations in terms of informal rights. Their gender, age and low socio-economic and cultural status also reflect how those with few locally recognized rights also have few things. At the other end of the scale we have met an emerging middle-class figure in the person of George. He enjoys high status as a local citizen and as a shopkeeper, and security and certainty through community recognition of his right to the land. In terms of the making and shaping of local rights, this is the opposite of what dominant and normative understandings of citizenship would assume. Here, statutory authorities would uphold and enforce formal rights to citizenship to protect the defenseless. But what we see instead is that the illegality of settlement drives individuals to develop their own, more meaningful 'rights' in the state of slum, through informal organization and production of common norms. These are endeavours to establish and define meaningful rights of their own to offset the sense of not knowing. In this way the search for shelter and land by individuals with unequal levels of resources opens up very disparate socio-economic spaces in Old Fadama. And the struggle to establish and affirm the rights that they can enjoy shapes radically different socio-economic subjectivities. These objective and subjective outcomes demonstrate the paucity of common conceptualizations of informal settlements in terms of homogeneity and the pervasive absence of agency.

The diversity of outcomes suggests that urban migration to informal settlements creates differentiated forms of rights that derive not from legal status but from combinations of different levels of resources, practices, social encounters and reflective processes that these resource levels allow. In this sense Accra is indeed a city of 'hope' to tens of thousands of migrants from the north of the country (Awumbila et al. 2014:17). The diverse trajectories demonstrate the importance of local and even micro contexts for the forming of informal relations of property and the substantiation of citizenship rights, which are detailed further in the next two chapters.

3
Gaining and losing land, and soft property

Pursuing issues of land-based development, this chapter explores processes of gaining and losing land in Old Fadama and diverse and fragmented relations of property that emerge involving different statutory and non-statutory actors and institutions. We see how the diverse relations of informal property in the state of slum reflect context-specific power relations and the shifting ability of different actors to establish themselves as land-controlling authorities. As we saw in the last chapter, a main concern for all who wish to settle in informal settlements is gaining access to land for shelter and accommodation. For the more ambitious, however, the issue is how to secure the backing for larger plots of land on which businesses can be built. It is with these land-related perspectives in mind that this chapter examines different types of land-based development, each with implications for relations of property and informal governance.

Property is commonly understood as a physical object or used as a synonym for absolute or private ownership. But outright owner-ship rarely, if ever, exists because it is always conditioned by the recognition of others – who may seek to exercise other rights and claims, leading to exclusion (Rose 1998). Rather than examining property as a physical thing, it is therefore approached here as a set of changing relationships concerning a particular object of value, in this case land for different uses. Establishing and losing property is thereby approached as a socio-political process about recognition that may or may not involve statutory institutions directly and which shapes context-specific relations of property. This perspective contrasts with the state-centrist approach that tends to assign power and legitimacy around landed property to statutory institutions and formal state law (for example, Shachar and Hirschl 2007; De Soto 2000). Micro-level issues pertaining to land are found to be a vital dimension of informal governance in the state of slum because they ultimately dictate whether settlement is possible or not, and define what is, and what is not, allowed to take place on the land, in the absence of statutory authority.

Changing power relations around land shape the ability to buy, transfer or sell land, the right to build upon and develop land, and ultimately the local right to control what happens to it, and who can and cannot stay.[1] The everyday negotiations, activities and efforts of all kinds of rural–urban migrants on the micro-level subsequently feed into a miasma of local understandings about claims to land and rights to benefit from it. All are in direct opposition to formal state law and the judicial ruling that all settlement is illegal, although, as we shall see, some negotiations still involve statutory institutions. The diversity of interests and power relations around land is such that there is no universal political authority in Old Fadama that is capable and strong enough to substantiate property rights in a uniform or systematic way once and for all. Rules may change and possession of plots may be ephemeral. But the occasional fickleness of occupation and possession does not mean that land issues are inherently violent or chaotic. Hereby, the myriad ways by which land is transferred in the state of slum defy dominant explanations of informal settlements as typically resource-weak and socio-economically homogeneous (Davis 2006; Mohanty 2006; Shabane et al. 2011), and as sites exposed and prone to violence by a conflation of poverty, lack of law and social marginalization (Lombard and Rakodi 2016; De Soto 2000). In the absence of the rule of formal state law and fixed, universal authority around land, what we see instead are micro-processes of consensus as well as competition, the importance of social recognition of land claims, and an array of different tactics and strategies used by different actors to gain access to and control over land. As we saw in the last chapter, possession of land also feeds into the effectiveness and meaning of local citizenship rights through social recognition. The dynamics at play concerning land in the state of slum suggest 'soft' forms of property that emerge and which contrast definitively with formal state ideals of fixed and legible relations.

The legal entanglement and significance of social recognition of land claims also mean that land access and distribution are not defined purely by market mechanisms and monetary value. Urban spatial differentiation in the global South is otherwise often explained in Marxian terms of widening social differences under capitalism and market-driven growth leading to class-based land struggles (Bailey 2014/15; Gillespie 2016; Harvey 2003). Attention paid to the shaping of informal and socio-political relations around property at the grassroots level in the state of slum consequently provides additional insights.

First, we see that spatial contrasts not only develop between the urban rich and poor, but within similar socio-economic groups in Old Fadama. Thus, individuals may have similar resources at their disposal but may simply not be able to take advantage of chance potentialities that sometimes open up for possessing land. Others still may be more capable of substantiating occupancy and possession, and be better skilled at developing the social and socio-political capital needed to gain the support of others. Thus, money can buy influence over land but it is not the be-all and end-all of decisions over land and the goal of attaining certainty of occupation grounded in local recognition. Second, spatial disparities within the slum and the informalization of land governance are, as we shall see, not only consequences of (discreet) mismanagement and neoliberal forces, but have developed because of direct and *decisive* government actions. This is exemplified by tracing the demolition of parts of the state of slum by city authorities. Following such demolition actions, stark contrasts in living conditions are produced between those who have directly experienced government bulldozers and those who have not. The result is a patchwork of complementary and competing relations of informalized property and land-based developments that have their own micro-level logics of support, resources and levels of precariousness (Stacey 2018).

Consequently, the socio-political relations of property observed in Old Fadama are more heterogeneous, multilayered and complex than are otherwise suggested by the dominant interpretations of urban land dynamics in the global South in terms of neoliberal conditioning. The different actors behind building in Old Fadama are not explicitly creating relations of property and rights in land. But they establish local ideas and norms about the control of land. In turn, they influence local behaviour, practices and the ability of statutory institutions to exercise *their* will and enforce the rights and practices *they* recognize and want to promote as grounded in planning and formal state law. In a Polanyian sense, furthermore, the significance of social recognition for land-based developments acts as a buffer against an unfettered commodification of land. This is because land-based developments at the grassroots level are driven and constrained by different webs of social and socio-political networks whose reach is limited. Hence, the local economy of land in the state of slum is not disembedded from its society but is a central constituent dimension of it (Mitchell 2002).

The corollary is diverse, 'soft' forms of socio-political relations around land that are fragmented and in flux. Hence, a snapshot of informal property in the state of slum could resemble a marble cake with overlapping dark, light and shaded areas that exemplify context-specific combinations of interests, resources and power around different building activities. The relations may be quick to form and dissolve, opportunistic and personalized, flexible and long-standing, and recognition in social and political forms may wax and wane. What they all share, however, is that they are non-institutionalized, actor-based, and develop under the noses of governments which are either unwilling or unable to control them. They all also defy conventional conceptualizations of land issues in informal settlements as either decidedly violent, chaotic or disorganized. Although gaining control over land can sometimes be a contentious and violent affair, the use of violence to wrestle land from others cannot explain the diversity of land-based exchanges that take place and the multitudinous forms they take in the state of slum. Old Fadama is therefore more than a site of unresolved contestations between different stakeholders and conflicting legal systems (Boamah and Walker 2016). Rather, it exemplifies how the historically unresolved issues over the land between different governments and the Ga customary authorities, and between 'modern' and 'traditional' institutions, have changed and been appropriated by new emerging systems and processes: recent migration has brought in new powers and created new socio-political spaces and opportunities for new power relations to emerge, following the grafting of the 'modern' judicial decision onto the area.

Studies have challenged narratives of chaos in informal settlements by examining practices of ingenuity around land-based developments. These include local mimicking of 'official' building standards and the use of approved materials to gain acceptance and legitimacy. The tactic of creating copycat versions of the formal cityscape in informal settlements promotes the notion of urban physical homogeneity and boundary-less spaces between legal and illegal settlements (Nielsen 2011). Local developments that copy the rest of the city, and local processes of cooperation that make land-based developments possible, induce an awareness that residents do actually belong and are part of the 'normal' city. Thereby, the shaping of local relations of property is closely linked to the local production of belonging and citizenship (Lund 2016).

Building and land-based developments in all guises reduce the ever-present unpredictability otherwise experienced by residents of informal settlements (Hansen and Verkaaik 2009; Lombard 2013: 814). The episodes of land-related development examined in Old

Fadama confirm these findings, showing that despite the 'widening, deepening, intensification' of local and global connections in African urban spaces, the impact on local development is notably uneven, even within circumscribed spaces and between otherwise similar groups of people (Fourchard 2011: 231).

On a broader level the evidence points to a clear divergence between state actors and institutions with the formal authority to control land but who cannot do so convincingly, and the developing ability of local stakeholders and non-state actors, who successfully develop and control land but lack the formal authority to do so. The processes of gaining and losing control over land are moreover similar in that both concern competition between stakeholders to establish rights, convince others and gain the recognition of those rights, and assert the ability to enforce them (Agarwal 1994). Still, the diversity of relational, situational and contextual dimensions means that one 'wasteland' or plot can differ considerably from another. In the state of slum, it is thereby less about questions of ownership status per se and what you *own* than it is about questions of who you are and who you *owe*, what is *owed* to you, and what you *owe* others. In brief, the monetary value of the timber and nails of the buildings and the purchase of land with no documentation are, in the longer term, less important than the socio-economic and socio-political relations that underpin your claim of possession. The cycle of building, the establishing of different social relations to substantiate land usage and control, and the loss of possession in the absence of formal documentation thus provide the dominant themes of this chapter.

Moreover, the chapter explores how people's experiences in rebuilding their lives following the loss of property to government bulldozers actively shape grassroots subjectivities and local agency. Here, we see how the social and economic activities of those affected are influenced by broader structural features and constraints of urban life. These include the dire lack of opportunities and alternatives offered by the public sphere, the persistent non-recognition assigned to informal settlements that relegates residents to the margins of the state, and government actions that produce and reproduce spatial disparities.

The next section briefly situates Old Fadama in the context of evictions experienced elsewhere in Accra in recent years. Then we look at the informalization of property relations, and local negotiations that lead to the freeing up of space. This is exemplified by looking at the building of relatively large complexes – a school and a hotel in Old Fadama. After this, we look at two examples of city

authorities endeavouring to regain lost space by bulldozing peripheral areas of Old Fadama, and the regaining of some of this space by
residents after demolition.

Old Fadama: some drivers of long-term settlement

Although in principle all sites of unregulated building in Accra risk
demolition by city authorities, the size of Old Fadama, together with
its economic, social and political significance and its geography –
hemmed in by water and main roads – has worked in its favour and
contributed to its longevity. These features feed into the popular
idea that Old Fadama is a law unto itself because, as one resident
commented, it is 'too big to go', a view that is vehemently denied
officially. Still, the experiences of tens of thousands of Old Fadama
dwellers who continue to live there defying the strategies of successive governments and developing their own systems of informal
governance, point to how desires to rid urban life of informality
are sometimes unsuccessful and backfire. In practice, therefore,
the continued existence of Old Fadama suggests that the hands of
successive Ghanaian governments have been forced, and that the
decision not to evict residents or totally demolish the site has been
involuntary. In turn, the popular notion of Old Fadama as *almost*
unassailable has driven business investments and made the site politically and economically important. The role of the site as a hub of
economic networks and source of employment adds further impetus
to its reputation for inviolability and reflects an interdependence
between formal and informal systems of governance.

The idea that Old Fadama is an exceptional case finds support
from incidences of demolition undertaken by city authorities in
Accra in recent years in other informal settlements. In September
2014, for example, around 5,000 residents in the informal settlement of Mensah Guinea were given three days' notice to leave
before bulldozers razed the entire area.[2] And in the same month,
the Ministry of Trade and Industry issued a thirty-day ultimatum to
all non-Ghanaian market traders to vacate thirty-five Accra markets
or face prosecution. This was part of a national campaign, following
pressure from the Ghana Union of Traders Association (GUTA),
to protect domestic markets.[3] Such actions show that under certain
circumstances crisis and political imperatives provide governments
with reasons and ability to remove designated 'foreign' street traders
or evict large numbers of squatters forcefully. But such manoeuvres

also contradict the liberal and more sympathetic gestures to informal sites of economic activity evident in the covenants supported by the same governments in international urban development fora.

As detailed below, in June 2015 several thousand Old Fadama residents living in perimeter areas lost their homes and businesses to government bulldozers, yet significantly the greater part of Old Fadama was left wholly untouched. The AMA objective in this instance was to reduce severe clogging of the Odaw River (see Images 1.2 and 3.3) and create a building-free buffer zone to reduce the risk of flooding. The background to this strategic clearance operation in Old Fadama was a calamitous and tragic combination of fire and flooding that occurred earlier in the same month at Kwame Nkrumah Circle, Accra. Here, over 150 lives were lost when a storm resulted first in flooding and then in a large explosion at a petrol station adjacent to the informal settlement.[4] The bulldozing and especially the calamity sent shock waves through Accra. This stood in stark contrast to congratulatory scenes just a couple of months earlier, after the mayor of Accra (Metropolitan Chief Executive), Alfred Okoe Vanderpuije, won the prestigious President Jose Eduardo do Santo African Best Mayor Award, in Luanda, Angola.[5]

Typically, demolition exercises are justified by city authorities with reference to public health and safety, as well as the continual and nagging need to decongest the city. In contrast, it is less usual for government to legitimize demolition exercises explicitly with reference to issues of illegal settlement, presumably because the city authority, in the form of the AMA, is wholly unable to halt everyday, informal and illegal building activities that occur all over its jurisdiction. Its continual referencing of public health issues suggests, therefore, government's basic inability to enforce statutory rights to land in the capital and promote the idea that it takes public health seriously.[6] At the same time, the intermittent episodes when the city authority demolishes informal settlements around the city provide a reminder of its willingness to breach the spirit of the different global pledges towards slum dwellers and, in the name of public health, to claw back lost urban space where it can.[7] Nevertheless, the overall, very poor environmental state of the Korle Lagoon complex and the negative health impacts it has had on surrounding areas for decades suggests strongly that issues of public health and environmental protection are not political priorities. It is against this precarious background of not really knowing what city authorities can and will do that insecure control over land by ordinary residents and investors alike takes place in the state of slum as they weigh up the pros and cons of developing land.

School building

The young population and the prevalence of young, working and single mothers in Old Fadama create a high demand for nursery schools, day care and child education. However, the legal predicament means that there are no public nurseries or schools in Old Fadama itself, and the demand has driven the growth of numerous private and NGO-financed institutions. One such is a school that started as a small nursery in 2007 and soon had some 400 registered students, with nearly 300 in daily attendance. Pupils are taught by four formally trained teachers among a total of twelve, and the school relies on occasional support provided by volunteer teachers from abroad (interview, headmaster, 23 August 2014). This particular school started as a hotchpotch of close-knit wooden shacks but today – with its cramped and hot classrooms housing old-fashioned wooden desks, chairs and blackboards – has the look and feel of an under-resourced government school. The pupils are uniformed in the Ghanaian state-school colours of yellow shirts and brown shorts for boys and brown dresses for girls. Pupils are provided with school dinners and there is a traditional hierarchical pedagogical approach to teaching, with classes based on age. The school is squeezed into a three-storey building that itself is jammed between a mass of shacks and winding paths just wide enough for bicycles to pass through. It does not receive any economic support from state coffers and is solely reliant on enrolment fees, donations and voluntary work.

Despite the problematic legal status of the settlement, however, the school enjoys a level of recognition from different state institutions. For example, the Ghana Education Service (GES) oversees the registration of pupils and accredits the curriculum. It is also registered as a private school with the Ministry of Education and as a business by the AMA, which means it pays business taxes. Thus, parallel to the legal stalemate and illegality of all building activities, statutory authorities still derive power in the settlement with an institutional presence through registering and taxing businesses. This supports a view of government pursuing a policy of normalization to make society legible and introduce 'a common standard necessary for a synoptic view' of urban development (Scott 1997: 2).

By summer 2013 the increase in pupils meant that a large extension to the school was necessary. To this end, the school contacted neighbours and encouraged them to 'do the right thing for the benefit of the children' by either moving their wooden shacks closer together, or by selling plots to the school to free up space. In this way leverage over neighbours to 'move around a bit' was gained by highlighting the vital role that the school played in the community (interview, headmaster; 23 August 2014). At the same time, global support in the form of a USA-based evangelical NGO was gained. This organization participated in negotiations with neighbours, provided the funds for building materials, and facilitated the purchase of plots for the extension. Their country representative explained their considerations:

[W]e had to get new land. I spoke to people and got to know [them] and one was willing to give up his land. The issue was that we had to go in for it [even though] we've seen in the past years that politics are at play and we keep on hearing the place will be demolished. [I]t was also hard to get another location. That was the interest. The charge was very, very huge for that small piece of land [but] we promised to raise the money in the organization. I kept asking and asking and [finally it was] OK. [W]e had the problem that the land [did] not belong to [the seller]. [So, we asked] who does it belong to? [And] are you going to give us documentation? [To which came the reply] Oh! are we going to sign some papers? [The point being that] I also knew the situation, I mean, I know that the land does not belong to the native owner there. So, there are loopholes in the system and that is where we came in. The issue [was] that it's about the children wanting to have a classroom who cannot be going through all this. So honestly, all we did was this; [the] guy should give us the land [and] we sign whatever. [P]robably, he came over there with his family first, and said 'this is our property' and he took it. So, he's willing to give it up, and nobody even came to question anything. [W]e know as an organization that anything can happen, but one thing was that it's a school! So, if they [the city authorities] break everything, [they] probably might leave the school for us, so that's the idea. [B]ut we know it didn't come right. We didn't go through the process and all that stuff, but it's something like ownership that has been handed over, and signed with legal documents. [A]nd this man has taken it over with this amount of money from us. [W]e have access to use his land.

[H]e had to do that because he has collected our money, and he
had to give us a receipt, and our donors were also asking about
the same things, [whether] there were documents for the land
and this and that. We told them this is the issue. [T]his man is
willing to give us his land, and somebody [else] is ready to pick it,
and build houses, and rent it out [if we don't take it now]. [W]e
don't even know who [the rightful owners are]. [S]o the system is
not right, because if you try, and you get to one person, the other
person will tell you this and that, and you will come in between.
[A]s soon as they know you are paying something, everybody
wants to take some, so we dealt with the person who said the
land belongs to him, and he gave an offer to sell the land [he was
occupying]. [W]e knew it didn't belong to him. [I]t belongs to
either the nation, or the AMA, or the government, or the Ga, so
we know that, but we needed the land to get the school running.
(Interview, country representative, 1 August 2014)

Here, obtaining land for the school took as a point of departure
the actual interests, claims and social relations around the actual
plot, and included a diverse group of actors with a common objective. Their involvement, and the compromises they made, embedded
the transfer of land and made it consensual. Although there is no
formal documentation what we see, however, are a series of efforts
to formalize the otherwise informal transferral, as the receipt of
payment and signatures provide images of 'legal documents'. The
rationale is that the paperwork will substantiate the new claim and
transform the transaction into a 'property right' that is recognized
by others (Campbell 2015). Emphasis placed on the fact that the
land is needed for a school and will benefit local children shows the
relevance of social capital in legitimizing building rather than the
financial dimensions alone (Pinson and Morel Journel 2016). The
development of the school also demonstrates how formal state institutions seek out opportunities to pursue and influence land-based
development in the settlement, and how they gain an institutional
foothold. Thus, the process of building 'illegally' sometimes offers
opportunities for state institutions to gain a presence which they
didn't have before. But by so doing state institutions become party
to the informalization of land governance and their tacit participation feeds into local understandings that statutory institutions and
regulators do recognize building activities in the illegal settlement,
when in fact they vehemently oppose it. At the same time, would-be
supporters of the school reason it will not be demolished. Thus, the

process of school building provides both formal and informal actors and institutions opportunities to accumulate power, benefit each other, and influence local development in non-institutionalized, unarranged ways in the state of slum.

Hotel building

A five-minute walk from the school, the construction of a large concrete hotel in the centre of Old Fadama was under way in the summer of 2015. Its progress was followed by many residents for numerous reasons. As it grew, there was increased awareness that it could become, when complete, the biggest and highest structure in the settlement by far (Image 3.1). There were rumours that the main investor behind the building was politically well connected or a parliamentarian, and that this was thwarting the AMA's desire to forestall the emergence of a colossus among buildings in the state of slum. The Ga customary authorities were trying in vain to halt the project for which their permission had not been sought. The story of the hotel's construction thus affords insights into processes through which different groups of statutory and non-statutory actors gain and lose the power to decide the fortunes of land and contribute to the informalization of its governance.

3.1 The hotel under construction
Source: author

The Ga traditional authorities have always had representatives living and working in Old Fadama to monitor land transactions and try to regulate building activities. Though this is a near-impossible task, they are occasionally on hand to inform and convince builders and developers that the land being built on actually belongs to the Ga. In their words, they seek acknowledgement, and collect token payments as a sign of respect for the ancient Ga land and customs. But they have neither the presence to keep track of all new buildings and constructions, nor the power to enforce sanctions when their requests to developers are rejected or ignored. The Ga representatives in Old Fadama therefore have limited ability to enforce their will, and their status as the customary authorities of the land is further weakened by divisions between different Ga clans themselves within the broader Ga traditional state that covers parts of greater Accra. While some factions claim that collecting money is 'tribute' that helps sustain an important and much-needed traditional Ga presence in Old Fadama, others say that monies collected are 'fees' and violate the sacredness of the site. Other Ga stakeholders hold that 'the wrong Ga people' are making money from such 'collections', which amount to land sales and speculation, and that proceeds are not forwarded to the appropriate Ga institutions (interview, Ga priest, 9 July 2014). Further, some builders refuse to make payments because they say 'Ga representatives' are not who they claim to be, but part of a swarm of parasites who seek to make money from land developments. These challenges reflect some of the ways by which the Ga customary claims over Old Fadama land are changing, being eroded and have become the subject of everyday debates about who has the right to control land use and development in the settlement. The uncertainty and lack of overall authority, however, provide ample space for micro land grabs and opportunism.

The story of the hotel is difficult to substantiate but several different sources agreed on the following sequence. Initially, the site of the hotel was allocated at least twenty years ago by a 'Ga chief' for a token fee. After this, a small 'chop bar' selling skewered and grilled meat in a wooden shed was set up by the occupier of the site but was destroyed by fire some time in the early 2000s. The chop bar owner started to rebuild with concrete blocks to lessen the risk of another fire, but after several years of stalled efforts to re-establish the business, she conceded that rebuilding was beyond her means and therefore started to look for a buyer. In 2014 the partially developed plot was 'sold' for a 'substantial' price to a local businessman and the chop bar owner 'ran away' with the money (interviews, residents, June 2016).[8]

The Ga representatives explained that they were not involved in the sale and found out about it only much later when they saw that the construction of the hotel had commenced on the site and spread to surrounding, previously unused land. In their view, although the chop bar owner did not have the right to sell the plot, there was at least an obligation to forward a portion of the money from the sale to them. As word spread, their Ga traditional superior also tried to halt the hotel construction because it was an affront to his authority; he appealed unsuccessfully to the AMA, arguing that it should, at the very least, ensure that recognized building standards were followed (interview, Ga representative, 3 June 2016). In the meantime, the issue of unregulated buildings and informal settlements in Accra had become the subject of increased popular and political attention because of the disastrous combination of fire and flood (described above) that occurred in Accra in June 2015. Despite pressure by the customary authorities and city government, the construction of the hotel continued until it was complete and, by late summer, was operational. As building progressed, developers gained the support of leading community members in Old Fadama and members of OFADA. Opponents of the hotel suspected that members of OFADA had been bribed but, still, the project gained local legitimacy and support was canvassed for it to be completed, as many locals were won over because the building site offered labour opportunities. Not least, the edifice made Old Fadama look like 'normal' parts of the city.

Eventually, the AMA pressured OFADA to issue an outright ban on all new concrete buildings in Old Fadama (see below) but this was not consistently enforced. Still, the ban exemplifies how the unofficial institution of local government in the form of OFADA was used by the city authority, and it introduced a dimension of formality and convention into OFADA's approach to controlling building. In this way, and regardless of OFADA's ability or willingness to enforce the ban, the organization's local image as a regulatory authority that worked alongside the AMA was boosted. The ban was hung in the office of OFADA and served as a warning that it had the support of the AMA. Moreover, OFADA adopted an approach to 'unlawful' buildings that was identical to that of the AMA, and mimicked AMA tactics to establish itself as a local authority over a given jurisdiction: it communicated the ban publicly and formally, warned of the consequences of non-compliance, and claimed the right to define perpetrators. This also hints to residents that the AMA is power-less to stop building activities without the support of OFADA itself, whose task it is to enforce the ban.

Meanwhile, the construction of the hotel fed into local under-standings of Old Fadama as 'invincible' and 'a law unto itself'. Some residents reasoned that the 'allowing' of the hotel by the Ga, the AMA and OFADA was a sure sign that investments in land in Old Fadama were secure because '*If such a thing gets built, then this place ain't going anywhere.*' Along the same lines, a proclaimed, leading community member came out in favour of the benefits that would flow from this hotel that all seemed unable or unwilling to stop. He suggested that *he* allowed the building to progress and justified that the hotel had a social role to play:

> As a leader of the community, I think my people also deserve
> that kind of thing. So I will not sack [force] the man not to
> invest. [So] that's where we agreed, that when you are going to
> do it, you make sure that you do it, not because you want money,
> but because you are coming to save the people of Old Fadama.
> (Interview, 3 December 2015)

In contrast to the case of the school, the story of the hotel is one of hidden economic and political interests that have managed to wrestle control over a site, substantiate their claim to the land though a series of negotiations in open defiance of statutory authorities and the customary landowners, and pursue the project to its comple-tion. The obscurity around obtaining the land for the hotel project meant it was not socially embedded in the way the school was but was justified all the same as having its own inherent social value. Significantly, although the project was haphazard and debated, the process was non-conflictual and reached consensus. And it was like the school in that it, too, was the product of the actions of very different stakeholders who together forged non-statutory, informal property relations.

These dynamics of informal governance around land are not inherently in opposition to institutions of formal government as 'weak state' theories would assume. Rather, what we see are unarranged dimensions of both complementarity and competi-tiveness between statutory and non-statutory actors. On the one hand, we see the authority of the AMA undermined as it fails to halt the hotel construction. But the AMA was not excluded entirely from influence because it 'outsourced' regulation of building to a

MEMO
FROM: THE COMMUNITY SECRETARY
TO: ALL STAFF
DATE: 29TH AUGUST 2015

SUBJECT: STOP ALL CONCRETE BUILDINGS

In response to the directive from the Accra Metropolitan Assembly, precisely from the Lord Mayor, to stop all concrete building within Old Fadama has taken effect from today, 29th August, 2015 and all concrete building ongoing within the community should seize.

Any individual or group of persons found building with blocks would be asked to appear before the AMA works Department to explain why court action should not be taken against him/her/them for building without permit.

In carrying out the said directive, OFADA will stop all concrete buildings within the community with inscription on new concrete buildings; STOP WORK BY OFADA.

Thank you

Frederick Opoku
Community Secretary

The ban issued by OFADA on all concrete buildings, 29 August 2015 (verbatim)

non-statutory organization in the form of OFADA. Although the efforts to halt the hotel construction failed, the process shows how statutory authorities contribute to the informalization of land governance, and conversely, how non-statutory, informal actors introduce formal elements into their organization to legitimize their own authority. The messy process exemplifies how sets of different actors not only endeavour to save face over projects they cannot control but how they try to convince others that they are in fact in charge of what is going on. Hence, although it appeared to all that the AMA had lost this battle, it was important for the institution to reaffirm that it was in fact fully in control. One result is that new processes of recognition emerged as, in this instance, OFADA and the AMA appear as 'partners' committed to enforcing building regulation (when in reality the process revealed that neither could halt the development). What we see in a broader perspective, therefore, is that statutory and non-statutory powers establish an unrehearsed contract to support each other to control building activity because none can actually do so single-handedly. In this sense the hotel resembled many other buildings in the state of slum that rendered obsolete government urban plans and the significance of state-recognized property rights. At the same time, the multi-storey hotel changed the single-storey, horizontal skyline of the slum and made it look more like other parts of the city undergoing construction and investor-driven development (Images 1.2, 3.1).

Clawing back control and loss of power

As a contrast to the successful defiance of government by the stakeholders involved with the school and hotel, the following section sketches the experiences of residents who lost land to city authorities while those buildings were being constructed. We are at another informal settlement just across the road from Old Fadama, closer to the city centre, and a few hundred metres away from the building activities for the school and hotel. Here, the urban landscape is also changing. But the concerns and conversations of settlers could not be more different and people are openly angry with city officials. A few days previously the city authorities demolished large swathes of constructions and, with it, obliterated and renounced the informal relations of controlling land that had been built up over many years. AMA bulldozers created mounds of debris, and well-trodden paths through the informal settlement are now erased. The area resembles a war zone, with small twirls of smoke rising from piles of burnt-out junk, jagged timbers poking up out of the ground, and people scouting around for bits and pieces of wooden panelling and tarpaulin to build shelters before nightfall.

Yaw

To recap, Yaw is ethnic Gonja from the north of Ghana, fifty years old, and married with four children under the age of fifteen. He has lived in the Old Fadama area for the best part of thirty years and for at least ten years has lived in an adjacent informal settlement, just across the main road from Old Fadama. This site is about the size of two football pitches and is known locally by supporters of the NDC political party as 'June 4th'. This is the now famous date in 1979 when supporters of then Flight Lieutenant Jerry John Rawlings broke into the jail where he was being held during his trial for planning to overthrow the government of the Supreme Military Council under General F. K. Akuffo. After being released in spectacular fashion, Rawlings quickly seized power and became head of state.[9] Popular opinion has it that shortly afterwards Rawlings built a platform on the site, made a speech, and told people to name the place 'June 4th', which since then has become a day of celebration for NDC supporters all around the country.

Prior to demolition the site comprised sprawling shacks and make-shift market stalls but was more visibly dilapidated than many parts of Old Fadama. It earned the nicknames of 'Sodom and Gomorrah' and the equally dubious Hausa name 'Kawou Kudii', which collo-quially means 'Bring the money', or 'Leave your bag', because of its notoriety as a hangout for bag-snatchers, robbers, drug dealers and prostitutes. It is common knowledge that it is a no-go area for most outsiders after dusk, and, as Adjua put it, '*Every blessed day people are complaining about getting their things stolen in that place.*' From a thief's perspective, however, June 4th is great for business because it is cut off from the main road, very dimly lit yet always busy, and has a mass of short cuts that serve many thousands of people walking to and from marketplaces at either end of the site. In the early hours of 4 July 2015, however, the residents of June 4th awoke to the sounds of shouting, sirens and machinery. Allegedly without any prior warning, a combination of city officials, the Ghana Police Service and Ghana's armed forces then went about dispersing people and demolishing shelters.[10]

We sit and talk to Yaw several months later, in November. He pulls up a rickety wooden bench alongside a large sheet of tarpaulin stretched over oil drums which now serves as his family home. After demolition the site was cleared of hundreds of tons of timber, corru-gated tin and plywood that made up the shelters and businesses of its 1,500 residents, leaving mounds of rubble and trash, while a flat section closest to the main road has become a makeshift lorry park. Looking around, Yaw explains that he lost a food store, a bar and the shack that he had lived in for years with his wife and children. He is well known in the area, with a reputation as a hard man who started at the very bottom, unloading yam from lorries in the nearby market. He eventually worked his way up and boasts that today he is a respected and reformed leader of the community. Many people address him as 'Chief' as we talk and they walk by. An old associate recalls how Yaw changed his ways after a group of yam farmers, friends of his from Gonja, lost a lot of money to a gang of thieves. Matters were settled in a wrestling match with a gang leader. Yaw's victory earned him the right to control a large patch of June 4th.

He explains that before the demolition he had many income sources and responsibilities. And as he became an influential figure in the area, he enjoyed the right to define the rights and obligations of others: allocating plots of land for market stalls, renting out buildings, receiving 'drink money' for solving community and individual tensions, collecting kickbacks from stolen computers, telephones and other goods, and organizing communal labour for cleaning-up exercises. All testify to the shaping of micro-level socio-political power relations that underpin Yaw's status as a local 'big man'. Since the clearance operations, however, he and many others have been starting again from scratch – although they are not sure how to go about it. This is because the physical destruction of the area also reduced and transformed the countless socio-economic relationships that grounded his position of power and ability to control the area. In a chain of bad luck and inability to turn things around, many contacts have dispersed to other areas of the city and numerous opportunities to earn a living and substantiate control have disintegrated. Besides the physical loss, there is therefore personal bitterness, anguish and a crisis in terms of what to do, who to become, and how to provide for one's family. As always, Yaw remains disjointed from formal systems of governance, but now is also isolated because local, informal power systems are broken. As he says:

> What plan must I use to get money for the family? Must I go and kill someone and take their money, or maybe I must go and steal and pull a knife on someone, or maybe rob someone at a gun point? I'm looking at all these things now and I feel ashamed at the options. I feel like dying because that will be that! (Interview, 19 January 2016)

Reflecting on the psychological trauma brought about by the demolition, he tells of two friends who poisoned themselves, taking days to die, and of another who 'died of shame' because he could not face having to start again after years of hardship. In the following months, however, a degree of 'normality' returned to June 4th. This suggested the limited ability of the AMA to keep the pressure up and substantiate authority over the area. The presence of law enforcers diminished and interest turned elsewhere, the people crept back in, and new potentialities opened up. The new space in the void of formal authority was filled with dozens of small businesses and lodgings that sprouted up again, and handfuls of people settled, albeit hesitantly. Clusters of pallets and cardboard shelters dotted around the site reveal where people once again sleep, cook, wash and establish small stalls for business. In one corner, a young man pins up posters of different haircuts and hangs a large mirror on a wall. He places five chairs in a row, turns on the radio, and thereby creates amongst the rubble a barbershop that can be dismantled again in five minutes. Another spreads out over the rubble about fifty pairs of newly washed second-hand jeans, attracting customers as they dry in the morning sun. All activities exemplify the staking out of new claims to urban land by old and new settlers, who both sidestep the will of city authorities, and establish their own impromptu system of micro-governance over the site.

As we talk, a friend of Yaw casually approaches a slow-moving lorry coming into the area. He talks to the driver, who offers a few cedis and is then beckoned to a 'parking space'. A girl behind a makeshift stall selling biscuits and tinned food seems oblivious to the logic of government and the supposed difference between June 4th and a regular market site 100 metres farther along and exclaims: '*Look at all the people here buying things. Now you tell me why we should not sell things on this playing field?*' Similarly, the presence of all the new activities that are slowly mushrooming on the site continually pushes the boundaries of what the AMA will allow and what they can get away with. Although the June 4th site is only a fraction of the size of Old Fadama, the reclaiming of space by squatters after the total clearance a few months previously reflects the inability of city authorities to convincingly govern urban land.

As the activities reflect, the formal rules that are supposed to govern land and define property rights are openly, actively and relatively easily compromised by unarranged actions by the ambitious and mischievous. Still, city officials wearing fluorescent vests occasionally walk around the area to convince settlers that nothing is allowed without their consent (see the AMA press release below). In the interval, people sometimes receive tip-offs about possible dawn raids, make deals with local police and officials to persuade them to turn a blind eye, and communicate with each other quickly and effectively to warn of fast-moving squads of police in the vicinity. They rally each other's support to contest the claim that the site

The Accra Metropolitan Assembly (AMA) wishes to remind the general public especially all those who are putting up structures on government reserved lands such as along the Odaw River, Korle Lagoon, Old Fadama, the East Legon Green Belt, Mensah Guinea, Railway Station (around circle VIP Terminal), the stretch from Avenor to the Sikkens Bridge, Agbogloshie, Glefe and Chemunaa where structures were removed last year and left fallow to enhance the ongoing dredging project to remove them immediately.

Furthermore, hawkers who have turned footbridges and the under-pass of over-head bridges into trading points are to stop these activities now. All those who are selling on pavements and roads in the Metropolis are being reminded that their activities are contrary to AMA Street Hawking bye-laws 2011. While those hawking in the middle of the road are breaking the above mentioned bye-laws as well as the Road Traffic (Amendment) Act, 2008(Act 761) Section 29(2).

All are again being reminded that it is an offence to dispose of refuse, especially e-waste in water ways.

In addition, the unauthorized parking of vehicles on pavements and roads especially by mechanical shops and car garage owners are to desist from such practices and remove all vehicles either on repairs or abandoned from the shoulders of roads. AMA officials will clamp and tow such vehicles and surcharge the offenders for the cost of removal.

Finally, removal of such structures shall commence from WEDNESDAY MARCH 22, 2017 and they should know that constructing without permit is an offence punishable by law.

NUMO BLAFO III HEAD OF PUBLIC AFFAIRS

Source: citifmonline.com/2017/03/21/ama-to-commence-mass-demolition-exercise-tomorrow/

Press release by AMA concerning the prevention of building on government-reserved land (verbatim)

3.2 Adam and his bridge
Source: author

belongs to government; they exclaim that they have nowhere else to go; they claim the moral high ground, and they partially dismantle and wrap up their stalls at dusk to make their stay look temporary. In these ways the wrangling about rights to settle continues and a non-commodified, social process of controlling land in the heart of the city continues. Settlers in Old Fadama reasoned that June 4th was only demolished because Old Fadama as a whole could not be, while others expressed worry that Old Fadama would be next.

The wall: boundary-making and new opportunities

But a couple of weeks before the demolition of the June 4th site, the AMA had in fact commenced demolition of a long swathe of structures on a perimeter area of Old Fadama on the bank of the Odaw river on 22 June 2015. This process reveals how city authorities' plans to contain the settlement inadvertently provided new opportunities for new relations of informal property to develop. In contrast to the clearing of June 4th, however, residents were given warning by AMA officials and OFADA members alike, and, before the demolition, officials visited the area and marked out the area to be cleared with tape and paint. The AMA emphasized that demolition was necessary because of the high risk of flooding that building, refuse disposal and subsequent clogging of the waterways posed not only for Old Fadama, but also for large areas of central Accra situated farther upstream (Images 1.2, 1.3). To deter future encroachments along the riverbank, a strip 100 metres wide was cleared along the water's edge for almost the whole length of the settlement on one side.

In the months that followed, a concrete perimeter wall 2–3 metres high that stretched for nearly a kilometre was erected to seal this strip (see Image 3.3).[11] The attitude of some AMA officials on-site towards residents was 'we told you so, you had a chance to move, and now were walling you in!'. In this way the responsibility was denied for any future, negative consequences that occurred as a result of the wall-building. Meanwhile, some members of OFADA increased their local standing and used contacts at the AMA to take charge of the clearing of the area. They managed to gain control over the flow of resources that the clearing and wall-building required, and provided youth and clients with labouring and driving jobs, which were in high demand. By so doing 'OFADA' portrayed the image that it was cooperating fully with 'government' in the form of the AMA and that it was undertaking tasks the AMA could not have otherwise fulfilled without local opposition. Importantly, the wall-building signified that OFADA recognized the AMA as a superior power. Hence, in different ways the process of erecting the wall exemplified formal and informal powers complementing each other, and by working together both were able to gain influence over local development and benefited from new opportunities that opened up. The demolition and wall-building that were appropriated by 'OFADA' interests

3.3 The perimeter wall under construction. The view is roughly north with Old Fadama on the left and mounds of garbage and mud dredged from the waterway on the right.
Source: author

bolstered local images of individual members of OFADA themselves as powerful actors, and of OFADA as an umbrella organization doing the work of the AMA. Meanwhile, the AMA established itself as 'responsible government' that was solving serious challenges and working with community leaders.

As the majority of Old Fadama settlers are originally from the north of the country, those affected by the clearing operations in the new buffer zone were offered between 200 and 300 cedi ($50–75) by public officials to 'return immediately, preferably the same day, to go back where they came from'. But this was invariably interpreted as a bribe, an insult, and an unnecessary confirmation that northerners were not welcome in the city, and as evidence that the AMA had no comprehension of the challenges returnees would face when migrating north after many years spent in the city. There were two dynamics at play here that impacted on each other. One was northerners' understanding and experiences of the north's historical social, political and economic marginalization, which, as they understood it, was now resurfacing as the AMA encouraged and 'bribed' them to 'leave the city' and go 'home'. From this perspective, 'northerners' were being picked on and were unwelcome in Accra. The other local perception, however, was that settlers were asked to leave not because they were northerners, but 'only' because they had settled on land in violation of statutory and customary rights.[12] Despite the differences the action of clearing the land and encouraging the settlers of both June 4th and the buffer zone to leave fed into popular understandings that certain sites were targeted for clearance because they were occupied mostly by northern groups and were 'easy targets'. Whether accurate or not, residents talked about this and agreed that it was so. It demonstrated that issues pertaining to unlawful and illegal settlement easily become embroiled in prevailing debates concerning the superior and inferior rights of different ethnic groups in different parts of the country.

The clearances for the wall were therefore not limited to questions of rights to settle but fed into long-unresolved questions about ethnic citizenship and regional divides within the country. Those affected talked about the 'marginalized urban poor from the north' being chastised by a 'southern-based economic and political elite', of 'government' and the 'AMA' acting as unaccountable powers who had little interest in or knowledge of life in the north. There were also gender dimensions to the clearance as women spoke of 'bullying AMA old men' dictating what 'young northern women' could and could not do.

The most obvious effect of the government's wall was that, for the first time, a clear boundary separated Old Fadama from its surroundings. Although the official view was that the wall was intended to 'put things right' by preventing further building, it was widely interpreted and utilized by residents as something else entirely. For them the wall signified a demarcation line between, on one side, the riverbank where no buildings or settlement were permitted, and, on the other, the illegal settlement where buildings were now tolerated by the AMA. From this perspective, the state of slum had acquired for the first time a fixed administrative and political boundary that recognized the limits of city authorities' influence. Ironically, as the community experienced getting 'walled in', the wall also generated a new 'safe' space where new erections could proliferate beyond the government's gaze, and it produced new, observable differences between the 'inside' and 'outside' of Old Fadama. Thus, the wall created opportunities for new building activities that were not possible before, including constructions that actually used it as an inside wall for new dwellings. In this way, government efforts to limit informal construction, discipline the squatters, contain the settlement and prevent its spread misfired.

Although it had been agreed between public officials and OFADA that a 10-metre buffer would be observed between the wall and the first line of buildings *inside* Old Fadama, where no constructions were to be allowed, this undertaking was never enforced and was anyhow quickly overtaken by the new dwellings popping up. Some OFADA members (in disagreement with others) gave 'permission' to build in the planned buffer zone, first to one, then to another, and then to a stream of others – to the point where extended lengths of the wall came to be taken up by new shelters and it was unclear who had given who 'permission' to build. In this way the initial clearance and rebuilding in the 'border area' inside Old Fadama allowed new rights and claims to land to be renegotiated and bargained for. And well-positioned actors within Old Fadama sold permission to build, exercised discretionary powers, and made some extra money. Individuals with few resources eyed opportunities to take advantage of the messy process to carve out a space for themselves. In multiple ways, therefore, the wall created new opportunities for some and restricted the previous, hard-won rights of others. The immediate area inside the wall became cramped as pathways were built on and closed off. Rather than undo and discourage settlement, the wall actually demarcated new ground where new buildings could rise up, and it sparked a fresh round of micro-level land speculation and new relations around land control (Image 3.3).

As building spread on the inside, so did the popular idea that the wall marked a new degree of recognition bestowed by the AMA on the settlement, and that building was 'safe' (allowed) as long as it was 'inside' and did not encroach on the waterway. One resident pointed out that although a lot of houses had been destroyed and Old Fadama had 'lost' land in the demolition, the wall now served as a *'convenient'* border that would protect residents from further bulldozing and prying. This view encouraged another resident to remark that it was a sure sign of Old Fadama gaining status, which, together with the hotel, meant the settlement was moving towards the status of the rest of the city. From these perspectives, the wall provided security and protection from undesirables, including the AMA! Then a community leader weighed in, explaining that '*now that Sodom and Gomorrah proper [the June 4th site] has been successfully taken out, it is now only Old Fadama that will be on the Ghana map to be integrated into the greater Ga-Mashie constituency*'. Others, however, were not so sure: it was the AMA that had decided where and when to build the wall and it was not the first time that areas of Old Fadama would be knocked down by decree, nor would it be the last.

For Adjua, things were different: the initial demolition cleared a space at the back of her rented room but this was quickly filled with new sheds and people moving in. In the months that followed the construction of the wall Adjua recorded eighteen new structures put up 'out back', most of which were the size of single rooms in spaces previously deemed unsuitable for building because of fears of flooding and well-used pathways. But builders now reasoned that the wall and dredging of the river would diminish the risk of flooding and make the old paths useless, and this made the area popular for building. Still, building near the wall also increased the risk of flooding, since new, overlapping roofs meant rainwater drainage was concentrated in fewer places. Moreover, the new building spree created fire traps because the number of rooms with shared walls increased, paths were narrowed, and living space was now enclosed by the high concrete wall. Clearly, the AMA absolved itself of responsibility for the negative consequences and the increased risks that followed the building of the wall. Similarly, OFADA was wholly unwilling or unable to enforce rules of its own. From the AMA's perspective, the wall was about establishing control over the area on 'their' side to reduce flood risks faced by a much larger area, as well as to discipline the unwanted inhabitants. It exemplified the way the AMA did not have to fully justify its actions to residents and could act with impunity and deny responsibility for its actions. It was something 'they had to do', and rendered non-valid any productive and enabling social contract with settlers.

For Adam, meanwhile, the wall meant a loss of much-needed patronage because there was no longer easy access to his footbridge. It was effectively cut off from the settlement and was now bordered by large piles of garbage heaped up by bulldozers (Image 3.2). To improve access Adam called persistently on OFADA for help and contacted the AMA to create a gate with opening and closing times. This idea was not only rejected, but resulted in members of OFADA setting about Adam's shelter at the end of the bridge and smashing it up, angry that Adam was 'causing trouble' and undermining the objective of the wall and the aims of the AMA. Shortly afterwards, however, a group of young people who relied on the bridge broke down a section of the wall to restore access from the settlement. So, just as the lack of formal authority provided Adam with the opportunity to build the bridge unhindered and develop a fairly comfortable living, the delicate balance of relations between city authorities and OFADA meant that it had to be sacrificed and give way to the wall.

Talking to Adam, it is clear he never envisaged himself as a provider of a key community service, and back in the north he certainly never dreamed that he would end up in the capital building local infrastructure in the form of home-made bridges over major waterways! His ability to do so demonstrates the social, political and economic space that is sometimes available to the ambitious in Old Fadama. At the same time, it's important to highlight that Adam's progress is not due to distinct competitive advantages over others, business acumen or higher levels of resources than those available to others in the settlement. Rather, it is shaped by the nerve and drive to put a good idea into practice and rally help where he could find it to succeed.

Access to the bridge, however, jeopardized the purpose of the wall of containing the settlement and making difficult encroachment onto the banks of the river. So its partial destruction by OFADA members reveals that, despite the leeway enjoyed by OFADA, it is beholden to the superior power of the city authority, which 'outsources' its 'dirty work' (destroying part of the bridge) to the informal organization. Thereby, the wall clearly became part of the local political complex of emerging and productive relations between statutory and non-statutory systems of governance. Both utilized the construction of the wall to gain leverage over local affairs in new ways. At the same time, the contests reveal the contrasting logics between the survival strategies of different urban squatters, the desire to control space by government, and the aim of OFADA to carve out a role for itself as a strong and obedient partner to the AMA.

The wall defined Old Fadama as a zone of exception that is separate, enclosed and excluded from the rest of the city and 'government', and where normal rules and rights do not apply (Agamben 2005). And it marked the emerging jurisdiction of Old Fadama and the state of slum, with its own logics derived from residents' endless outmanoeuvring of formal state law. Hence, it demarcated the point where 'government' control and responsibility ended, and where government accepted it had limited control over what happened on the other side.

Changing claims, rights and spatial disparities

Exploring land-based developments demonstrates that processes of gaining and losing land are not only about its material value and market mechanisms but extend to the making and changing of rights, and social and political power. Even though all the building activities share the feature that they defy formal state law, they are different from one another because they are based on different power relations and resource levels. The tentative norms and rules that are established in one place (for example, around the school and hotel) are different to those in other settings (for example, in June 4th and around the new wall). Similarly, access and occupation proceed with reference to a range of discursive strategies, actions and systems. Gaining land can be due to a quick opportunity that is grabbed and means that others lose out, or it may be the result of months of bargaining and arrangements. For people aiming to establish businesses or build in the settlement, the diversity means they have to come to terms with a process that is often open ended, messy and experimental (Hoffman 2017). The diversity of processes linked to land-based developments is an important part of the fabric of the 'state of slum'. The informal governance of land in Old Fadama is therefore unsystematic and may be ephemeral because there is no overarching regulatory authority, system or power to establish 'once and for all' land-based rules. Effort by city authorities to enforce their rules and systems, clear areas and demarcate boundaries can evaporate almost as quickly.

The variety of building and occupation processes explored shows that access to housing is not always driven by positioning in political and patronage networks (Paller 2015). Rather, what we see on the micro level is how relatively resource-weak individuals can also enjoy the ability to create new places and networks, if they can take advantage of micro-opportunities and potentialities that open up as different land systems compete. Hence, actors in search of land for erecting basic shelters may use the process of government actions to carve out new spaces for themselves as new cracks open up. This is what we see in the 'revival' of June 4th: new settlers strive to define their own socio-economic niches and establish a place for themselves within it alongside and in competition with returnees like Yaw. The micro land grabs around the wall meanwhile testify to ordinary people following a logic of 'if it doesn't work it doesn't really matter', and 'if it goes it goes, if it don't it don't'. Hence, they take advantage of the inability of the AMA, Ga traditional authorities, and OFADA to regulate what goes on. The gaining of land and governance of local and micro-spaces are social processes that involve establishing facts on the ground in the hope that others can be convinced, or that they will buy into and accept what is going on. The process is not always successful but demonstrates the shaping of pliable informal relations of property that involve both statutory and non-statutory actors.

As we saw in the last chapter with George, the success of settling in Old Fadama can depend on establishing and nurturing productive relations within the community and gaining recognition. When it comes to larger developments the resource demands are expectedly higher. Stakeholders have to outwit as well as negotiate with competitors and convince a range of different actors that their initial claim over a plot of land is substantial before they can pursue building activities. Similarly, difficult demands are also experienced by government when it chooses to clear an area and evict people, in that demolishing shelters and shooing people away is only half the story. In the long run, if people do not respect the fact that building and settlement is not allowed, or fear that the bulldozers will return, or are not convinced that settlement in the area will not be tolerated, and if government does not use the necessary resources, then people will trickle back to a contested area and slowly start to rebuild. The control and possession of land, by squatters and government alike, therefore demands considerable and constant effort and resources to create and undo 'rights'. On the one hand, relatively simple moves by ordinary people such as putting up a stand, a stall or a tarpaulin for temporary shelter can influence others to do the same and establish mutual recognition. Subsequently, within a short space of time constructions can take shape that send the signal that here it is OK to stay and government cannot or will not assert statutory rights to land for one reason or another. On the other hand, relatively routine measures by government to bulldoze and clear land can quickly undo years of individuals' social and economic investments.

After securing a plot, a common activity for many Old Fadama residents is repairing and patching up shelters, houses, shops and other places of work and habitation. Assistance by neighbours and friends adds to micro-level endorsement of a right to stay and live in Old Fadama. Mutual support and recognition are thus engrained in a range of everyday activities that perpetuate the diverse informal property relations that all rely on. These can be challenged, however, in the event of calamities such as flooding and fire – common occurrences due to the combination of low-lying areas, cramped conditions, rickety wooden structures, widespread use of kerosene stoves, and a dearth of building regulations. Fire and flooding sometimes lead to the freeing up of much-needed building space, and those affected will sometimes try to raise roofs, expand walls or move away from dips in the ground that are prone to flooding. After calamities some may have to move elsewhere and end up not returning to rebuild as they initially planned. In such cases the social grounding of plots can evaporate, land becomes vacant for reclaiming and reselling, and new webs of social relations and socio-political networks that underpin occupation sometimes take shape. Some plots and new building activities are contested or may be fought over, while others may be transferred or exchanged without a hitch – swapped, loaned, leased, rented or re-rented. Some cleared land may be clad in new, well-functioning buildings as new interests with access to better resources gel together and realize projects. In other places, plots fall into disrepair or remain hot spots and 'wasteland' where local squabbles play out for years afterwards because stakeholders are unable to outmanoeuvre or agree with each other. While all land use in the settlement openly defies the will of government, the diverse power relations and resource levels behind different kinds of building create and change spatial disparities. As with fire and flooding, the demolition exercises undertaken by city authorities similarly dent, change and redefine resource levels, creating new disparities as houses are reduced to splintered timber and debris and new opportunities for others open up. However, one key difference between demolitions and fire and flooding is that the former mark the power and will of the 'state' to claw back control and enforce statutory rights, even if in practice they impose only a temporary halt on building and settlement. Controlling and occupying land – the staking out of claims and the substantiation of rights – are consequently a precarious affair that produces winners and losers and an uneven socio-political topography of claims and rights in the state of slum.

Conclusion

Government demolitions of informal settlements are often legitimized with reference to responsible government, a will to improve the city and protect rights. Yet formal levels of government often cannot control the social or local political consequences of demolition and forced evictions. People are left to fend for themselves, 'government' absolves itself of responsibility, and citizen rights are undermined or ignored. In these ways struggles over the control of urban land which purport that eviction is necessary in order to uphold the rule of law produce strong images of 'state' in which claims of a democratic, fair and just state are eroded (Sundar 2014).

One obvious feature of government demolitions and forced evictions therefore is not so much a determination to secure statutory property rights as purported. Rather, it is the urge to obliterate sites of illegal settlement with an almost total disregard for the social, environmental and human costs. The cycle of gaining and losing land is characterized by ordinary people circumventing the objectives of government to assert statutory rights to land, and efforts by government to clear land and undo the social, economic and socio-political investments made by ordinary people. Settlers, entrepreneurs and non-governmental supporters organize and in ingenious ways endeavour to create social facts and social documentation on the ground in the hope they will gel into socio-legal norms and locally accepted rights to land. Locally, these dynamics produce multiple, informal and fragmented relations of property based on a wide range of loose, context-specific webs of relations. There is no universal set of rules or authority that convincingly governs land issues in the state of slum. Instead, the relations of property that develop and endeavour to underpin land usage comprise a mosaic of statutory, non-statutory, formal and informal stakeholders. In turn, the diversity of interests, and competing and emerging systems of land control, undermine efforts to spread a single set of rules. Thereby, informal systems of property relations take shape. These are not established or fixed through specific institutionalization processes undertaken by politico-legal authorities, but develop through ad hoc social engagements and encounters between ordinary people that try to substantiate precarious claims to land.

The actions undertaken by both statutory institutions and settlers to gain control over land exemplify resource levels and context-specific relationships between formal and informal institutions that range from mutual and tacit support to intense competition. The regulation of the school, for example, shows that despite the illegality of the settlement, the AMA utilizes expansion to gain influence. Yet at the same time the AMA appears powerless to intervene and is actively undermined by the building activity itself, as is also the case with the hotel construction. Conversely, we have seen how informal organizations of governance in the form of OFADA utilize formal institutions of government to gain local influence and introduce formal elements of management into their organization. In the case of the wall and the clearing of the June 4th settlement, moreover, we see how government efforts to contain settlement inadvertently fuel the informalization of property relations and provide new opportunities for building, which OFADA itself is unable to control convincingly. The absence of state support for badly needed infrastructure, the dearth of public services in Old Fadama, and people's experiences of not getting the help they need all feed into a lack of anticipation for what the 'state' will bring in the way of improvements. Thus, local initiatives such as school-building gain a sense of urgency, and establish understandings of justification along the lines of 'if we don't do this nobody will', and 'it's important that we all support this'. In these ways land-based developments create new loose networks of social support. The building projects and land-based developments discussed in this chapter are suggestive of an important structural challenge of urban development more generally in Africa. There is a wide gap between the way ordinary people validate land rights through social relations and investment, and the endeavours of government to do the same through the logic of formal state law.

4
Shifting yam and marketplace citizenship

The yam and vegetable markets of Agbogbloshie serve as main breadbaskets for Accra and beyond and support thousands of livelihoods and countless supporting small businesses and services. The yam market is widely known as a Konkomba area because it is predominantly managed by loose networks of Ghanaian Konkomba comprising thousands of individuals. These link up with others who farm, trade and transport yam mainly in the north, north-east and southern parts of the country, many of whom are also ethnic Konkomba. Since its inception, however, the yam market in Accra has been plagued by its 'temporary' status and, despite its obvious popularity and the whole area being a hub of enterprise, has had long-standing contentions with the AMA and different Ghanaian governments. In this way, the issue of the yam market's temporary status and plans for its relocation have become embroiled with the political and legal contentions concerning the plight of Old Fadama. The pressure to move the market has now haunted it for many years and meant there has been a long-standing political unwillingness to optimize the market potential of the area. Nevertheless, it has grown to become the largest of four major national trading points for agricultural produce in Ghana, and in terms of movement and handling of produce is now the second-largest yam market in West Africa.[1] Consequently, this chapter focuses on the experiences of Konkomba working in the market under the perennial conditions of not knowing its fate, and as forged by the stalemate and pressure from statutory institutions to move. Exploring this dynamic gives insights into socio-political and socio-economic conditions that produce local identities, and understandings of citizenship rights as experienced from below. Thus, what we see is how the political and legal conditioning shapes the state of slum and produces context-specific rights of citizenship and belonging.

The original idea laid out by government when the market was established in 1981 was that it should only be temporary. Many years later, and with the legal entanglement as well as increasing developmental challenges coming from a burgeoning Old Fadama, city authorities started to push for the market to be relocated to a site outside city limits. The plan to move was based on the simple and optimistic logic that 'if the market is moved the people will follow'. The immediate results of the contentious stalemate over whether the market should stay or go are considerable traffic congestion in the area, loss of market potential, and mounting infrastructural challenges that go unheeded. The challenges have mounted up as the population of the area and the number of informal businesses have also increased. Moreover, everyday disturbances risk flaring up and can be accentuated by narratives peddled by politicians, media and ordinary people alike, who depict the area's challenges and the stalemate in ethnic terms.[2]

As with Old Fadama, the yam market exemplifies a case of government inability to solve myriad challenges that have slowly unfolded and accumulated as a result of decades of indecision, passing the buck, and a lack of coherent, comprehensive and realistic planning. Consequently, the yam market has taken on a life and logic of its own disjoined from formal regulation with a multitude of sociopolitical and economic activities governed by its own rules, norms and customs. These diverge from the logic of sections of government that push for the relocation and have developed largely out of government's reach.

The city authority in the form of the AMA uses the threat of relocation as a political tool to wrestle control over urban space, people and resources, but is not powerful enough to pursue the objective of relocation. Indeed, the idea of moving the market appears certain, ambiguous and impossible to execute at the same time. The complexity and massive costs involved are sidestepped in utterances that highlight the plan to relocate, which remains a central component of political rhetoric and is not ruled out. This is a point where the trajectories of the yam market and Old Fadama diverge, because while the question of relocating the market has continued as a political priority, in recent years the issue of clearing the whole of Old Fadama has waned. This is despite ongoing political and public support for closing Old Fadama, which appears more and more as an unrealistic and unviable policy option. As we saw previously, the removal of Old Fadama has given way to government actions centred on containment, law, order and 'normalization'. For governments and city authorities alike, therefore, the persistence of the yam market in its present location is another embarrassment and exemplifies another failure to follow through with city plans. Similar to Old Fadama, the plight of the Konkomba yam market also reveals governments absolving themselves of responsibility for the myriad social, cultural, economic and political challenges that have followed in the wake of the stalemate. Instead, a hotchpotch of shifting and non-institutionalized relations with stand-offs and easing-offs between market stakeholders and government actors and institutions has perpetuated the stalemate year after year. Meanwhile, the thousands of people who work in the market and the thousands of others who rely on it have had to get used to working under very difficult and insecure conditions. On an everyday level they experience constant pressure to vacate the area under looming threats of imminent market closure. Traders experience loss of produce and trade from warnings of confiscation, hassle, obstruction, delays, high costs and the permanent sense of unknowability concerning the market's plight. The negative impacts that the continual uncertainty about moving and staying have had on market life and the organization of trade are difficult to underestimate and extend to social and political life.

This chapter shows how the conditions of uneasiness reproduce historical understandings of regional divides between the north and the south of the country. Particularly, we see how the imbroglio regenerates understandings of ethnically defined citizenship and of Konkomba as a second-rate, rurally based settler group who do not belong in the south and the capital city, homeland of the native Ga. The pressure to move and experiences of not being wanted in the city produce ideas of Konkomba yam stakeholders as 'us', and levels of government as 'them'. The pressure to move thereby alienates the group from what they perceive as 'government', and it hardens lines of division between the Konkomba and the Dagomba, the largest ethnic group in Old Fadama

One advocate of moving the yam market out of Accra, for example, emphasized that 'Konkomba' unwillingness to move was based on the group 'not really having anywhere to go'. This does not mean that the Konkomba in the yam market have lost their formal rights as Ghanaian citizens and do not belong in the city. Rather, their present-day experiences of opposition, of not being consulted about the relocation, pressure to move from Accra, and hearing from public officials that 'you have to go', feed into the negative histories of marginalization and discrimination the ethnic group experienced in the north in the 1980s.

The narratives and sentiments about ethnic affiliation mean that the issue of relocating the market and its temporary status are not merely about moving or not moving, but become embroiled with contentious political issues of citizenship rights. This touches on whether government should actively support the right of a designated 'settler' group to settle on the land of 'natives', against their will. Moreover, the question of improving market infrastructure touches on ideological concerns and political ideas about the role the state should play and the use of public funding to finance the betterment of market conditions. For some opponents, market improvements should be left to private investors and market stakeholders. As a consequence of the stalemate between market users who don't want to move, governments and city authorities that want them to, and the general increase in economic activity in the area, the physical condition of the market has deteriorated. Several traders spoke of high risks of crime in the market areas, especially after nightfall, which again reinforces images and ideas of the market area as 'backward', 'underdeveloped' and an unwanted aberration that spoils aims to modernize the city. The labour-intensive, unmechanized nature of yam production and distribution as well as the 'muddy' nature of yam trading provide further evidence for opponents that the yam business is incapable of diversification, development and modernization and does not belong in a 'modern' city environment.

For the market people themselves, however, the market is also something to be proud of and a source of inspiration, as it is an area that not only has survived despite the odds, but has flourished to become a key economic hub for Accra. It is here that urban life starts for many migrants, and for the lucky, careers and educations are kickstarted with the money made by labouring in the market. Through everyday interactions and encounters, social status is attained, power relations are affirmed and communities and local identities are shaped. All this takes place under the gaze of government but goes against government plans.

First, the chapter discusses the approaches of studies of citizenship that provide the analytical frame for the empirical material. Next, some of the everyday activities of the market are described from the perspectives of traders and managers. This includes their experiences of working with the doubt about whether the market will be relocated in the near future and the unknowability about how long they will remain where they are. Afterwards, the contentions about the issue of relocation and how they feed into historical animosities and lines of division between the north and south of the country, between ethnic affiliations and categories of settlers and natives, are explored and elaborated.

Citizenship

Citizenship is often equated with a series of rights and status bestowed by statutory institutions on individuals who are full members of a community and which protects an ability to be '*equally able to determine the conditions of* [your own] *association*'.[3] Marshall draws attention to three important dimensions: political rights, which include political participation and suffrage; civic rights, including the protection of, access to and fairness of a legal system; and social rights, which are the '*distributive rights to social entitlements that define the obligations of the state to citizens as well as obligations between citizens themselves*'.[4] Ideally, citizenship allows individuals to define the rules of the polity of which they are members, and to decide on leaders to represent their interests. If not, they should at least be able to hold leaders to account. The historical attainment of citizenship is thereby often equated with formal, national status bestowed by governments (Honneth 1995). This focus can, however, deny the role and significance of a whole range of forces, including non-statutory institutions and actors and social networks, which in legal pluralist contexts like Old Fadama and the Konkomba market impact heavily on the actual ability of ordinary people to enjoy their formal status and rights.

Understanding the actual citizenship status of settlers and workers in the market therefore demands looking beyond the formal rights of residents (such as the ability to vote freely, and to delegate power to holders of public office), to consider local processes and conditions that make their rights less or more meaningful. Because marginalization often takes place regardless of one's national citizenship status, it is useful to look at how effective citizenship actually is. This directs attention to citizenship as a dynamic status that can be lost or gained through social actions and encounters (Heller 2009: 125; Isin and Turner (2002). The actors and institutions involved in this process of recognizing, supporting and substantiating citizenship rights in the market are many, but include local chiefs and elders; home-town associations; religious leaders; street gangs; local, national and global NGOs; political actors; and voluntary organizations such as charities. In an everyday capacity, moreover, we find it is frequently neighbours, friends, family and one's immediate network who stand up for each other's rights, and who in turn recognize and contribute to the norms and customs of the broader community they live in. The recognition of rights in the market is a process that is purely informal, non-institutionalized and often implicit, yet it produces strong images and understandings of status, local rights and belonging. The significance of local over national citizenship, which is common in Africa, reflects the fact that the sovereign power of the Ghanaian state is incomplete. In terms of citizenship, the Ghanaian state therefore competes with, and loses ground to, diverse local groups and networks around the market that have something better and more tangible to offer and simply provide the necessary resources.

Market organization and governance

The yam market is the first port of call for many young rural–urban migrants after leaving home towns in the north of the country to seek new opportunities in the capital, and for George, Yaw, Adjua and Frederick it was the first place they earned money in Accra, while for Jemima it remains the only place where she has worked. Young men typically embark on the ceaseless loading and unloading of yam lorries by hand, or the pushing of handcarts full of yams to different buyers and sellers, while females take up work as head-porters. Close to the yam market are scores of smaller vegetable stalls that stretch along both sides of the main road. It is in this area of Agbogbloshie–Old Fadama that youth hook up with old school friends, acquaintances, distant relatives and drop-outs from home towns. They get the run-down on where to stay, who to befriend and who to avoid. Up-to-date details of casual and fleeting labour opportunities currently on offer in the markets and surrounding areas are exchanged with news and gossip about home towns.

In high season the yam market is jam-packed from dawn with open trucks stacked to bursting point with fresh yams. For want of parking space drivers may have chosen to overnight close by on bits of waste ground, such as the one freed up by the recent clearing of the June 4th settlement (Chapter 3). Heavy congestion on nearby roads is a daily occurrence as overloaded and often decrepit lorries queue to enter the market through a gap only a few metres wide. The market area has no specific parking areas or holding or loading bays for market traffic, no weighing station, walled areas or security at the entrance. It is wholly un-demarcated. The 'in-road' to the market is muddy, potholed and filled with rubble and sand by market labourers. On either side of the opening from the main road are kiosks and abandoned, stripped and smashed-up vehicles. Farther in, one-man stalls offer imported tinned food and consumables – notably pasta and tinned tomatoes – plastic household goods, poor-quality building materials, and haircuts, truck, car, motorbike and bicycle repairs, seamstresses and tailors, beers and soft drinks. Lorries sway unexpectedly as they fall into the potholes as they rumble slowly in, and girls hurry past with head loads and raised hands as if they can hold back 10 tons of yam. After the lorries come motorbikes that take advantage of the openings. They speed up to avoid getting stuck in the mud before the openings are filled again by the mass of people and hawkers on the main road. Now and again a wobbly four-wheeled barrow stacked high with yam pushes past with one boy at the front and two boys at the back. They shout at each other to get moving and for all others to get out of the way. If they lose momentum the barrow too will sink into the muddy furrows left by the lorries.

We sit and watch the hectic scene most of the morning as we talk to Antony, the daily secretary-cum-manager of the yam market who has worked there since the beginning in 1981. He can be found there most days and his main tasks include organizing the coming and going of the many lorries, collecting 'rent' money from the yam traders, keeping an eye out for petty thieves, and rallying youth groups for communal clean-ups and chores around the market area. He ushers us into the 'office', a rented space on the ground floor of a two-storey building of bare concrete. It is just inside Old Fadama and offers good views of the lorries that have to pass by to enter the market. It's not like any 'normal' office because it's completely empty and stands as a concrete shell apart from a scuffed wooden table and three plastic chairs. There are no cupboards, filing cabinets, shelves, pictures, calendars, computers, pens or paper, toilets, kitchen, kettle or much else one would expect to find in the office of *the* busiest agricultural market in the country, which handles thousands of tons of yam every month. There is no electricity and the bare walls are adorned with scribbled telephone numbers. A colleague of Antony joins in the conversation but first sweeps out the mud and dust that has blown in through gaps in the walls where windows and doors should be.

As we sit talking it becomes clear that the appearance and work-ings of the market office are very much influenced by its temporary status and indefinite political status. The office is empty not because it isn't needed or used, or because of a lack of resources, but because the yam traders and informal management are fearful of impending eviction and confiscation of property. As one elder said:

> [Because] there is a threat we are moving away, people that have the mentality to develop [do not do so]. We cannot stay because

at any time we can be forced to move away. You see how nasty
and filthy the whole place is? The drainage is poor. Everything
is poor. So, when someone tells you its temporary here, how can
you develop the place? (Interview, James Kpajal and Roland Naji,
27 July 2014)

The elders describe the market as a Konkomba place and
emphasize that 'we' are threatened, 'we' cannot stay, and 'we' are
treated differently from other areas of the city. The empty office
provides an alternative and more subtle expression of informality
contrasting with common manifestations of the urban informal
sector as constant hustle and bustle. It is as it is because it is the
product of the decades of cajoling and indecision by successive
governments, which unwillingly accepted its continued existence.
For the Konkomba market elders, it represents a hard-won, semi-
autonomous space and expresses local determination to persist in
spite of 'government' plans to eject them and the market from the
city. As Antony put it, '*This is where we meet and talk and discuss market
issues. This is our place. We do things on our own here, and this is where we
decide things.*' For Antony the fact that there even was an office was
a sure sign that the market was successful in its own right, and in
warding off a hostile external environment for nearly forty years. All
involved with the yam market had been told countless times by politicians and media alike over many years that relocation was imminent
and that they could not expect any notice as enough warnings had
been given already. It was on the understanding that they could be
moved at any time that the market management agreed not to keep
anything in the office. James and Roland, two colleagues of Antony,
have been involved in the yam trade for decades too. Both started
as small-scale producers on family farms in the north and over the
years combined family-based production with market trading in
Accra. Now, the two represent loose groups of small-scale farmers,
drivers and traders. James explained:

There is no permanent office. There is no place for all [the]
documents to be kept safe. You have to have it all under your
arm in a bag because one day it will be ransacked. We have been
meeting [AMA] security people and once in a while there is a
problem, and you come early in the morning and [suddenly, the
office] is heavily guarded and you cannot enter, and therefore it is
very risky to keep your documents here. (Interview, James Kpajal
and Roland Naji, 27 July 2014)

Since the plans for relocation emerged around 2010, they and others have become adept at operating in an environment that could be ransacked at almost any time. They also focus efforts on lobbying government to support relocation to a site other than that proposed by government, which, they argue, is wholly unpractical. Antony explains:

The first place we had was just across the road but it was too close to a school that was always being disturbed, so they reported us to the education authorities and they asked us to leave. So, we contacted our MP. This was around 1980. The matter was taken up in parliament and then when the conflict [ethnic fighting in the Northern Region] occurred, the city council released part of the land to establish the market. So that was how the place was given to us. There was no contract. It was only that we should accept it as a temporary place from the government who released the land to us. (Interview, 27 July 2014)

The former Konkomba yam market was also very close to timber and yam markets that were under Dagomba and Nanumba control. As such, the moving of the Konkomba yam market to its present location was designed to diffuse emerging animosities between the different ethnic groups in the capital that were already playing out in the north of the country (Longi Felix and Mbowura 2014). The lorries entering the market hold between five and seven thousand yam, and from early morning they are unloaded by hand. Teams of youth toss the yam one at a time along a chain where they are stacked on the ground in piles of 100. After the stacks are sold the yam on top are dabbed with paint of different colours to identify buyers. Female head-porters stack up to thirty-five yam, which may weigh as much as 100 kg in total, in their large metal bowls. Others help lift the load onto their heads before they scurry off in twos and threes through the market crowds to the buyers' destination of choice. Rates of porterage are negotiable but are about 50 cents for a fifteen- or twenty-minute walk with a full head load.

The straggling yam market comprises an open space about the size of a football pitch filled with countless piles of yam guarded by mostly female traders who sit on low wooden stools. The traders are partly shielded from the sun, dust and rain by battered, sun-bleached parasols (Image 4.1). Around one side of the market are dozens of small wooden sheds and shacks that face the market and act as a demarcation line separating the housing and shacks of Old Fadama.

Awnings at the front face the market and are used by labourers, drivers and market women as shelter for chatting, sleeping and looking after youngsters. When it rains all huddle together under-neath to seek shelter. Attached to each shed are between twenty and fifty sellers who 'belong to a shed' and pay a commission to the owner to occupy a selling pitch nearby. A single yam is collected every day by Antony and colleagues from each of the sellers as rent-in-kind. The collected yam is then resold to cover different market expenses and a percentage is forwarded to the Konkomba chief of Accra and his elders. The individual yam sellers also pay a yearly levy to the AMA. The trading of yam is gendered, with men gener-ally taking care of buying and selling large quantities to individual women traders, who sit together in small groups selling smaller quantities. Jemima buys from both middlemen and directly from farmers and sells about thirty to 100 yams at a time to local and regular customers, who come by weekly or fortnightly. Trading is impossible without a high degree of trust between different buyers and sellers across scales and networks that join up extended family members, growing areas and points of sale (Grant 2009).

The challenges experienced in the Konkomba market every day link up with much wider institutional challenges that the Ghanaian yam trade faces, and which impact negatively on trade, surplus and capacity across the country. For example, it was only in 2012 that the

4.1 The Konkomba yam market
Source: author

Ghanaian government took steps to formulate a supporting policy framework (the Yam Sector Development Strategy). This did not address the underdevelopment of the yam market in Accra specifically, although it did identify numerous sector-wide challenges. These included a range of managerial and technocratic-related obstacles such as limited access to finance and investment, a dire lack of storage and preservation capacity along the commodity chain from farm to market, near-non-existent food, health, safety and other qualitative standards, and a dearth of processing, value-addition and export promotion opportunities.[5] The lack of universal standards, for instance, means that yam quality is negotiable and favours experienced and powerful traders at the expense of the vulnerable. And poor road networks and lack of storage and warehousing facilities lead to post-harvest loss as well as rotting, damage and petty theft at markets sites. In all, the many negative logistical and infrastructural features of the yam trade increase risk, costs, uncertainty and unreliability.[6]

Jemima

Under one of the parasols sits Jemima in a spot she shares with five or six other yam-selling female friends. All are Konkomba and, like the others, Jemima has her cash wrapped tightly around her waist in a knotted cloth and her phone is at hand. Despite spending up to ten hours a day in the market, six days a week, for the last sixteen years, in roughly the same spot, none of the sellers has other belongings with them. Similar to the working conditions in the office, this makes it easy to move or flee within minutes and reflects the temporariness of the market space. In the event of a 'raid' the traders prioritize their personal safety and are forced to leave behind the tons of yam that surround them, which anyhow would not be possible to transport.

Jemima is from Saboba in the Northern Region. Her uncle owns a small storage shed in the market and helped her get established as a trader. Her husband trades large quantities of yam and her eldest son unloads lorries and works a hand barrow. She explains about getting established as a trader:

> In this market in particular, you must know someone or pass through someone before you start. In addition, you do not just come here because you feel like coming to Accra, and see people

selling, and you then start selling yourself. [You have to] go
through the process and procedure of acquiring a place [to sell].
That person [you go through] must own a shed. [They] control
who sells in front of the shed. (Interview, 21 January 2016)

Jemima explains that the yam trade is inherently unpredictable
and its sensitivities are worsened by the looming threat of eviction.
The need for trust is related to the chronic lack of credit that many
traders experience. She says her customers generally do not have
sufficient cash to cover the amount of yam they want and trust
issues often mean that a sale does not go ahead. In turn, she herself
rarely has enough cash to cover the amount she wants to buy from
middlemen higher up the commodity chain. The threat of eviction
and constant 'scares' increase the need for trust, make it difficult to
establish stable relations with customers, and make access to credit
from formal institutions such as banks near impossible. Despite
years in the trade, she says it is not possible for her to access credit
from banks and she has to rely on socio-ethnic networks. It is risky
to make unsecured deals with unfamiliar customers as *we do not
know if we can find each other again if we are moved without notice*.
She adds that the absence of sufficient storage facilities around the
market is also a major problem. This leads to unnecessary losses
and risks too, because it is normal that customers reserve quantities
of yam in advance before returning to pay and collect, which may
be several days later or longer. Informal trading agreements state
that sellers are responsible for the yams until they are collected and
so any losses from rot, damage or petty theft that occur while the
yam await collection in the open are borne by the sellers. Thus,
Jemima and her friends experience first-hand how the uncertainty
around the relocation impacts negatively on her business and translates into credit and storage shortages, interrupts supply, raises
risks and costs, and makes it difficult to provide necessary services
to customers.

Pressure to move, promises to stay

Over the years, there have been many leading political voices urging
'The market should go!' In October 2009, for example, the then
major of Accra, Alfred Okoe Vanderpuije, warned market traders
to prepare to be relocated.[7] And in January 2014, national media
proclaimed on the basis of an AMA press release that

> Friday, February 28, 2014 will see the end of the Agbogbloshie market and all foodstuffs located at Old Fadama as a team made up of officials from the Ga West Municipal Assembly, Accra Metropolitan Assembly, National Security and the Police Service will begin relocating all traders.[8]

However, this day came and went without any signs of relocation on the part of traders or city authorities. Afterwards, the market settled down the best it could with suppliers, traders and customers alike not knowing if the statements were just more empty threats or whether a forced relocation had only just been averted. Fresh calls to move the market were aired when the area experienced street fighting in April 2017 after a disagreement between youth escalated into 'ethnic' clashes. This led the Inspector General of Police to state that *'One major solution to this is for us to ensure that the people are relocated.'*[9]

Government plans to move the Konkomba yam market to the peri-urban site of Adjen Kotoku are traceable to the then NPP government of John Kufuor in 2007. Storage areas and in-roads were completed at the new site in 2012 and a number of other facilities and improved infrastructure including a new senior high school, a fire station, a police station and a health clinic have since been completed (Image 4.2). The grand plan is to redevelop what is at present a sparsely populated site outside of Greater Accra to draw rural–urban migrants away from Old Fadama and Agbogbloshie. But the site, located nearly 40 kilometres from central Accra, and which can easily take over an hour to drive to, has proved widely disliked and governments have been unable to coax people away. Indeed, the idea of shifting trade to the new site is deemed unthinkable by many traders, who have, in effect, boycotted the new site, which stands idle (Image 4.2).

The lingering issue of moving the market has meant that an important part of its character is that it defies government and persists despite not being wanted by the AMA in the city. But while utterances over the years from different state institutions point to an impending relocation, the people who actually work in the market are left guessing as to what the lack of decisive steps towards either relocation, upgrading or something else actually means. Opposition to the move is voiced not only by the many different daily users of the market, but also stakeholders at the proposed new site at Adjen Kotoku, who do not want their relatively quiet home town area transformed into a second, sprawling Agbogbloshie. So the government has experienced difficulties in reaching political agreement about the move and obtaining the land needed for the relocation from the customary authorities at the proposed site. As a related issue, there have been deep-seated disagreements about the amount of compensation that should be paid.

Up to 2018, however, the principal idea that migrants will move away from Old Fadama when the market also moves continues to be a dominant and popular position amongst politicians at each end of the spectrum. Nevertheless, this simplified version of reality has not materialized because it anticipates a voluntary diaspora to the sparsely populated peri-urban site, which fails to consider the numerous drivers that make the present location popular and convenient. As a friend of Jemima said, laughing, 'not one yam has ever been sold at that place'.[10] Government logic holds, however, that a relocation is both desirable and necessary to lessen congestion in central Accra, and would redirect the waves of seasonal migrants that come to the market to work (Afenah 2012). As of 2018 the proposed site remained empty and idle, symbolizing the high level of detachment between city authorities and government interests in favour of relocation, and a mass of different agricultural stakeholders who want the market to stay in the capital. Antony said:

Yes, the letters were given to us to move [in February 2014] but you know Ghana. We had a pleasant encounter with the movement team and they put a hold on it, but in my mind, I know this place is temporary. We have been given the place at Adjen Kotuku but we feel if we go there, we will not be able to make the market, and the mistake is, people of Adjen Kotuku are also agitating [against us moving there]. The government has not paid for the land or any concessions and therefore we don't see why [we should move]. And then the people behind [the move] have given us a bad image. You know when people talk about Konkomba market they don't see it as people selling yams, they just think we are a bunch of hooligans that have come to settle there. Some people from Adjen Kotuku came and saw the market and said they wanted it, but not the squatters. [But how can we stop people moving?] We are not accepting the fact that if we don't move then one day we will be forced out of this place, so why not move people to other grounds where the land is more accommodating, and we will not spoil it? You know, when it rains here the water cannot move away or sink into the ground. It cannot seep anywhere, so this makes the place very muddy

4.2 Rows of sheds stand idle at the planned site for the Konkomba yam market – Adjen Kotuku
Source: author

and smelly, so it will be better if we could get a place outside, but then again too we think of the proximity to our customers. You know Adjen Kotuku is far, very far, and it's not at all practical. (Interview, 6 July 2014)

The sellers and informal managers spoke of numerous other challenges with the proposed site: Antony explained that many vendors only buy small quantities of yam but also purchase many other goods and services that are available in the Old Fadama area while they are there. In the event of relocation, he reasoned, they would therefore still have to shop in Accra and it would be highly inconvenient and expensive for vendors to travel to both places. He feared the long distance to Adjen Kotuku would put them off.

He continued:

[Government] is not listening, they are not listening! It's an impractical solution. Even the land there, it's been encroached upon! [There are squatters living there.] You know the size of it and the way it's been constructed? You know we need a big car park, and people can't stay there. We need places where people can stay for two or three days and then they are gone. So, we need some kind of sleeping places and toilet facilities and washrooms, and a place of other kinds of vendors. It looks like none of these things are there!

Clearly, there was a strong sense that government had planned and built the new site without taking Konkomba knowledge, experiences and interests in the yam trade into consideration.

James adds:

[It was] the idea of the central government. We were not consulted. It was a rush. [It was like] *We will move you there whether you like it or not. We are breaking this place and moving you there!* (Interview, James Kpajal, 27 July 2014)

For these stakeholders and the many traders and labourers they talk to everyday and represent, there has been a complete lack of dialogue about the move and wholly inadequate planning. Further, they reason that the numerous concerns they raise about the new site show that moving the market actually has very little to do with wanting to improve market conditions and develop the yam trade. Rather, they see relocation as a political strategy to get Konkomba out of the city and clear the market area for modern commercial and investor-driven property developments.

For James and Roland, the government only chose the new site because of a lack of alternatives in the Greater Accra area and because the local government institution in Adjen Kotuku, the Ga West Assembly, offered to sell land.[11] Other opponents of the move in the market claim that the site was built purely to showcase Ghana as a modern and attractive marketplace for investment. From this perspective, the new site was built to demonstrate to foreign dignitaries that the AMA was actively combating urban sprawl and taking congestion seriously with the opening up of peri-urban sites. Whether accurate or not, such accounts of the relocation fed into existing apprehensions that the Konkomba-driven yam trade was simply not wanted in the city.

Nevertheless, nearly six years after completion there were still no vendors at the new site and the place was totally desolate. The uncertainty about whether the move would ever take place dragged on and was a constant cause of stress and anxiety for the hundreds of traders whose livelihoods are grounded in the yam trade in Accra. Next to Jemima are four Konkomba friends who are all traders and have between two and five family members working in the yam market as well. I asked each of them how long they had worked in the market and they laughed as they answered that they have over 100 years' experience between them. One said about the move:

> You know your mind is always telling you that you are moving. We were last given three months [to move] but look at this whole place. *How can you move such a place in three months?* (Interview, 22 January 2016)

A second said they had only been told to 'go' and were occasionally shooed by AMA officials but had received no concrete information about how the proposed move would proceed:

> [Yes] they gave us three months but that is now passed and they haven't come to tell us anything, *there is no 'how'*, so we are just sitting on it. They can come any time and say move. *You know if you want to move us then move us! If you want to leave us then leave us!* (Interview, 22 January 2016)

Hence, despite the enormity and complexity of relocating the market, the regular traders that comprise its backbone are at a total loss as to how it will happen.

A third added:

> It [came] to our notice they should eject us from here. We are told that [they could come] any time, that they want to get us, that they've got a loan from outside, and want to dredge the lagoon, and make it a tourist centre, and all that. But mostly you can't see [anything]. Someone some time may come in [every] one or maybe two months [and tell us to leave]. Then they will stop and we [will stay]. And in some year to come, especially after the elections, they will threaten '*You are going, you are going!*' Then it goes down when we get to the election [and] it dies off. Nobody mentions it again. All the politicians come to campaign: '*There, there, you can stay here, you can stay here. When I win I will come and make it good for you!*' [It is something] both sides [of the political spectrum] promise. Any politician and party will say '*Oh, when we win we will make your market.*' (Interview, 22 January 2016)

The fourth said, 'They are just deceiving and using us for politics to win their elections.'

Jemima continues:

They [the AMA] are always coming with a letter demanding
that they want to move the market from here. It may happen that
[we] will be moved, and it can happen that [we] will not. I am
ready for whatever is going to happen. [But] no one knows when
they will be moving us! [And] we cannot sleep. We are always
thinking about the idea of moving [even as we are still here] and
they have not moved us, things are very difficult! How much
more so if they move us? How is the patronage [trade] going to
be? [P]eople will not go there [Adjen Kotuku] at the end of the
[working] day. The market and the yam business will collapse!
(Interview, 22 January 2016)

Jemima and her colleagues also worry that the relocation would
lead to price increases as everything and everyone connected to the
yam market would have to travel farther and incur numerous extra
expenses. They would obviously prefer to stay where they are as
it is here they have their friends, family, co-traders, networks and
customer bases built up over many years.

Staying and going, and perceptions of difference

As seasoned sellers, Jemima and her friends share an awareness
that many of the difficulties they experience are due not only to the
bungled relocation plan. They are based as well in governments not
acknowledging what they as traders actually do, how they contribute
to the development of the city, and what the market actually means
for the area. Thereby, they feel estranged by the pressure to move,
seeing their everyday participation in the market as contributing to
the development of the city. On the one hand it is impossible for
them to do what government says and move their trade because they
have to stay where the trade is. Yet on the other, staying where they
are gives their trade the appearance of a protest that actively defies
government, which they do not want either. As such, their ongoing
participation in the market places them in a no-win situation, where
to earn a living they have to defy the simplistic rationale of government. This produces a sense of 'us' versus an unhelpful 'them'. In
turn, staying put and carrying on expresses the desire to not give in
to government cajoling, which they do not see the logic in anyway.
In this way the continuation of yam market activities by Konkomba
in Accra demonstrates its detachment from 'government logic' and
reflects the impotence of city authorities to enforce their will. The

persistence of the market moreover exemplifies the inability of individual suppliers, traders and customers and of government to set in motion and orchestrate the considerable resources that a move would entail. This is similar to the impossible task the government faces in executing the eviction order. What we see instead are efforts by city authorities to encourage movement away from these areas and occasionally make life difficult while perpetuating 'myths' that the market will be moved and settlement in Old Fadama will not be tolerated. The combination of unwillingness and inability reproduces popular ideas of the Konkomba ethnic group as 'difficult', and of 'government' as 'incompetent' and 'unreliable'. While the pressure to move plays out, however, Konkomba elders have pursued ideas to develop another site of their own choice. As James explained:

> Our late chief and some elders [have] acquired some land [which is more suitable for the market]. If you look it's a Konkomba community, and for that matter we have reserved a space for a market which the new chief wants us to develop. [This is] closer to the Konkomba community than moving to Adjen Kotoku which is far away [and our site is] closer to the newly constructed road [the N6–Nsawam road]. [So we want] our *own* market which we *own* and where no government can come and say, *Go here! Go there!* You know, most of the farmers are illiterates and therefore they cannot do this money transfer thing [electronic transferral of money that requires a bank account] so they work with cash and theft is a real risk. The new site we have chosen would be much better and safer. You can come and sell, and stay with your brother, uncle and so on, and then you take the car from here to sell in Accra. (Interview, 27 July 2014)

What we see here are efforts to solve the problem without the interference of government and where Konkomba can control things for themselves. James reasons that gaining political and economic backing for their proposed market is made more difficult owing to the widespread support in Ghana for a development model based on liberal, market-based growth without state interference. In Roland's view, this means as well that there is a reluctance to modernize the agricultural sector as a whole, which the yam trade is an important part of:

> It's not that politicians don't want to support the idea, it's that *you* are doing *your* trade and we are farmers who come to sell *our*

produce. So, it's the case that they [government] leave us on our own. That is it. It is like we are peasant farmers. (Interview, 27 July 2014)

For Ubori Bio, a Konkomba chief of Accra, the decades of deadlock and indecisiveness around the relocation, together with the lack of support for the market, have been sure signs of successive governments not wanting to recognize the significance of the Konkomba-controlled yam trade. He said:

We always go to AMA [and] as for the mayor, he did not hide anything from us, and all he told us is that considerations about the movement of the yam market are constant. The market *will* be moved from that area. And so we asked him, *Then if that be the case, you should show us where you will send us to* [Where should we stay?] And he answered, *There is no place for your people, and even if we give you people another area, there will be a time we will move you again.* Based on [this] and what we also heed from other sources, we decided to find a land for ourselves so that we can buy. It is very sad and painful that we the yam farmers in the Northern Region do not get any help from the government. It's only around Tamale that the farmers at times get support [inputs] from the government but the rest of us, we [still] do the farming with our hands [even though] we produce yams in large quantities and supply Old Fadama. (Interview, 27 July 2014)

Thus, the choice of leading Konkomba stakeholders to ignore Adjen Kotuku and build their own site is based not only on infrastructural and practical concerns, but also on deeper and pressing political issues concerning their status as a settler group with historically inferior rights to land and citizenship. A main concern is therefore that *any* relocation will be conditional and, ultimately, temporary. Experiencing the wavering uncertainty, veiled threats and overall lack of government support consequently reignites ideas of Konkomba historical grievances, regional developmental disparities, and ethnically defined marginalization. The sense of unfairness shared by different Konkomba stakeholders is made worse by the regular extraction of different fees and taxes by the AMA, which, the chief suggests, amounts to at least $750 a day (based on the market receiving on average fifty truckloads of yam daily during harvest times and paying one cedi to the AMA for every 100 yam).[12]

The chief shares the viewpoint of Antony that the relocation plan is not really about developing the market in a better place, but about removing Konkomba from valuable urban land that can be sold off expensively for redevelopment. He frames the struggle in ethnic terms between the 'rural' Konkomba and an unaccommodating 'urban' government, between the Konkomba as a 'settler' group and Dagomba as a 'native' group that controls Old Fadama, and between Konkomba and 'Ga' as the customary owners of the urban land. The chief said:

> [Destroying] the yam market will move everyone from the area and the name Konkomba will be gone. Dagomba just don't want to hear the name *Konkomba market* so it's all about tribalism and politics, and they are trying to claim the ownership of that place from us. Today, if you go to the yam market and you ask for the chief, they will send you to the Dagomba chief's house, and the fact is that Dagomba don't like us at all, and want us to always be under them. Now, we *the Konkomba* have bought a large piece of land [for our own market and] if anyone wants land there to build on, we can sell it to that person to build, and we welcome everyone to that area. [But] not long [afterwards] the Dagomba came [and said] they wanted to appoint a chief there who will be next to me. [Now] they have even [installed] a chief there, who they say is there to look after the area! Is that how people should behave towards each other? The new area where government wanted to relocate us [Adjen Kotuku], the Dagomba have already built a house and [installed] a chief *there* waiting for the market! (Interview, 12 December 2014)

So, while the uncertainty about relocation of the market continues there are other contests that play out over rights to land, ethnic affiliation and differentiated citizenship. These not only concern the current market site but fan out and produce new struggles about rights of settlement in possible future sites of relocation. In this way chiefs of opposing groups make claims to land areas and endeavour to carve out traditional jurisdictions, which mimic northern customary institutions, but which are over areas they have previously had little or no attachment to. From this perspective, the denial of Konkomba ambitions for the yam market by city authorities is also a denial of the traditional authority of their elders. According to the Konkomba chief,

Wherever we go the Dagomba will follow us or try and get there
first! This will happen even if and when the market is ever to be
relocated to a new site, whenever that may be ... (Interview,
12 December 2014)

The emerging struggle over new locations demonstrates how
long-established and contested northern traditions about rights to
resources and conditional settlement are reworked and imported
into urban and peri-urban areas. The Konkomba in the yam market
claim independence from the Dagomba in Old Fadama on the basis
of arriving *there* first, or as the chief put it, '*As everyone knows, we
the Konkomba were here [in the market] before they came to settle.*' This
is a rebuttal of the historical argument of settlement played out in
the Northern Region, where it is the Dagomba that claim control
over the Konkomba on the basis of being the first to settle there.
Latent contentions between Konkomba and Dagomba in the market
spill over to the membership of OFADA as well, which, the chief
says, was established by Dagomba alone and which the Konkomba
were invited to join only *after* the organization was up and running.
'OFADA' is thus understood by the Konkomba chief as a Dagomba
interest group that does not want to acknowledge Konkomba as a
legitimate stakeholder in Old Fadama affairs. He explains he has
even called for it to be dissolved in favour of a new overarching organ
where all groups and leaders can be fairly represented. The want
of their own market and experiences of lack of cooperation with
OFADA suggest negative relationships between ethnic diversity and
successful collective action to secure public goods (Habyarimana et
al. 2009). For the Konkomba elders and market traders, diversity
potentially jeopardizes trust and increases risk, and makes it difficult
to impose sanctions on transgressors.

Conclusion

Rural–urban migration and the related, vexed issue of government
addressing or not addressing the severe infrastructural concerns of the
market in Accra reproduce well-established lines of division between
older categories of native and settler (Boone and Kwame Duku
2012). A condition of permanent uncertainty and unknowability has
taken hold around the knotty issue of relocating the Konkomba yam
market and in different ways reproduces images of the ethnic group
as northern, rural and subsistence-based. In turn, the entanglement

undermines everyday Konkomba understandings of the worth of their relations with city authorities and the social contract they are entitled to as Ghanaians. Hence, the impasses estranges Konkomba from city authorities as well as the dominant 'native' groups of Ga in Accra and Dagomba in Old Fadama. The experiences of Konkomba stakeholders in the market therefore reproduce long-standing experiences of political and social disparities between the north and the south of the country, and inequalities in terms of rights to resources, of belonging, and of differentiated citizenship as experienced by categories of natives and settler. In an everyday capacity many experience the pressure to move as them being treated as 'nobodies from the north'. The impasse in moving the market and related questions of citizenship status and production of local identities that it gives rise to are also entangled in broader questions of 'state' and 'market'-driven models of development. The resultant spatial inequalities between an undersupplied, neglected and harassed market area and resource-rich, privileged areas of 'modern Accra' also fuel the reproduction of social categorizations and distinctions. These are used popularly to explain and sometimes justify propositions such as that 'northerners' do not belong in the 'south', and thus must accept a much lower level of resources and basic rights if 'they' choose to stay. Thereby, the features of 'temporary' status and 'illegal' settlement that comprise the state of slum are often lost in popular and simplistic notions of mutually exclusive ethnic groups.

Notions of mutually exclusive ethnicities and communities that hark back to the colonial period in rural northern Ghana are thereby reproduced in present-day urban settings and in the state of slum as part of the struggle of historically marginalized groups to progress and modernize. We see this as Konkomba organize and produce a collective identity around the yam trade to overcome the uncertainty, unknowability and risks they face and improve on protection, security, trust and representation. And we see how the opinions of leading Konkomba stakeholders concerning the yam market reflect how deep-seated experiences and ideas of social and socio-political relationships in home towns shape obligations to and expectations of the ethnic group in the city (Thorsen 2017: 300).

Thus, the governance of people, space and resources is commonly talked about and understood in ethnic terms, even if it is not immediately apparent whether ethnicity is a defining element. A key consequence is that the plans to 'modernize' the city by relocating the market are ethnicized and embroiled in broader and deeper historical struggles over differentiated citizenship and nagging contentions about rights to resources. As the intractability of the market relocation plays out, the physicality of the market deteriorates and 'us' and 'them' categories sometimes harden. The persistent disdain of different state institutions towards the market means it is framed as an anomaly and as an unwanted and misused space. In turn, notions of the yam trade as 'traditional' are reaffirmed, as are the popular ideas that the market is managed shoddily by 'backward northerners' who are incapable of diversification, and who are just 'waiting to be moved'. The empty office, the gridlock of dilapidated trucks and the hand-drawn barrows stuck deep in the mud are thereby expressions of jarred and disjointed urban development. They do not reflect weak institutions and weak resource bases but ill-conceived urban planning, modern-day forms of alienation, and entrenched positions by successive governments.

The plight of the yam market consequently exemplifies how urban planning failures relate to identity politics and undermine social contracts with citizens. Thus, the issue of moving is complex and is not only about relocation. It reflects a stalemate between statutory institutions that are unable to force through their will to relocate or find viable alternatives, and market and Konkomba interests who are similarly unable to develop the market or relocate to a site of their choice. Although it is difficult to ascertain whether, when, or how a relocation will actually materialize (or the extent of agreement about the relocation within and between the AMA and government), the plans to move the market remain a mainstay of public and political rhetoric despite the widespread unpopularity and the seeming unfeasibility of the plans.

Since first being told to move long ago, traders have endeavoured to make the best of a bad situation. However, its temporary status and the long-term threat of relocation impacts negatively on the market's physical and business conditions, as well as everyday activities and management practices.

Yam facts

- Ghana is the second largest producer of yam in West Africa after Nigeria, and produced some 6.3 million metric tonnes of yam in 2011 worth ca. $1,600,000,000. Of this, just 0.3% was exported, worth about $18 million
- More than 50% of Ghanaians are employed in agriculture, which covers about 68% of the land mass and accounts for about 23.1% of Ghanaian GDP
- Yam is mostly producing on small scale farms under 2 acres and is a major staple in the West African diet
- Ghana figures number 83 in world rankings of 'merchandized exporters' with only a 0.07% share of global exports
- There is limited evidence of yam, as a non-traditional export crop, gaining inroads in new markets, and trade with neighbouring countries is 'negligible'. For example, just 26 tons of yam were exported to Burkino Faso in 2007, increasing to 140 in 2011
- Brong Ahafo and the Northern regions produce about 62% of the total production in the country
- Annual yields range from 0.8 to 1.7 metric tonnes per hectare, but are decreasing since 2009 because of decreased soil fertility following an intensification of cultivation
- To improve production the "Fertilizer Subsidy Programme" under the Ministry of Food and Agriculture supplied over 114,000 tonnes of chemical fertilizers to farmers in 2011
- Yam production is labour intensive, non-mechanized and rain fed. Land is cleared annually with fire and machete, and seeds are planted in mounds dug with a short hoe, which is also used for weeding and harvesting
- Yam is normally planted in November and December and harvested as 'new yam' from June, where the tuber is removed leaving the root intact. Alternatively, the tuber is left to grow as 'dry yam', and harvested the following November, and sold through to May
- New yams are prone to gluts, have low starch levels, high water content, perish easily, and make up about 80% of all yam because farmers need immediate cash. Dry yams are starchier and hardier, are more sought after as the season progresses, and make up the remaining 20%

- Harvesting comprises of manually digging the yam up and carrying them in headloads to the nearest roadside
- Yam rot is common and can lead to losses of up to 20% of a yield
- The Konkomba market in Accra trades on average about 900 tons of yam a week, with intra seasonal peaks of 1100 tons in March, and nearly 2000 tons a week in August
- Varieties of yam include white yam (*Dioscorea Rotundata*), trifoliate yam (*Dioscorea Dumetorum*), yellow yam (*Dioscorea Cayenensis*), and the main landraces such as Pona, Larebako, Muchumudu and Dente

Source: Yam Sector Development Strategy, Ghana. GoG 2012.

5
Solving problems and emerging authority

We are taking a walk around the perimeter of Old Fadama with Adjua to get an idea of the settlement's size and the condition of outlying areas where, over the last few years, bog, bush and mangrove swamp have yielded to reclaimed and cleared land used for temporary shelters. Already, many dwellings have been lost to sporadic tidal rises in water levels, or water that flows from the city down the estuary and onto the land. Currently the flat area is open, muddy, and strewn with rubbish and larger discards from vehicles and dwellings. The smells and sights of the area make it seem as if we are in the wilderness, and it is difficult to fathom that we are close to central Accra. Obviously enough, we are way outside the reach and authority of the Ghana Environmental Protection Agency, even though it is housed in new high-rise offices only a couple of kilometres away. We are similarly outside the mandate it holds from the Ministry of Environment, Science, Technology and Innovation, a title which expresses the purity of 'high-modernism' (Scott 1997). Together with the filth we therefore sense first-hand the failure of the 'state' to rationalize social organization, and there are jarring contradictions between the claims of authority and order by government ministries, departments and agencies, and the actual living and working conditions of ordinary people not far beyond the shadows of government offices

In one area there are large, wooden, ranch-like pens that have been built to hold cattle and goats. Despite the absence of green fields, the bleating goats and the wandering cows give the urban landscape a rural feel. Across from the pens is a U-shaped broken wall that serves as an abattoir. Here, there's a cow with its back to us, kneeling on its front legs with its hind legs raised. It looks relaxed and composed until we realize it is headless; and then that its head lies a few metres away, next to a bloodied man in shabby clothes holding an old axe. The blood oozes from the cow's body and runs into a pool of oil from a discarded gearbox, then farther into puddles of mud and other sludge. Next to the man a lazy fire consumes rubber tyres and wood, with several goat carcasses on top of the smouldering pile. The goats are turned every few minutes until the heat singes off their fur and seals their orifices. Afterwards, the grimy carcasses are carted away to be cut up and cooked at venues all over the city.

Farther down towards the sea, on the other side of the estuary, a steady stream of cesspit tankers filled with raw sewage empty their sloppy loads onto the beach at Lavender Hill. The Hill – a source of national embarrassment – symbolizes all that has gone wrong with Accra's urban planning. The ebb and flow of the tide is more efficient and systematic than government efforts to manage human waste, which is carried out into the Gulf of Guinea, whose waters support the livelihoods of thousands of local fishermen. Their daily catch is transported back to fish markets dotted around Accra, and then consumed by city residents, thus completing an ecological cycle. The density of Old Fadama, the concentration and visibility of its many developmental shortfalls, and its location in the capital all make it obvious that it has not attracted sufficient political interest or the momentum needed to solve its problems. Meanwhile, the steady increase in Old Fadama's population has meant there is a growing demand for all kinds of basic amenities, services and utilities by residents who seek to make their lives more manageable, livable and safe. Besides the pressing issues of sanitation, waste management and health, residents demand a degree of law, order and security, a regular water and electricity supply, and a reduction in the risks of fire and flooding, to name some of the most basic requirements. The escalation in residents' needs and demands, and the dearth in delivery of much-needed services and regulation by government, has fuelled the growth of diverse institutions, organizations and businesses that endeavour to cater to these needs. The loose networks that sometimes provide these services and emerge as public authorities may stretch between local stakeholders and global supporters, and in the process, they contribute to the everyday informal governance of public services in Old Fadama.

The increase in rural–urban migration and failure of local efforts to offset the immense developmental and infrastructural needs add to urban inequalities based on resource access and distribution. Hence, what we see are sharpening and often glaringly adjacent urban contrasts in levels of sanitation, cleanliness, regulation, and the general appearance of public spaces. The entrenched position of governments towards Old Fadama results in a creeping informalization of public services and governance. Thereby, local actions to overcome the challenges of absent basic services are not only responding to their non-delivery; they also display important societal and political dimensions (Swanson 1977; McFarlane and Silver

2017). For Old Fadama residents the enduring and widening disparities translate into everyday experiences and reminders that they are deprived of basic rights and services, and constrained to live in a filthy and unhealthy environment.

The subject matter of this chapter is the socio-political dimensions of informal governance and related, emerging social contracts that follow diverse local actions and innovations to offset the dearth of basic services. We see how the provision of basic resources and the benefits that accrue from them result in local understandings of obligations, privileges and local rights, as well as notions of who has the right to what, who can supply what, and what is or is not permissible. Context-specific understandings of social contracts are made that produce new power structures as well as reproduce existing lines of social division 'imported' from rural home towns. The actual organization and management of service delivery debunk the dominant myth of 'urban development', which is habitually explained by adducing modernist theory with its assumption of a teleological unfolding that supposedly mirrors Western 'progress' (Ferguson 1999). The emergence of ambitious yet under-resourced, non-statutory organizations that try to distribute resources and provide services also defies negative characteristics of slum areas – disorganized, ungoverned and ungovernable. On the contrary, diverse activities, innovations and resilience under difficult and changing conditions demonstrate local agency with an often greater ability and reach than is on offer from statutory institutions. As discussed previously, efforts to improve the settlement and utilize the limited reach of city authorities also afford micro-opportunities for well-placed actors to carve out new roles for themselves and gain privileged access to resources.

The explorations of everyday experiences of what people *need*, what they sometimes *get*, and who supplies what, contribute to understandings of impromptu urban governance and emerging power relations on the periphery of the reach of statutory institutions. Local subjectivities and rights are produced because the people who enjoy the delivery of services support the actors and institutions that provide them, and these emerge as public authority. At the same time, the providers recognize the claims and demands of residents as valid and as something to which they are entitled. Thus, residents of Old Fadama experience routinely that the sustainability of their everyday life does not depend on 'government' but on close and productive affinities to networks of actors. In this way, ordinary people participate directly and indirectly in the shaping and making of informal power relations around the distribution of services.

Hence the exploration of relations between those demanding and those providing different services exemplifies how political space is filled and 'government' is once again reduced to the role of an unresponsive and inept player out of sync with local realities. This sentiment develops and takes hold with the local realization that establishing basic and decent conditions for survival and living cannot be taken for granted as a fruit that will fall from government's tree (Chenwi 2013).

There is an uneven drip-down of resources that find their way to Old Fadama through patronage networks, but for most people the basic management of their everyday lives rests on local and close support. In this way the delivery of various resources to improve life becomes the subject of local processes of politicization that change authority and increase the governance capacity of the actors, institutions and organizations in question. The structure of service delivery and its governance in Old Fadama is unsystematic and comprises a mix of many private and individual businesses, as well as statutory actors and institutions, NGOs, etc. In this chapter, however, the focus is on one of the most prominent organizations involved in resource and service delivery in Old Fadama, the Old Fadama Development Association (OFADA).[1] OFADA is not an all-powerful entity, its resources are severely limited, it often faces opposition, and there are many tasks it cannot do. Still, relations between OFADA and residents to improve livelihoods do exist. They are not impersonal or formalized relations but nevertheless exemplify the making of 'rights subjects' and non-statutory governance between agents that share the desire to improve living conditions. And looking into the operations of OFADA, regardless of their success, provides insights into the development of obligations and non-statutory social contracts in informal settlements. Thus, their operations exemplify informal governance as a socio-political and cultural process that plays out as ordinary people and changing groups of local community leaders try to improve their living conditions, which are shaped by the broader developmental 'crisis' of Old Fadama. Hence, the focus is on how the legal entanglement and the political conditioning of the state of slum drive the non-state provision of public services. This contrasts with dominant approaches that typically focus on the informalization of non-state provision of basic resources as stemming from decades of 'neoliberal' and market-based reforms (Cammett and MacLean 2013).

The next section situates Old Fadama and the development of OFADA in the wider context of local government and decentralization reform in Ghana. Afterwards, the organization of OFADA is described and two different types of mutual recognition, which emerge as the association delivers services and establishes itself as a public authority, are analysed. The first focuses on internal relations of recognition between the population of Old Fadama and OFADA, and examples of efforts to improve security, justice and stable rights of tenure. The second focuses on external relations of recognition between OFADA, the Accra Metropolitan Authority and international operators such as NGOs that shape the tentative jurisdiction of OFADA.

Local government reform and the de facto government in Old Fadama

The emergence of OFADA and its ambitions to become the de facto institution of local government in Old Fadama can be understood in the wider context of changes to governance structures that have taken place in Ghana. Since the late 1980s, Ghana has pursued an ambitious national programme of local government reform with the decentralization of a range of political responsibilities to the local level. This has resulted in the creation of some 216 districts as newly demarcated administrative units. As in many other developing countries, the impetus for reforming the structure of local government stems from a combination of local, national and global pressures. For Ghana, it was the government need to establish legitimacy and political stability after years of military rule in the 1970s and 1980s, together with pressure from the international community to reduce the size of the public sector, and a desire to improve service delivery and financial management, that brought decentralization in a new Constitution inaugurated in 1992 (Biswal 1992). Article 240 states that district assemblies, created in newly established political administrative areas, '*shall be the highest political authority in the district, and shall have deliberative, legislative and executive powers*'. Further, '*Ghana shall have a system of local government and administration which shall, as far as practical, be decentralized*'.[2]

Since, domestic momentum for decentralization, and particularly an understanding that local control over local affairs is effective and optimal, has taken hold, and the setting up of local government institutions and district assemblies has been ensured by both of the leading political parties: the New Patriotic Party and the National Democratic Congress (NPP and NDC).[3] International endorsement and strong donor support for decentralization have provided continued momentum, too. Support is based on the assumptions that a restructuring and deconcentration of relations between the state, market forces and civil society will lead to 'good governance' and improve democracy, government performance, service provision and civil society capacity.[4] However, the extent to which decentralization actually fulfils these objectives is widely debated. Of Ghana, as of many other global South countries, critics have asked whether representation, accountability, transparency and other credentials of a healthy democracy have actually improved, or whether, instead, in some instances, local government reform has intensified existing contests over resources and solidified unequal power relations (Ayee 1997; Bierschenk and Olivier de Sardan 2003; Boone 2003; Heller 2009; Stacey 2015). Nevertheless, all over the country, the goal of maximizing *local* control is an objective for many community, home-town and youth movements (Lentz 1995; Owusu 2005).[5] It is also a means to attract government funding from the Common Fund (treasury), bring about infrastructural developments and investments, attract donor and NGO activities, and realize the political ambitions of local actors. It is against this background, as well as a proliferation of civil society interests seeking to deepen democracy, that OFADA claims credentials of representing the community and providing basic, everyday support in ways that 'government' does not.

Under 'normal' circumstances Old Fadama community leaders would be able to make a strong case to the Ministry of Local Government and Rural Development (MLGRD) for the area to be demarcated administratively as a municipality, or at least as a district.[6] Its large population, economic potential, political significance and, not least, developmental needs would all support the case. But, in practice, its legal standing – or lack thereof – means that Old Fadama cannot be recognized by government as a new political administrative area and attain 'district status' and the trappings that go with it. Therefore, Old Fadama is stuck with its inferior status as a mere 'ward' under the much larger local government structure of the Accra Metropolitan Authority. The AMA itself comprises ten sub-metropolitan district councils made up of seventy-two communities and seventy-six electoral areas, which are headed by the mayor of the city, the metropolitan chief executive (GSS 2013). This administrative set-up means that Old Fadama's population has only *one* formally recognized representative on a local government institution. In national politics Old Fadama is also at a representative disadvantage because it is part of the much larger constituency of Odododiodioo, which has a single member of parliament. Consequently, there is a stark mismatch between the size of the population, the developmental needs and challenges, and demands for representation and for residents' voices to be heard from Old Fadama, on the one hand, and the very limited levels of formal representation enjoyed by the settlement, on the other. The lack of formal representation does not go unnoticed by residents and community leaders. This political condition feeds into popular understandings of Old Fadama as politically isolated, ignored and excluded from 'normal' avenues of political representation. In turn, the political conditioning contributes to the intractability of Old Fadama's nagging developmental imperatives (Afenah 2012; Obeng-Odoom 2011).

OFADA organization, membership and representation

Various factors – the legal stalemate, pressing developmental needs, and increased interest from global NGOs – explain the emergence in Accra over the years of several organizations seeking to facilitate the provision of basic services to the population of Old Fadama. Among these are People's Dialogue on Human Settlements (PD), which worked for productive relations between Old Fadama residents and government. To this end, People's Dialogue aided the formation of a national organization, the so-called Ghana Federation of Urban Poor (GHAFUP), as well as OFADA in 2004. OFADA claims to be the most prominent and influential player in the governance of Old Fadama. After years of stands-offs, occasional demonstrations and violent confrontations, the organization claims to reflects a new, wider trajectory for urban struggles that have been recognized else-where in the global South. These focus on attaining basic rights and services by overcoming long-standing disputes with governments (McFarlane and Silver 2017).

OFADA acts as a loose umbrella body and is made up of some sixteen people from the different ethnic and religious communities that reside in Old Fadama, with many known locally as chiefs or sub-chiefs of their respective communities. To avoid domination by the largest ethnic group (Dagomba), ease the administrative burden, and make the organization accessible, membership is not based on election. Instead, each ethnic or religious group has a right to representation regardless of size. Several OFADA members combine the development of the organization with the pursuit of individual ambitions – party-political, business, traditional or NGO-related: thus, George the pharmacist acts as the 'public relations officer' for OFADA, while Frederick is assigned the position of 'community secretary'.

Leading members of OFADA present their objectives for Old Fadama as a mix of individual, personal ambition and a broader, community-wide project that confronts and betters the cumbersome and unhelpful 'state'. Frederick, for example, is highly influenced by a bombardment of global, donor-related and governmental discourses addressing grassroots and community-based development that Old Fadama has been subject to. He has read up on, internalized and mastered the correct 'development-speak' so as to present and justify his projects to the outside world as productive, inspiring and worthy of finance. He has learned this from years at college, and writing countless applications to global foundations, charities and NGOs. Entrepreneurs like Frederick interpret 'government' as fundamentally unhelpful and absent while adopting government and donor terminology to undertake some of the everyday tasks that, from a normative perspective, government should be tackling. Frederick and many others in Old Fadama have literally given up trying to hold government to account and now do things in their own way with language, actions and plans borrowed from government and the international donor community.

OFADA members have experienced decades of broken promises about development, progress and improvements. And they have taken advantage of the absence of formal government to carve out niches for themselves as agents of local development. In a broader perspective members like Frederick and George are influenced by forces of globalization that promote a universal language of rights and narratives of progress and democratization, and by their own individual experiences of hardship.

OFADA members are predominantly from northern Ghana, male, numerate, literate, and aged between about thirty and fifty. According to a leading member, an ideal member should take an active interest in and have a proven ability to solve community problems; have resided in Old Fadama for a 'long time'; and be locally known and popular. But as OFADA membership is not a salaried job the desire to solve community challenges runs parallel, as we have seen, with the drive to gain influence over local affairs, and establish status. Thus, OFADA membership can provide gatekeeping opportunities and access to more powerful political actors in Accra and beyond and can confer privileged knowledge of development projects, income-earning opportunities, and access to direct resource flows. I experienced gatekeeping first-hand while collecting data, when, after initial visits to OFADA and Old Fadama, I was advised by a leading member that it would be a 'very good idea' if I started to contribute to 'OFADA coffers' on each visit, and was warned not to enter Old Fadama without first having a meeting with an OFADA-assigned 'official'. Other OFADA members were clearly oblivious that such requests were made, so refused repeatedly to accept any payments, and insisted I should come and go in Old Fadama as I pleased.

Despite the outward portrayal of ethnic and party-political neutrality, some community leaders and residents complain that OFADA is dominated by the Dagomba. As we saw in the last chapter, Konkomba leaders particularly sense that OFADA is an organization mainly for Dagomba, and that Dagomba enjoy privileges and access to resources that they don't. The fact that the OFADA office is situated close to the home of a powerful Dagomba chief in Old Fadama, in an area which itself is often the site of Dagomba customary celebrations, drumming and rites of homage, strengthens this impression. All these social-situational coordinates strengthen understandings that this is a Dagomba-controlled area. For OFADA's opponents, the setting up of the organization represents the importation into the city of long-established rural institutions of inequality along native–settler lines, according to which the control of land and positions of traditional authority are reserved for Dagomba, while Konkomba are categorized as traditional and inferior subjects (Jönsson 2007). Another, more salient feature of OFADA as an exclusionary organization that reproduces social stratification is its total non-representation of women, though Old Fadama's population is divided equally between males and females. It is also alleged that OFADA is closely aligned to the incumbent National Democratic Congress (NDC) and, in an ethnic-traditional dimension, to the Andani lineage of the Dagomba. Circumstantially, the claims of party-political allegiance find support from the composition of OFADA and the affiliations and local political influence of some of its members (Paller 2015). However, OFADA members vehemently deny this presentation, especially the internal ethnic dimension, and outwardly at least the organization promotes the ideal of inclusiveness and independence from any particular ethnic and political interests.[7]

OFADA members are assigned positions that mimic those of formal government organization, with a financial officer, administrative officer, community secretary, waste manager and public relations officer, all of whom are overseen by an executive committee. There is also an ad hoc multi-ethnic Task Force with a leader, who can rally up to fifty men via text messaging. Ordinary members elect eight executives, who in turn elect a chairman. OFADA endeavours to meet at least fortnightly in their well-kept, one-room office in Old Fadama. The OFADA office hosts all kinds of meetings, gatherings and comings and goings. It is used weekly as an impromptu meeting place for visiting nurses who advise on health issues, and is also attractive as a cool, dry place with a large TV. The financing for the office came through donations and internal generation as ubiquitous food vendors and operators of amenities such as public toilets and showers were encouraged to contribute a 'tax' to 'community coffers'; public officials, including the constituency MP, chipped in with money and building materials. In this way OFADA has come to represent a wide range of civil society interests that have supported the construction of its office, and in turn this has allowed the organization to claim that it represents a wide spectrum of the community. However, although it does enjoy a degree of local legitimacy and has sometimes worked closely with the AMA, its status is also disputed locally (as, for example, by Konkomba elders) with stories of unjust practices, exclusiveness and closed decision-making. Support for the setting up of OFADA also substantiated the developmental profile of People's Dialogue and this NGO's engagement with pressing urban challenges as addressed in the Millennium Development Goals and Sustainable Development Goals.

Public tasks and the provision of services

While going about normal daily business, OFADA members monitor numerous aspects of community life. Following in their footsteps, we saw on different occasions how they look out for new constructions that block pathways; call on emergent businesses; ensure broader access roads are kept clear of containers and vehicles; caution young people riding motorbikes carelessly. If they spot leaky pipes they contact volunteer plumbers; they identify fire hazards and endeavour to 'keep the rubbish moving' to minimize problems with vermin; they look in on recurring domestic disputes and shoo children to school; they follow up on complaints of theft and damage to property, and pursue disagreements over rental payments; they give newcomers advice on building; after heavy rain they inspect low-lying areas for flooding; they rally communal labour to clear blocked waterways and ensure unsafe buildings are demolished after outbreaks of fire; they also organize the collection of contributions to cover medical bills, funeral expenses and support to families when a deceased person must be returned to what is often a remote northern village; and in some instances they cover bail money when it cannot be raised by relatives.

In exchange for these services OFADA gains the recognition of residents, who approve and comply with their rules, so shaping informal social contracts. More than anything else this is based on the commonly held attitude that to make life bearable and livable in Old Fadama it is necessary to make the odd effort beyond your own doorstep. This desire for an overarching social contract is similarly asserted when OFADA communicates its successes to communities through its members and public relations officer. In January 2015, for example, OFADA announced that its constant proposals to government to improve services were paying off. The constituency MP agreed to forward a quantity of electricity poles, which, together with a transformer and electricity meters (gleaned from good relations with an electricity company), were welcomed by residents. The supply of electricity and access to it on the household level in Old Fadama are generally outside the immediate control of the Electricity Company of Ghana. The 'grid' is such that a limited number of houses and businesses have their own registered meters, while countless other neighbouring houses, shops and shacks tap into these through makeshift connections, and contribute to the bill that is paid by the registered user.

The company is unable to regulate the plethora of unauthorized users and chooses instead to make sure that the utilized power bill is settled. It also warns of the dangers of illegal connections, while increasing the electricity capacity of Old Fadama by occasionally providing extra poles and meters. The improved electricity infrastructure supported by the local MP resulted in an increase in sporadic lighting around the settlement and residents' sense of security. It was claimed by OFADA members as a success in 'upgrading' parts of Old Fadama towards an acknowledgement by city authorities of a right of residence. Still, the recent demolitions of nearby areas showed the unevenness of relations with 'government', and the precarious standing of incremental improvements.

OFADA claimed credit for the extra electricity and improvement, which also reduced the risk of fire, while recent proposals sent to city authorities by OFADA include plans for gutter systems, a health clinic and schools, all of which Old Fadama sorely needs. In this way OFADA can derive local legitimacy from claiming as well as demonstrating its ability to acquire resources from outside that solve community-wide challenges. Moreover, local interpretations of OFADA's claimed successes feed into popular understandings about development and the improving status of the settlement. A note-worthy example is the claim that OFADA and People's Dialogue are central to the stalling of the eviction order, and that large-scale eviction now looks unlikely. This claim is based on the 2009 census of the settlement, which apparently prompted government realization that large-scale relocation or eviction was not feasible because of the large population count (Farouk and Owusu 2012). But as we saw in the introduction, the apparent shift away from the eviction option has multiple roots, including the political and economic significance of Old Fadama, the dissonance between eviction and democrati-zation, an increasing awareness of the plight of the urban poor in civil society and global discourse, and pro-poor statements made by Ghanaian governments in international fora, often referencing the MDGs and SDGs.

Waste management

As reflected in the opening vignette, the acute issue of the manage-ment of waste and the dearth of health standards concerning everything from human waste, animal carcasses and vermin to household rubbish, and to the refuse and cast-off materials created by hundreds of small businesses, probably demonstrate best how government's legalistic approach not only diminishes the quality of everyday life in the settlement but results in an impasse that poses a real risk to the general health of a much broader public. The legalistic approach has inadvertently resulted in the transfer of waste manage-ment, a mundane yet essential task of government, to casual actors and non-statutory institutions that have very limited capacity. The AMA, however, is also stretched, as only 70 per cent of the daily generated waste in its jurisdiction is collected, and some 60 per cent of its internally generated revenue is used on solid waste management (UN-Habitat 2011; Songsore et al. 2014: 22). There are, however, contrasting approaches to waste and the environment around the city that highlight stark urban disparities. While city authorities refuse, for example, to organize the collection of *any* waste from Old Fadama, their water tankers can be seen regularly spraying clean the pave-ments and roads in more affluent residential areas around the city.

Drainage, sewerage and household waste collection in Old Fadama thus depend solely on improvization by individuals, neighbours and communities, or ad hoc private-sector or NGO support. Consequently, the extent of 'waste' and filth in and around Old Fadama makes clearly visible the absolute inability of statutory and non-statutory powers to deal with the issue. Nevertheless, local efforts provide some evidence of organization and success. As one young supporter of OFADA described the process:

> Whenever this environment is dirty, we come out and do community cleaning. We clean the whole place, so we make sure that cholera and other germs do not destroy our lives. ... The chairman [of OFADA] will give a 'dong dong' and go around and announce, this particular day, we need to clean our environment. If we don't come to clean, and he sees it, he will say come and clean and stop working. (Interview, 21 July 2014)

Participation in such activities is an element in the system of informal governance in Old Fadama but is often not considered by the participants themselves as a decisively political act. But all the same, it has important socio-political consequences as agreeing to clean up after a demand from OFADA substantiates the authority of the organization. Although OFADA stands out as an organizer of public services, and there are countless other smaller enterprises and institutions, many important tasks are never addressed. The most ubiquitous of the public services offered is the loose network of several hundred public shower and toilet facilities, which are crammed between stalls, shacks and rooms all over the settlement. Together with OFADA, these businesses attempt to find common solutions to the perennial challenges of drainage, flooding, sanitation, blockages and sewerage control. To this end, micro-loans from the NGO Slum Dwellers International have financed public toilet blocks and bathhouses (Gillespie 2013). And OFADA has purchased waste bins from the AMA for distribution to shower businesses, toilets and food stalls. This is in order to encourage the phasing out of plastic and rubber bins, thus curbing fire risk. OFADA also contracts local smiths to produce suitable metal bins and negotiates delivery of large metal containers that are placed in earmarked locations for regular collection by private companies.

Occasionally the AMA provides local businesses with waste bins when they register with the authority, but this mark of recognition, and the sale, rather than the supply, of waste bins, means that there is no systematic collection. The suspension of waste management by the city authorities has thereby created space for non-statutory actors to organize and gain local legitimacy as residents recognize the much-needed services they provide, while government suffers in the popular view as it has wholly failed to ensure a basic level of public health. Despite OFADA's efforts, the lack of regular, organized collection means that household waste is either dumped on the banks of the lagoon or alongside artery roads, or burnt. Latrines run directly into the lagoon and pose constant health risks. In Accra in 2014, for example, the accumulation of waste, poor sanitation and seasonal flooding (compounded by a strike by contracted rubbish collectors) contributed to what became Ghana's worst cholera epidemic for thirty years. Nationally there were over 17,000 confirmed and suspected cases, and about 130 deaths.[8] Cholera did not affect Old Fadama directly but city authorities were overstretched and OFADA organized communal labour to clear open drains and channels. At this time, in close proximity to the vegetable markets, were numerous mountains of garbage along the main roads bordering Old Fadama. The suspension of statutory governance afforded the opportunity for OFADA to establish itself as a responsible actor in the management of waste. This helped instil discipline and norms about waste in the community, and supported the idea that OFADA stands for good social values, is 'looking after' public space, and contributes to a positive social environment (Owusu 2010). In turn, the ability to organize communal labour facilitated socio-political relations between labourers and OFADA and established a degree of recognition of OFADA by the city authorities. These examples of what OFADA does show how local resources are mobilized to shape informal governance. Rules and control about public space are made that increase the credibility of OFADA and its capacity to solve serious developmental challenges. As city authorities 'do nothing' because of their legalistic approach, OFADA steps in and develops its ability to reduce local health risks. Here once again we see how formal and informal governance increase the reach and capacity of each (Helmke and Levitsky 2004).

Regulation of building and construction

As examined in the previous chapter, the types of building in Old Fadama and the resource levels of those who build vary considerably, and OFADA endeavours to implement a basic set of rules for the whole settlement. Primarily, these are designed to reduce the great risk of fire or flooding, and to increase safety; every year dwellings and lives are at considerable risk. The combination of adverse factors – population density, narrow alleys and lack of access roads, the abundance of wooden shacks built back to back with shoddy electrical wiring and overloaded meters exposed to weather, the use of open kerosene stoves or charcoal fires for cooking, and an irregular water supply – often proves lethal (Image 1.1). Many building activities are driven by the involvement of small-scale, jack-of-all-trades building contractors who are hired to construct one- or two-storey concrete houses with tin roofs. But most ramshackle wooden dwellings, typically made from plywood, are hammered together by the plot holders, often with help from friends and family. All types of shelter and building may take several years to complete, or remain unfinished and exemplify the open-ended process of establishing a safe dwelling while demonstrating, over months and years, 'housing as a verb' (Turner 1972).

To reduce risk, OFADA and others strongly advise the use of concrete for flooring and cement blocks instead of wood for walls. Constructions in particularly low-lying areas are discouraged to avoid flooding, and any semi-permanent constructions such as stalls and makeshift shelters that create bottlenecks or protrude onto access roads are pushed back or removed. To avoid subsidence, builders are advised to dig concrete foundations at least one metre deep, and buildings over two storeys high are discouraged, although, as we saw in the case of the hotel, the skyline of Old Fadama is being pushed up owing to land pressure and new investments coming in.

In the case of a new building, OFADA as an organization will try to enquire into the transfer or purchase of land, from whom it is rented, what permission has been sought, how many people are moving in, and the line of business of the new residents. If an existing building is sold, OFADA encourages the parties to have an OFADA member witness the deal to avoid cheating, multiple sales and subsequent disputes. OFADA does not document construction, occupation or local understandings of ownership, but as a regular activity, members will patrol the settlement, in loose conjunction with Ga representatives, and scout about for 'infringements'. After taking due cognizance of the local clout that developers enjoy, OFADA will give notice for any 'irresponsible' or 'illegal' buildings to be adjusted or removed, and a red cross is marked on the door and walls (a practice widely used by AMA all over Accra). After a given period, the decision may be taken to raze the building, if necessary and possible.

We saw how, after fire has gutted an area, OFADA aims to oversee the marking out of new plots with stakes that follow the external walls of the destroyed houses. OFADA strives to regulate the process of rebuilding and to prevent internal encroachment and opportunism, and it will facilitate the transfer of plots in the event of previous occupants not being able to afford rebuilding. The efforts of OFADA to plan, organize and manage property development in Old Fadama are not always successful and there are often instances where the guidelines are opposed or simply ignored, and the emerging authority they want to establish is not respected. They often lack the resources to carry out objectives and are plainly not told or aware of all that goes on. Nevertheless, the role OFADA plays as makeshift surveyor, regulator, construction engineer and urban planner – together with its efforts to reduce the risk of fire and flooding, manage waste and filth, and demarcate access roads – have all meant that areas of Old Fadama are now improved and safer than before. In effect, OFADA endeavours to establish itself as a regulatory authority for construction and takes advantage of the absence of government to do so. Consequently, the emergence of OFADA as a non-statutory form of governance in Old Fadama runs parallel with an increased ordering and systematization of the physical landscape that arises from other efforts. This does not follow statutory rules but is a mix of what people can get away with, what OFADA can enforce, and what the AMA can demand. The result is generally experienced positively by residents, with some areas resembling 'planned development' and more 'normal' parts of the city as concrete buildings in straight lines phase out wooden shacks; pathways enjoy street lighting; and designated alleys are widened. In these ways OFADA tries to carve out a governance role for itself and create closer relations with settlers, who look to broader powers to recognize their settlement, and who want safety and security. Although government does not approve of settlement, many of OFADA's actions earn its tacit approval because they improve living conditions and reduce risks.

Policing

OFADA's role as facilitator of local development is inseparable from its provision of security and policing, including effective sanctions against undesirable behaviour. The regulation of social behaviour by customary leaders in specific ethnic groups is replicated in their role as task force members under the broader framework of OFADA. In this way the delivery of policing as a basic service by OFADA builds on and adds legitimacy to already existing relations of consensus and representation within communities, typically based on age, gender and social status. Generally, OFADA members will endeavor to take serious incidents such as gang fights, stabbings, beatings, rape and domestic violence to traditional superiors; they, in turn, are likely to escort suspects to the nearby police station, just outside Old Fadama, with whose officers they work closely. Still, residents spoke of Old Fadama as a place renowned for theft, as a potentially dangerous place, especially after dark, when robbery is common, and where gang fights and vigilantism are common, which all exemplify the limits of OFADA authority as well as the limits of the power of individual community leaders. Yet policing by 'traditional' actors offers opportunities to prove themselves as trusted negotiators, community leaders and emerging authorities. And when disputes are settled under the auspices of OFADA or with help from OFADA members, the local credibility of the organization is established. One resident explained how a local chief solves issues in the following way:

> Recently there was a fight between groups of Dagomba and Nanumba. We even lost some lives. If such things happen, we gather together, all of us and the chiefs gather, and every chief will do their bit to solve it. If the issue is too big the police will be called. Maybe the perpetrator will be made to pay compensation and things will be shared together. Sometimes it will be announced at the mosques that what has happened was bad and should be stopped. (Interview, 21 July 2014)

Another resident explained:

> [W]e have established chiefs here. Most of the ethnic groups that are here, they have their chiefs, their leaders that lead them. [We] share agreements [about] how to develop Old Fadama, or about some challenges, how we sweep our roads, about sanitation, a lot of things. ... [O]ur leaders have to call all of us. They will make announcements, and all of us will gather, and then they will bring out some ideas [about] what are you going to do, and it will help us in this community, and we will all share ideas. And finally, they have to make sure that what we have discussed should be put into use, so that all of us can benefit from it. I think because of the leaders that we now have in Old Fadama it is very hard to see somebody just misbehaving. [It] may be thirty minutes [until] I

will be called to the chief's palace [where] I will be disciplined! We are living together and we know each other very well. We have all agreed to it – that we have to have elders, and because of these elders, whenever the government or the Accra Metropolitan Authority wants to come and do something here, they too [communicate] the message to our elders that they are coming to do something. So because of this I think the leaders are playing an important role in this community (Interview, 10 July 2014)

Hybrid authority and new subjectivities

As an organization endeavouring to police and establish civic norms, OFADA mimics the social and moral codes that are also communicated by individual ethnic and customary leaders. In this way, OFADA establishes itself as a hybrid non-statutory authority as it promotes secular norms and those promoted by different ethnic, traditional and customary leaders. Dagomba chiefs, for example, earn respect by looking out for residents and serving the community, and in return receive customary 'drink' money, which for OFADA translates into its dependence on collections, donations and internally generated revenues. The reliance of OFADA on discretionary and practical payments for its services therefore acts to reproduce the traditional and customary feature of paying homage to authority through gift-giving, drink money and symbolic donations. In this way, a lack of official and regulated financial support drives the informalization of OFADA's operations and activities, while the involvement of highly revered traditional figures means interactions between OFADA and residents may also be formal and follow coded conventions. In day-to-day problem-solving activities, the boundaries between what 'OFADA' and 'traditional' actors undertake to improve the settlement are often unclear as each uses the other to establish authority and compliance.

The delivery of services by OFADA is also reciprocated through the payment of 'taxes' by local businesses such as food vendors and operators of public toilets and showers in the area, and it receives contributions from powerful local notables. Still, OFADA members emphasize that all payment is voluntary, as they are unable to enforce it. Previously, they experienced limited success in establishing a flat-rate tax base, coming up against residents' variable willingness or inability to pay, and the impossibility of enforcement. Since then, the resilience and persistence of the organization have depended on the implicit acceptance, by OFADA and residents alike, that the tasks and obligations performed should be paid for somehow, and should not fulfil particular individual or sectarian preferences but be directed towards a shared public good. Again, this does not go uncontested (and allegations of bribes against OFADA members are common), but in contrast to the hackneyed approach to the area adopted by government, the results of OFADA's various activities are visible and appreciated. The status of traditional leaders therefore stands to benefit from their OFADA-related activities.

The standing and influence over local affairs enjoyed by traditional leaders can improve by another route: by way of business investments in housing, by becoming landlords, renting out accommodation, or by establishing toilet and shower businesses, among many other possibilities. Their involvement in land-based developments requires them to make decisions and formulate rules about the use of dwellings as well as scarce resources such as electricity and water. Influence over such resources gained from investments thus overlaps with their traditional status and contributes to their 'traditional' role as a controller of land and people. As one resident described a chief's influence:

If you want to build a room, you need to have his permission.
All matters concerning your room, you have to consult this
person. He has this position because he was one of the first
people who came to Old Fadama. If anything happens in the
society you can go to him. He is in charge of the whole area.
He gives orders. Everything he wants will be done. If there are
any conflicts between the different tribes, he is the one who solves
them. If there is any violence, he is the one making sure that it's
under control. (Interview, 10 July 2014)

Mutual recognition between traditional leaders and residents, on the one hand, and between OFADA, as a secular and regulatory organization, and residents, on the other, thus produces public authority that projects and is a combination of both 'modern' and 'traditional' registers. The various strategies employed by OFADA members to gain influence and legitimize control over local affairs add to local notions of OFADA as an institution of local government. In the absence of Ga chiefs who claim customary rights to the land but do not reside in Old Fadama, Dagomba chiefs validate their role as significant powers with influence over land issues. The Dagomba chiefs are not explicitly claiming ownership of the land.

But as we see from the quote above, their land-related activities are decisive in undoing the relevance and customary authority of Ga chiefs, who are outside of OFADA. The result is the emergence of new land-control mechanisms and customs that successfully bypass the limited customary power of both Ga chiefs and government. Again, their activities are not wholly successful and accepted but still demonstrate that the land-related actions of OFADA, its members and its power base rework understandings of property, authority and social contracts. As the influence of different stakeholders changes, so do local jurisdictions of authority and the socio-political contexts of the rights on which they are based.

External dynamics of recognition

People's Dialogue was central in the creation of OFADA and plays a key role today as mediator between residents, OFADA and AMA. The organization's activities are traceable to 2002 when representatives from Shack/Slum Dwellers International (SDI) visited Old Fadama to counter the eviction proposed by the High Court order of the same year.[9] According to People's Dialogue and SDI, their actions stalled and overturned the eviction after negotiations with city authorities as representatives of the area (Farouk and Owusu 2012). At this time the NPP government opened itself to the possibility of relocating residents and agricultural market traders (Gillespie 2013: 210). Vital to People's Dialogue's strategy was its census of the area, using locals trained as enumerators. This was designed as a first step towards improving local economies, to assist in the relocation, and to ease community concerns. To this end, in 2003 the Ghana Federation of the Urban Poor (GHAFUP) was formed and initiated savings groups.[10] Increasingly detailed censuses were carried out in 2004, 2006/07 and 2009, with government backing and People's Dialogue providing logistical support and experience from other countries. The population of 48,000 determined by the 2006/07 census increased to 79,000 in the 2009 census.[11] To push through plans for either relocation or eviction, successive governments had argued on the assumption of a much smaller and decidedly transient population.

The new knowledge of the size and demographics of the settlement contributed to the government reconsidering its objective of large-scale eviction (Farouk and Owusu 2012). People's Dialogue thus improved the organizational capacity and level of awareness of OFADA and it brought international experience, awareness of human rights agendas and knowledge of international agreements to slum dwellers. This suggests elements of global citizenship as international institutions take up the plight of Africans and develop knowledge of rights and development, challenging and transcending obligations to government that rest on national identity (Grant 2006). Frederick and other OFADA members are clearly influenced by such global agendas, which with the involvement of organizations like People's Dialogue and SDI help to define Old Fadama as part of a global problem. This also contributes to the global profile of these international NGOs as facilitators of urban development with a human face, although we have also seen that OFADA, as a civic structure of informal government, is also exclusionist and enjoys discretionary powers (Roy 2009).

Contests around and within OFADA have also influenced members to break off and pursue their own developmental ambitions. Frederick's NGO, for example, has numerous projects and proposals on the go covering sanitation, youth training and gender awareness campaigns, and his project group is applying for funding from agencies situated all over the world, which may or may not involve OFADA. As he explains:

[T]here are a lot of World Bank smaller projects and funding possibilities around here [in Old Fadama]. It could be that I want to prove a point, that if this can be done [here, it] can be replicated in the other slums all over Africa or all over the world. [Y]ou could see a lot of the same kind of self-help groups and other things spring up here and there to help themselves because nobody else will help you. It's better. You must understand that there is a city authority and for that matter so many agencies [that] have taken a very fixed position, and that you must do something to change them, and that for us, as an organization, we are putting up [numerous] proposals. (Interview, 23 April 2015)

NGOs often claim that city authorities and government alike tacitly accept the persistence of Old Fadama because they have been led to accept their obligations to a global human rights agenda. In reality, however, it is more likely that this forbearance is enforced by the complexities that any large-scale movement entails, as well as disagreements within government. Still, the acceptance of the near-impossibility of relocation weakens the claim of community-based organizations that their activities have forced government to recognize the civil, social and political rights of squatters in slum settlements. A senior planning officer at AMA, for example, explained the balance in the following way:

> We will recognize them [Old Fadama residents] as residents of the city, but we will not recognize them as landowners. I don't know if anybody will recognize them as landowners, but their interest [is] as stakeholders [and] as residents of the city, and [with] the current houses they are building. I know in future that if we get adequate funding and if the project comes on stream, we should be able to build different types of houses that can be accessed by low-income people so that everybody can be catered for, so there are so many different packages and models for that area. [A]s for eviction, it's been out of the question for some time. The relocation is on board and after the relocation there will be fertilization and upgrading of the area [sic]. (Interview, 30 July 2014)

However, interactions and relationships between different government departments and utterances from public officials about Old Fadama may be contradictory and open to numerous interpretations, claims and counter-claims. When asked if Old Fadama is covered by the social services department, for example, a senior manager answered that officially 'they were not supposed to go there', and in the past the mayor's office had warned the department not to deliver any services. Yet social services had 'forced their way in' to support the neediest (notably post-natal aid for single, young mothers), and now visit the site on a weekly basis.

Other senior officials at the AMA played down interactions with Old Fadama and especially OFADA. Some claimed they had heard of OFADA but did not know who they were and had no dealings with them. Other officials appreciated that OFADA and People's Dialogue organized and carried out tasks the metropolitan authority could only undertake with great difficulty. Others still replied that they liaised with 'influential individuals' from the settlement but not under the auspices of OFADA, or simply dismissed the status of any institutions based in Old Fadama on the basis of it being an 'illegal squatter camp'. One senior local government official answered angrily that 'the whole lot should be driven into the sea'. This array of responses suggests unsystematic, changing and personalized relations between Old Fadama, formal government institutions and leading local government figures. Nevertheless, People's Dialogue

highlights that relationships between the settlement and governments have definitely improved. As the executive director explained:

> I can assure you it's the same parliament of Ghana that has
> been very, very progressive, and in fact the most impressive
> and forward-looking response to the crisis of Old Fadama. In
> fact, there was a parliamentary hazard [bill] in September 2008
> [and] in that pamphlet you will realize that the government of
> Ghana, the parliament, had a whole loan that was contracted,
> and on that day the floor of parliament was full of [positive]
> discussions around Old Fadama and the Korle Lagoon.
> (Interview, 22 July 2014)

Despite the positive evaluation of government, considerable
doubt remains on the part of OFADA (as well as residents) as to if,
when and how the current, ambitious plans of government might
be implemented.[12] In all, the chronic ambiguity around the future
status of the settlement and the agricultural market (Chapter 4)
has meant that awkward and multiple dynamics of recognition have
developed. These are invariably interpreted differently and selec-
tively by all stakeholders, while the people most affected (residents
and traders) are left second-guessing as to their fate. And while
OFADA members invariably claim they have cordial and productive relations with AMA, the organization does not figure in recent
city policy documents.[13] Interactions shift from confrontation to
begrudging acceptance, from improvised and discretionary cooperation based on individual relations to mutual accusations of
institutional obduracy. Actors in both statutory and non-statutory
institutions of government thus develop contrasting and contradictory stances towards each other while each try to gain the upper
hand. Competition and cooperation between OFADA and the
metropolitan authorities determine how governance proceeds, but
not always how it is interpreted, and who is to blame or take credit for
locally experienced successes and failures. By interpreting interactions with government as a validation of its claims to be a legitimate
local authority and facilitator of local development, OFADA and
OFADA members have made some tangible gains from the permanent state of temporariness. Meanwhile, city officials try to stay
within the law while also acknowledging the need to work with who
they believe to be the most influential actors and local organizations. More powerful figures may exercise discretionary powers for
the delivery of material support to OFADA to consolidate political

backing. In turn, OFADA and People's Dialogue will claim that ad hoc gains are due to increasing respect for human rights and democratization, and their constant pressure.

Conclusion

In the absence of any systematic provision of public services by government, an assortment of actors set out to ensure that Old Fadama residents and businesses have access to the various services and resources they need, and can carry out basic activities. Social contracts are not made between a singular authority and the population, but between different groups of residents, actors and organizations that sometimes compete and sometimes cooperate to establish and exercise authority, and claim and acquire rights. Although not everyone cooperates with OFADA, accepts its role as a regulatory force or agrees with its members, its overall objective to improve living standards in the settlement enjoys widespread approval. Similarly, the dire developmental needs of Old Fadama provide countless opportunities for those who are able (and capable) to muster the necessary resources to deliver the services demanded by residents. Rights, authority and non-statutory social contracts therefore emerge through everyday pleas by ordinary people for different services that are sometimes delivered by OFADA and its members, who in exchange may assert other obligations. In this way, OFADA and other loose groups of influential actors not only resist the authorities that want them to leave, but become authorities in their own right, enjoying the tacit recognition of government as they mimic state practices of governmentality and gain local legitimacy.

The focus on non-statutory providers of services detracts from studies based on the idea that the 'state' is the sole provider (Post et al. 2017). The operations of OFADA have developed in a context of low and unreliable 'state' involvement and distribution of resources and services. At the same time, there is a low degree of 'state' penetration and direct involvement in the urban settlement, where services and resources are very much in demand. As such, OFADA both 'supplements' what formal institutions of government do, and acts independently of them (ibid.).

Public revenue in the form of tax or labour, and public authority such as policing, building regulation, waste management and recognition of property transfers, are evident all over Old Fadama. The provision of these services often has a sporadic or episodic character and OFADA has only a very limited hold on the overall physical and institutional condition of the site. This demonstrates the many pressures under which OFADA operates, its limited resources, and the fact that many residents' lives are far removed from OFADA's immediate control. Nevertheless, OFADA operates like a state institution and governor in the state of slum as it marks out its jurisdiction through different activities and by negotiating with settlers and endeavouring to lever them into compliance. As the organization tries to provide a broad range of public services, it exemplifies the emergence of local government from below, but whether OFADA will succeed or not is uncertain. What is clear, however, is that when the loose organization undertakes functions 'normally' fulfilled by local government, and when it collaborates with city authorities, it serves to actually increase their capacity as well as extend its own reach. But at the same time, relations between OFADA and levels of government are not clear cut, and the discretionary powers that OFADA sometimes enjoys in the settlement undermine the authority of the AMA (for example, in allowing building activities). So, the activities and efforts of OFADA point to how parts of the population in the illegal settlement come to rely on informal networks and suppliers. This develops because there is a serious deficit of services and a lack of control by levels of formal government concerning the provision of basic services.

Initially aided by a global NGO, OFADA seeks ad hoc solutions and has also developed capacity and organizational ability without government approval or support. OFADA thus exemplifies the diversity of urban change that flows from new relationships forged between non-statutory local and global stakeholders. As we saw in the cases of land governance in the last chapter, there is a sharp contrast between the locally produced institutions that enjoy the power to govern but do not have the legal backing to exercise authority, and statutory institutions that are assigned the formal authority to rule but do not have the power to do so. The lack of universal authority over Old Fadama therefore provides ample space and opportunities for able and ambitious local actors to organize and frame themselves as an institution of local government.

Although the internal structure of the organization ensures some form of representation along ethnic lines, OFADA is an exclusive organization with limited participation, influence, accountability and representation. Further, there is evidence that social stratification along lines of age, gender and ethnicity is reproduced and reworked by the organization through its developing relations with government and the population, leaving OFADA's 'conduct of conduct' wanting (Watts 2003; Myers 2017; Storper and Scott 2016). Nevertheless, opposition to OFADA appears to focus on the unjust proportion of influence it commands rather than on what it actually tries to carry out.

Conclusions and policy perspectives

Processes of marginalization and new geographies of exclusion have long been linked to inadequate and mismanaged urban planning in African capital cities. In recent decades the drivers include the gentrification of urban areas, the negation of and marginalization of all that is 'informal', market-based development under an all-encompassing neoliberal agenda, and the persistent diminishing of interest in low-end and social housing. All occur amidst seemingly unstoppable rural–urban migration and all have contributed to the development of the informal settlement of Old Fadama as a state of slum.

The main argument pursued, however, is that a state of slum is conditioned by the legal entanglement which suspends everyday governance by statutory institutions. This means that context-specific dynamics of informal property, citizenship and governance are established at the micro level. These socio-political dimensions of the state of slum are driven by the inability of statutory institutions to enforce statutory rights, and the needs of ordinary people to ameliorate precarious and uncertain living and working conditions. Therefore, the state of slum is not a product of a weak state or failed state institutions, but exemplifies persistence on the part of statutory powers to uphold the sovereignty of the judicial decision that settlement in Old Fadama is illegal. The corollary is a creeping informalization of governance that is supportive of the judicial decision. These findings challenge dominant and normative approaches, which would posit that formal and informal processes of governance are mutually exclusive and dichotomous.

The corollary is a state of slum characterized by decades-long developmental neglect and ambiguity, and a suspension of formal governance. A range of alternative socio-legal logics have developed in competition with 'state' logics, which influence how governance, urban struggles, inequalities and democratization proceed. For ordinary people living in the illegal settlement of Old Fadama an everyday consequence of living with, and under, the legal entanglement is that their legal status as national citizens is secondary and there are no definitive systems of land regulation. Essential to citizens in the state of slum, therefore, are the gaining and maintaining of social and socio-political recognition. This substantiates tenuous claims to land and produces locally recognized rights to services and resources from informal providers. It takes place every day as ordinary people partake in relationships with neighbours, patrons, kin, community leaders and others to establish rights of recognition to reduce uncertainty.

Residents' perception of 'government' is generally negative with experiences ranging from the predatory (extracting taxes and levies) to the coercive and conclusive (evident in ad hoc bulldozing operations) to the ineffective (trying to stop building) to the negligible (vain efforts to contain waste). Yet governments tacitly accept the settlement because they are ultimately unable to do anything substantive about it. The state of slum cannot be totally eradicated, relocated or recognized. Instead, resource flows are discretionary and politicized to coincide with national cycles of electioneering and local government canvassing. Political promises are made and then broken, and residents' negative perceptions of 'governments' are confirmed anew until the election cycle starts again. Through different everyday situations, encounters, relations and practices the actual citizenship of residents is thus produced and given meaning at the micro level. Residents buy into informal social contracts with different actors who *are* able to provide them with what they need, right now. In turn, the actors and institutions that cannot provide such things are disregarded.

Thus, questions of accessing and controlling land in Old Fadama reflect structural disjuncture and discontinuities between, on the one hand, the will and aim of statutory powers, and on the other, local strategies, tactics and opportunities. Rather than the rule of a singular and coherent set of laws, it is therefore local people's observations and experiences of what is actually happening to the land mass around them, who is doing what, what is allowed and by whom, and who can provide what, that are the key sources of meaningful knowledge, certainty and common purpose about how to settle. This may mean they are obliged to seek the approval of OFADA before building, or get permission from Ga representatives, or seek out the support of neighbours or a powerful local patron, or something else entirely. The range of mechanisms, strategies and tactics to gain local recognition reflects shifts and changing power relations over land at the micro level.

As we have seen, the legal entanglement and political conditioning of Old Fadama impact both positively and negatively on the capacity of formal government and statutory institutions to act. On the one hand, emerging 'partnerships' between statutory and non-statutory powers can increase the reach and governing capacity of both. But in other instances, the opposite is true – for example, when OFADA defies the aims of the AMA, and tacitly supports building activities in designated border areas against the plans of the AMA. In these cases, it is the non-statutory powers that increase reach and governing ability while the credibility of statutory powers is compromised. Hence, together with broad disjointedness between 'state' and 'society', we also see micro-processes of complementarity and competition between different statutory and non-statutory powers that reshape the governance capacities of both. The informalization of governance in the state of slum thereby shapes, and is shaped by, formal governance institutions, and shows that urban informal settlements are not discrete places or particular spaces (Barnett and Parnell 2016).

SDG perspectives

We have seen that informality and illegality are not distinct sources of entanglement for urban growth but are drivers of social, political and economic organization and development. Therefore, their significance has to be considered seriously if grand plans for making cities more inclusive and sustainable are to be achieved.

With the end of the Millennium Development Goals (MDGs) era in 2015, a mixed set of development actors and organizations aimed to keep urban issues at the forefront of developmental ambitions. As a result, the Sustainable Development Solutions Network (SDSN) was set up in 2012, overseen by the UN and comprising policy, academic and civil society expert groups, which, through the Sustainable Cities Thematic Group, drafted an 'Urban SDG'. This was finally approved by the UN General Assembly as Sustainable Development Goal 11 in September 2015, with the commitment to '*Make cities and human settlements inclusive, safe, resilient, and sustainable*' and as one of seventeen goals to be pursued from 2015 to 2030 (Barnett and Parnell 2016). The follow-up to the MDGs in the form of the SDGs was similarly inspired by the UN-Habitat III New Urban Agenda. Paragraph 2 of the 2030 Agenda's political declaration aims to achieve '*sustainable development in its three dimensions – economic, social and environmental – in a balanced and integrated manner*' (Mcgranahan et al. 2016). Related, the UN-Habitat global summit (Habitat III – UN Conference on Housing and Sustainable Urban Development) in October 2016 resulted in an increased realization that ambitions directed at sustainability and urbanization had to be developed and pursued simultaneously, given that they were deeply interrelated processes. The SDGs came into effect in January 2016, and the UNDP now supports the Ghanaian government in integrating the agenda into national policies and plans. Ghana is also committed to similar long-term social, political, economic and environmental improvements as formulated in the African Union Agenda 2063, which is moreover integral to the SDGs. The urban goal of the SDGs is an improvement on the preceding urban MDG, which aimed for '*a significant improvement in the lives of at least 100 million slum dwellers*' but which was criticized widely as a vague and largely meaningless objective (Earle 2016).

As the SDGs become part of various national strategies, policy frameworks and planning initiatives, their ultimate success will rest on how they are implemented and received at the grassroots level and how they are experienced by ordinary people. During data collection for this book there was no obvious evidence in or around Old Fadama of any concrete measures taken to implement Goal 11 or increase the resilience, safety, sustainability and inclusiveness of its population in integrated ways. However, given that Old Fadama is undoubtedly one of the areas in the country in most need of decisive action to obtain these attributes, it is highly relevant to address how informal governance can be used constructively to realize the goals.

Faith in formal planning

The grand ambition of development thinking that complex social realities can be improved by implementing one-size-fits-all solutions is commonly critiqued. Such solutions are typically directed at institutional improvements related to management, administration, planning, monitoring and evaluation, and decision-making, yet they rarely consider the power relations at play in the actual sites of implementation or across and between different scales (Kaika 2017; Obrist et al. 2013). Also, we have seen how politically convenient and 'cheap' solutions such as obliterating the homes of thousands of people and walling in Old Fadama may provide what appear to be quick and convincing fixes, but often rebound and accentuate many different kinds of challenges.

In the case of the SDGs, solutions abound that do not consider the local social and political conditions under which the challenges arise. They reveal that despite the grand title of the 'New Urban Agenda', which was welcomed by UN Habitat III as a paradigm shift, there is still much (unfortunately) that is not new. The premise remains that substantial improvements to everyday life will result from more streamlined decision-making processes and clearer linkages between levels of government. Similar to the MDGs, moreover, is a methodological bias in the SDGs towards quantitative indicators and techno-managerial solutions, which besides not addressing power relations risk losing sight of any important qualitative changes and carry the risk of the politicization of methodologies concerning the measurements of achieved goals and objectives. In this optic, the building of the wall around Old Fadama and subsequent dredging of waterways would be evaluated as positive outcomes because insecure areas would be contained and the risk of flooding in central Accra would be reduced. Yet the social costs as well as heightened risks for residents in Old Fadama would in all likelihood be smoothed over.

Thus, the difficulty lies not only in achieving the SDGs but in evaluating and assessing how outcomes are measured. This has directed research attention to definitions of success, and how results and indicators reflect smudged versions of complex realities and only one side of the story. Related, there are challenges of identifying and recognizing the relevant stakeholders who should be involved in the process of fulfilling and measuring the urban goals. The risk is of singularly focusing on '*what is readily measurable rather than what is actually relevant and important*' (Simon et al. 2015). In a scenario of upgrading and improving Old Fadama, this risk translates into leaving out those in most need of support, those that suffer as a result of 'improvements', and those that are already marginalized and 'invisible'. Instead, projects are judged as successful on the basis of who appears to have benefited, and the 'visible'.

From what we have seen it is likely that traditionally powerful social categories, well-placed community leaders and patrons close to the political centre will be those most likely to benefit from any future 'improvements' and likely to be measured in any assessments. Conversely, individuals, groups and social categories excluded from existing interventions (on the basis of age, gender, political affiliation or ethnicity), and those who may not even be aware of specific policies and plans affecting the area in which they live, are more likely to be excluded from improvements as well as experience omission from government evaluations of success. The examples of the perimeter wall being erected, the bulldozing of areas of settlement and the ambiguity about the relocation of the yam market show that existing policies intending to 'improve' and 'upgrade' the area do not benefit those who need it most. These and many other interventions have created new processes of alienation, misery and uncertainty. In sum, the question of whether plans and policy are successful or not is inherently linked to the technicalities and politics of measurement. Measurement methodologies have to reflect key issues of who is affected, who has participated and who has not, who has been recognized and consulted and who has not, and who has been assessed and why.

Power

The formula of Goal 11 alludes to a social reality without unequal power relations. This is apparent as none of the key concepts related to the urban target (more resilience, safety, inclusiveness and sustainability) are actually within the immediate reach of those that are most affected and need these things most. The attributes cannot be accomplished by marginalized residents on their own or without substantial grassroots support from more powerful actors and institutions. Hence, in the contexts of Old Fadama and Agbogbloshie, young headporters' ability to gain these attributes would be determined and most probably influenced negatively by their unfavourable positioning in broader power relations. While on a broader level the legalistic approach towards and political conditioning of Old Fadama provide ample evidence of a strong trajectory of state unwillingness to support the marginalized, and not only Old Fadama residents per se. On the contrary, the empirical evidence points to governments and city authorities doing much in their power to make life situations *more* difficult for all so that they will move away, back to where they came from (for example, by targeting the vulnerable and refusing to manage waste and provide schools, health facilities and basic infrastructure). The various efforts of different governments to 'contain' and 'discipline' Old Fadama, together with years of attempting to move the yam market out of the city without necessary logistic support, have consequently increased people's exposure to vulnerability, socio-environmental inequality and degradation. What city authorities actually do reveals a combination of inability and unwillingness to tackle and comprehend the complexity of the city as a lived system. It is much easier to pursue aims of containment and pass the responsibility on to the next government.

This means there is an ingrained lack of readiness to deal convincingly with the long-term, pressing and accumulating challenges, and to undertake holistic approaches to urban development which involve '*governance, infrastructure, markets, and social systems*' (Earle 2016). However, the dearth of much-needed holistic approaches to the developmental challenges of Old Fadama cannot be explained away by reference to a lack of capacity (as normative developmental thinking could propose). Rather, short-sightedness and 'holistic inertia' are driven by the legal imperative that means the settlement and settlers are not recognized. Thus, government approaches to Old Fadama are not only not characterized by the necessary level of integration between social, economic and environmental dimensions, but are marked by singular efforts to not recognize residents' rights and needs. Actions, strategies and tactics are therefore centred on maintaining and reproducing unequal power relations between an undisciplined, messy world of informality, and the righteous, ordered world of formal government (Koster and Nuijten 2016). Amongst many examples, this is clear from the plight of young head-porters who live in deplorable conditions and are regularly chastised and threatened by city authorities; the massive failure of waste management and collection in Old Fadama; and the long-term denial of support for the economically vibrant yam market.

Physically, the fact that governments do not undertake much-needed holistic approaches is most evident in the failures to clean up waterways, where despite numerous efforts in the last decade amounting to around $100 million, the different projects have '*no communality of shared knowledge among all stakeholders concerned with urban environmental health, livelihoods and ecological sustainability in [the] low income areas such as within the Korle-Lagoon Complex*' (Songsore et al. 2014: 3). This particular finding not only points to the dire need to integrate social, economic and environmental interventions, but for governments to seriously consider the political dimensions of degradation. On the basis of past relations between governments and Old Fadama, it is therefore unlikely that improved decision-making and capacity around policy implementation will result in changes that are actually needed to reduce vulnerability. In the case of Old Fadama, underdevelopment is the result of political imperatives and legal decisions pursued over many years with considerable vigour. Hence, the optimistic New Urban Agenda depoliticizes questions of development, power relations and political-legal realities, and glosses over the institutional and structural drivers behind people needing to improve their safety, resilience and levels of inclusiveness and sustainability in the first place (Kaika 2017).

Local rights and the rule of law

As ordinary people in Old Fadama seek out land for housing and businesses, and look to others to provide basic everyday needs such as security, sanitation, electricity and waste management, etc., different social contracts and rights are developed across the settlement in a non-uniform way. These are based on divergent socio-politico-economic mediations with emerging authorities that have differing abilities to provide people with what they want and need. Thereby, heterogeneous categories of rights subjects are produced that enjoy to varying degrees the objects of their rights. In turn, different authorities are also produced that to varying degrees can satisfy people's demands. As we saw in the case of George, the ability to enjoy rights often rests on social recognition and demands different social investments. Ordinary people have to manoeuvre and nego-tiate to enjoy rights and by so doing they are active agents of local change as they participate in the shaping of local power relations and understandings of rules and norms. Residents and allocators of different resources in Old Fadama often organize and plan for their own gains but they also have to contribute as well. In this way loose systems of informal governance emerge which generally share the aim of solving the many common problems faced every day. The making of local rights and informal governance thus acts to reduce uncertainty and improve living conditions.

Statutory mechanisms that supposedly ensure representation, infrastructure, rights, safety, security and recognition, etc., are therefore of limited significance to many residents as they try to overcome numerous everyday struggles. People turning their backs to formal state law and government is most obvious in the process of accessing and substantiating claims to land. Here, the influ-ence of the 'rule of law' is insignificant compared to how claims are transformed into rights on the ground and based on local and social recognition. In practice, whether rights to land are recog-nized locally depends on answers to questions like: How did you get this land? Who are you? What kind of person are you? Who supports you? Who do you know and what are you doing? The answers help define the level of support one enjoys and the ability to benefit from settlement.

By exploring and exemplifying these processes, *State of Slum* argues that different forms of citizenship, property and authority wax and wane at the margins of formal state law and amount to an informalization of governance. The forms that citizenship, property and authority take are varied and based on context-specific understandings of socio-legal norms. These gain and lose local legitimacy and meaning and are beholden to their own loose webs of social, political, economic and cultural actors. They often follow different and varied logics and mean that the 'rule of law' regarding the substantiation of 'rights' is but one, often minor, force. There are other emerging systems that decide, define and enforce access to resources.

The different governing rules that residents make and follow are developed through local practices and contests and often contrast sharply with government rationale. Simply put, following the 'rule of law' regarding land is not only impractical but is, by definition, illegitimate in Old Fadama because it would undermine all the land-based developments and investments that people's livelihoods rest upon.

So, in the state of slum, the principle of the rule of law has not brought about a reordering of social organization as dominant developmental thinking expects. Rather, the application of formal state law is a main cause of the considerable developmental challenges and structural deadlock the settlement faces today. In short, recognition of the sovereignty of the judicial decision that settlement is illegal has meant that the rights of settlers are not recognized. The vexed issue of illegal settlements is something that many cities in Ghana experience and is not something that will go away with better policy management. If not addressed it will continue to pose significant difficulties for the implementation of the urban SDG as well as future urban development plans. The whole issue of improving and developing Old Fadama is highly contentious, simply because it is ruled illegal by the highest court in the country and the settlement has a pending eviction notice served against its residents. It is therefore difficult to envisage how the urban SDG ambition to ensure '*access for all to adequate, safe and affordable housing and basic services and [to] upgrade slums*' can proceed without a solution to the legal entanglement. Related to target 11 is target 11.3 dealing with 'Land Use and Participatory Planning', which aims '*By 2030 [to] enhance inclusive and sustainable urbanization and capacity for participatory, integrated and sustainable human settlement planning and management in all countries.*' In Old Fadama, a clear challenge is therefore whether it is even possible to pursue these noble aims without undermining the judicial decision and the rights of the formal landowners. In a nutshell, can improvements to the settlement by statutory authorities proceed without recognizing the rights of people to live and settle on land that does not belong to them?[1] This is an elephant in the room that practitioners of 'slum upgrading' often choose to avoid.

There are many grand plans to improve Accra and the overall quality of Ghanaian urban environments but much, if not all, is linked to state-centrist thinking and the ideas that government plans are widely accepted by those affected, and that all live and work on the normative 'right' side of the law. Highlighting the significance of 'Urban Rules and Regulations', for example, Habitat III emphasizes *'The outcomes in terms of quality of an urban settlement [are] dependent on the set of rules and regulations and its implementation. Proper urbanization requires the rule of law.'*[2] Similar are World Bank publications about Ghana's urban challenges, one of which states, *'Ghana should strengthen and clarify property rights through land market formalization; make land use regulations and administrative procedures more market friendly; and coordinate land market reforms with increased provision of affordable housing'* (World Bank 2015). This is all easier to say than do. Both are based on the convenient, very popular yet flawed 'quick fix logic' emphasized by the development economist Hernando de Soto, whose work assumes that formal state law and the 'rule of law' can be made universally legitimate. Further, that governments are able, willing and powerful enough to implement and execute *coherent* bodies of law and regulation, and that the 'right' people will receive titles.

In the context of Habitat III, the myopic aim is a normative goal of 'proper urbanization' (which is not defined). The call for a singular set of rules and regulations is in line with dominant developmental thinking that informal property should be formalized and codified and will spur efficient land markets and reduce uncertainty. However, this is based on a simplified version of reality where the 'correct' and 'legitimate' owner-occupiers of urban land can be identified and recognized by government, as an important step towards creating a singular set of rules and regulations around land. As we have seen in Old Fadama, there are multiple and changing claims to land which can be individual-, group- and network-based. There are no universal sets of rules or dominant controllers of the land. What we see instead are changing socio-legal configurations and loose webs of land-based interests. The Agenda thus rests on a development model which assumes the formal 'state' is in charge, and equates legality with legitimacy, formalization with certainty, government with governance, and authority with state institutions. None rings true in Old Fadama.

The Agenda pictures cities as sites of considerable market-based potential and inclusive growth, with positive feedback developing between urban growth, social cohesion and responsive governance (Barnett and Parnell 2016). There are many (political) issues the Agenda conveniently fails to consider, including: Why has the rule of law so far failed to diminish inequality in so many cities? What happens to those that are not included in formalization drives and left behind? And can the Agenda diminish the underlying drivers of exclusion?

To increase chances of success, SDG-related policies and interventions have therefore to consider and invest energies in comprehending and solving the specific challenges of different sites. It is difficult to foresee the long-term plight of Old Fadama. But a major concern for this and many other illegal sites of settlement in urban areas is that political and legal entanglements, together with a lack of recognition, will continue to translate into political disinterest and urban degradation. This will continue to leave the solving of insurmountable environmental challenges to ordinary people.

Policy perspective

We have seen that the developmental and governance challenges of Old Fadama are highly complex, serious and have considerable and interwoven economic, social, political, legal, cultural and environmental dimensions. In terms of policy perspectives, therefore, it is likely that any set of recommendations or instruments will only be as good as how they relate to other dimensions and their components. In brief, there are no quick or monochrome fixes to solving the political-legal entanglement of Old Fadama, or its many related developmental challenges that in different ways evolve from it. Similarly, tackling the so-called informal sector with more or fewer laws, different types of laws and better knowledge of laws is likely to fail, as will short-term, politically convenient ideas of improving administration and enforcement of laws that govern people, land, space, property and economic behaviour (Hansen and Vaa 2004). The caveat here, and what we have seen, is that any purely formal *political* solutions imposed from above will not only fail but will amount to pushing the problem farther ahead. So, 'Old Fadama' will not be 'solved' by the continuation of disjointedness between, on the one hand, public policy that endeavours to 'address' different challenges, and on the other the socio-political and political economy of lived lives in the area. It is with this high level of complex and interrelated challenges in mind that the following modest, practical and reasonably realizable recommendations are made to statutory authorities.

1. Establish and sustain a realization that solving the impasse of Old Fadama and the yam market demands interdisciplinary and holistic approaches
2. Communication with different stakeholders in the settlement and market should be systematized and improved to address the perennial uncertainty and unknowability that people live with
3. Any 'partnerships' with non-statutory institutions of governance (such as between the AMA and OFADA) should follow basic standards of accountability and transparency. To this end, non-statutory actors should be persuaded to follow a basic code of conduct
4. Establish an authoritative council of different experts and stakeholders to undertake a holistic analysis and provide *evidence-based* advice to statutory authorities on how to address: a) the legal imbroglio concerning settlement in Old Fadama; and b) the vexed issue of the future of the yam market.

Notes

Introduction

1 UN-Habitat, for example, retains the traditional name Korle Dudor and follows it with 'Old Fadama' in brackets. UN-Habitat (2011: 5).

2 After the biblical story of God's wrath and destruction with fire and brimstone.

3 In India the inventiveness employed in avoiding legal restrictions is commonly known as *jugaad*.

4 The widely used term 'neoliberalism' generally refers to a belief in market-based policies as the best way to ease poverty and increase economic growth. For a discussion of the term's many uses, see Thorsen (2010); Pinson and Morel Journel (2016).

5 None of the residents of Old Fadama I spoke to claimed ownership over the land they occupied.

6 World Bank figures from 2003 estimated that about 15,000 land dispute cases were pending before courts in the Greater Accra Region alone. Obeng-Odoom (2014).

7 The word albatross refers to a heavy burden similar to a curse that cannot be broken and alludes to the poem 'The Rime of the Ancient Mariner' by Samuel Taylor Coleridge (1798), and the song by Iron Maiden of the same name (1984).

8 For a detailed discussion of debates around urban 'neoliberalization', see Pinson and Morel Journel (2016).

9 Still, it is well documented that forced evictions carry a high social and human cost. See, for example, United Nations Human Rights, Office of the High Commission (ONCHR): www.ohchr.org/en/Issues/Housing/Pages/ForcedEvictions.aspx, accessed 4 August 2018.

10 For a detailed discussion, see Ansell and Torfing (2016: ch. 1).

11 See, for example, Fukuyama (2013).

12 Potts disputes the finding that urban populations in Africa are generally increasing (Potts 2012).

13 Almost all the interviews were conducted in English. Where this was not possible they were undertaken in local languages (Ewe, Dagbani and Konkomba) with competent translators.

1 Origins and destinations

1 Consider the period from February 1966 to June 1979. In February 1966 the highly centralized government under President Kwame Nkrumah and the Convention People's Party (CPP) was overthrown by the National Liberation Council (NLC) in a coup led by the military. The NLC oversaw constitutional reform, multiparty elections that were held in August 1969, and the transition to a representative democracy.

The military handed power over to Kofi Busia and the Progress Party but in January 1972 Busia himself was ousted in a second military coup led by Colonel I. K. Acheampong of the NLC, from which the Supreme Military Council (SMC) emerged. In turn, the SMC was deposed by Flight Lieutenant J. J. Rawlings and the Armed Forces Revolutionary Council (AFRC) in June 1979.

2 Although Asante and Ewe groups are likely to be split along NPP and NDC lines, governments since 1992 have been fairly balanced in ethnic terms. Fridy (2007); Langer and Ukiwo (2007).

3 Cooke et al. (2016:1). Concerning education, the Northern Region's school attendance in 2005/06 was 54.7 per cent for both sexes aged between six and twenty-five (with a distinct bias in favour of male education). The national average was 86.1 per cent (92.5 per cent in Greater Accra). Ghana Living Standards Survey 5 (GLSS 5), September 2008. The mortality rate for under-fives in the Northern Region is nearly 60 per cent higher than the national average, 171 per 1,000 against 110 for the country as a whole (Codjoe 2004).

4 The Human Development Index (HDI) merges life expectancy, education and per capita income into a single figure.

5 This Oxfam report is by the present author.

6 The total population of the three northern regions was about 4.2 million in 2010, of a total national population of some 24 million. The northern regions together have fifty-seven political constituencies, while Greater Accra alone has thirty-four.

7 Total fatalities in the 1994/95 conflict range from 2,000 (DANIDA 1995: 2) to 20,000, given by the USA Department of State: *Country Report on Human Rights*, 1996.

8 The depiction is convenient but inaccurate. The Konkomba, for example, are often depicted as a minority, settler and stateless group, despite being today a majority in many locations and having a significant number of traditional authorities. The Nanumba, moreover, despite being frequently categorized as a majority chiefly group, are in fact a minority in their area of residence. See Jönsson (2007).

9 Austin (1964: 34). Here, from Stacey (2012: 30).

10 Many other slum areas of Accra also face a high risk of flooding owing to topography, proximity of rivers and encroachment, including Alajo, Kpehe, Kotobabi, Avenor, Kokomlemle, Ussher, James Town, Gbegbeyse and Mpoase (UN-Habitat 2011).

11 Timeline aerial images of Old Fadama are available from Google Earth®.

12 The latest figures from 2009 estimate that some 22,500 tons of imported e-waste to Ghana 'was unsellable and bound for the dump' (UN Environment Programme, www.smithsonianmag. com/science-nature/ burning-truth-behind-e-waste-dump-africa-180957597/, accessed 4 August 2018).

13 The study was by the *Blacksmith Institute/Green Cross*. See 'Toxic waste "major global threat"', www.bbc.com/news/science-environment-24994209, accessed 4 August 2018.

14 See, for example: Ann Adjasah, 'AMA running foul of the law?', *Daily Graphic*, 22 April 2015, www.graphic.com.gh/news/general-news/ama-running-foul-of-the-law.html.

2 Seeking shelter and freedom

1 An earlier study by the Ghana Statistical Service (GSS 2003) estimated that 40 per cent of all children work while some 88 per cent of these are unpaid workers. See Kwankye et al. (2009: 6).

2 The proportion of children aged five to seventeen in child labour in Ghana's northern regions is 22.8 per cent in Northern Region, 33.5 per cent in Upper West, which is the joint highest in the country, and 31.7 per cent in Upper East. GSS (2014a: xi).

3 Many informants mentioned ethnic conflict and the fear of violence as reasons for migration, although this contrasts with enumeration findings of 2 per cent giving ethnic violence as a reason for migration (Housing the Masses 2010: 2 and 9).

4 For a background to the dispute, see Anamzoya and Tonah (2012).

5 *Kayayei* (sing. *kayayoo*) is a Ga term describing the portering services of young women.

6 A survey of 100 female head-porters found 5 per cent aged 8–9, 25 per cent aged 10–14, 33 per cent aged 15–19, and 37

per cent over 20. Awumbila and Ardayfio-Schandorf (2008: 174).

7 Polygamy is commonly practised in northern Ghana.

8 The Children Act 1998, Act 560.

9 George does have opponents that consider him a 'fraud' but this is irrelevant in the context of understanding how images of generosity are produced to reduce the uncertainty of settlement.

10 This is reminiscent of Beckett, who writes of having 'dabbled with every kind of sleep'. Beckett (1955).

3 Gaining and losing land, and soft property

1 From Uphoff (1989: 295), who defines legitimacy as 'a conviction on the part of persons subject to authority that it is right and proper and that they have some obligation to obey, regardless of the basis on which this belief rests'.

2 Nathaniel Yankson, 'AMA pulls down illegal structures at Mensah Guinea in Accra', Myjoyonline. com, news.myjoyonline.com/news/2014/September-5th/ama-pulls-down-illegal-structures-at-mensah-guinea-in-accra.php, accessed 4 August 2018.

3 Nationally there were several large-scale forced evictions between 2003 and 2006. See Afenah (2012: 531).

4 'A year after the June 3 twin disaster', Graphic Online, 1 June 2016, www.graphic.com.gh/features/features/a-year-after-the-june-3-twin-disaster.html, accessed 4 August 2018.

5 Emmanuel Tornyi, 'Congratulations: Vanderpuije

wins best African mayor award',
Pulse.com.gh, www.pulse.
com.gh/news/congratulations-
vanderpuije-wins-best-african-
mayor-award-id3723516.html,
accessed 4 August 2018.

6 'Accra slum dwellers suspect
cholera demolitions are a pretext
for profit', *Guardian*, 20 October
2014, www.theguardian.com/
global-development/2014/oct/20/
accra-cholera-ghana-mensah-
guinea-slums-demolished-
commercial-profit, accessed 4
August 2018.

7 For example, the Millennium
Development Goal 2015, Target
7D, which is to 'achieve, by 2020,
a significant improvement in the
lives of at least 100 million slum
dwellers'.

8 Despite persistent attempts it was
not possible to establish contact
with either the investor behind
the hotel or the previous chop bar
occupier.

9 See Biswal (1992) for a political
history of the period.

10 Citifmonline. 'Agbogbloshie June
4 market demolished', 4 July 2015,
citifmonline.com/2015/07/04/
photos-agbogbloshie-june-4-
market-demolished/, accessed
4 August 2018.

11 The clearance proceeded more
calmly than the razing of the June
4th site, although many claimed
that more land was levelled than
originally agreed.

12 There are numerous informal
settlements and 'Zongo' areas
all over Accra where northerners
have settled and lived amicably
for many years, so the popular
claim that northerners do not
have a right to the city is factually
incorrect.

4 Shifting yam and marketplace citizenship

1 GRG, 'Yam sector development
strategy', 2012.

2 See, for example, 'Konkombas,
Dagombas at Agbogbloshie
clash: 2 dead', Myjoyonline,
www.myjoyonline.com/news/
2017/april-11th/konkombas-
dagombas-at-agbogbloshie-clash-
police-military-called-in.php,
accessed
4 August 2018.

3 Marshall (1950). Here from
Munro (2001: 296).

4 Ibid.

5 GRG, 'Yam sector development
strategy', 2012.

6 Losses from farm gate to market
are between 10 and 20 per cent.
Ibid..

7 'Be ready for relocation, Accra
Mayor advises wood dealers',
Modern Ghana, 13 October
2009, www.modernghana.com/
news/243510/4/be-ready-
for-relocation-accra-mayor-
advises-wood-d.html, accessed
4 August 2018.

8 'AMA relocates Agbogbloshie
market', NewsGhana, 30 January
2014, www.newsghana.com.gh/
ama-relocates-agbogbloshie-
market/.

9 'Konkomba–Dagomba feud:
Relocate yam market – Inspector
General of Police', GhanaWeb, 12
April 2017, www.ghanaweb.com/
GhanaHomePage/NewsArchive/
Konkomba-Dagomba-feud-
Relocate-yam-market-Inspector-
General-of-Police-528346,
accessed 4 August 2018.

10 Informants directly involved in
the yam market were strongly
against the relocation while many

residents in Old Fadama actually supported the idea.

11 The redevelopment of Adjen Kotuku is reported as costing about $37 million (172 million Ghanaian cedi). E. Smith-Asante, 'Adjen Kotoku market: investment gone waste?', *Daily Graphic*, 29 June 2015, www.graphic.com.gh/features/features/adjen-kotoku-market-investment-gone-waste.html, accessed 4 August 2018.

12 Besides the fees directly related to the market, the owners of the shed pay about 120 cedi annually, while many also pay income tax.

5 Solving problems and emerging authority

1 Parts of this chapter focusing on OFADA are based on Stacey and Lund (2016).

2 Quoted in Ferrazzi (2006: 3).

3 Ghana's system of local government is formally non-partisan and political parties are not allowed to endorse candidates for local elections, nor are candidates allowed to run on the basis of party political membership.

4 From 1994 to 2004, the UNDP supported decentralization in 100 countries and the World Bank *World Development Report 1997* highlighted direct links between decentralization and economic growth. See Treisman (2007); Manor (1999); Crawford (2004).

5 The District Assemblies Common Fund (Section 252, 1992 Constitution) reserves a minimum of 5 per cent of national revenue to be shared by all assemblies on the basis of a parliament-agreed formula. Successful petitions have to convince the ministry of developmental potential and market access, and have a minimum of infrastructure, a reasonable production base, and a minimum population of 80,000, *inter alia*. Owusu (2009).

6 The Ministry for Local Government and Rural Development invites applications from parliamentarians and civil society actors every four years for the carving out of new districts.

7 A previous OFADA member is now an MP for the NDC, the present OFADA chairman is also the NDC constituency secretary, and OFADA's current public relations officer planned to contest a northern constituency for the NDC in the 2016 elections.

8 Press release, US Embassy, 21 September 2015, <ghana.usembassy.gov/pr_092114.html, accessed 4 August 2018.

9 Shack/Slum Dwellers International (SDI) works in thirty countries.

10 GHAFUP has since developed a national network of community savings groups (Gillespie 2013: 210).

11 The increase suggests a present population of about 100,000.

12 Current government plans are contained in UN-Habitat (2011) and GRG (2012).

13 For example, see UN (2011).

Conclusions and policy perspectives

1 The issue of land rights also involves the difficult and

contested issue of compensation
for the customary landowners.

2 'Technical report by the Bureau
of the United Nations Statistical
Commission (UNSC) on the
process of the development of
an indicator framework for the
goals and targets of the post-2015
development agenda.' Here from
Simon et al. (2015). See also
Habitat III home page, habitat3.
org/the-new-urban-agenda/,
accessed 4 August 2018.

References

Ackah, C. and D. Medvedev (2012) 'Internal migration in Ghana: determinants and welfare impacts', *International Journal of Social Economics*, 39(10): 764–84.

Acquah, L. (1958) *Accra Survey: A Social Survey of the Capital of Ghana, Formerly Called the Gold Coast, Undertaken for the West African Institute of Social and Economic Research, 1953–1956*, Accra: Ghana Universities Press.

Afenah, A. (2012) 'Engineering a millennium city in Accra, Ghana: the Old Fadama intractable issue', *Urban Forum*, 23: 527–40.

Agamben, G. (2005) *State of Exception*, Chicago, IL: University of Chicago Press.

Agarwal, N. B. (1994) *A Field of One's Own: Gender and Land Rights in South Asia*, Cambridge University Press.

Ahlvin, K. (2012) 'The burden of the kayayei: cultural and socio-economic difficulties facing female porters in Agbogbloshie', *PURE Insights*, 1(4).

Amanor, K. (2001) 'Land, labour and the family in Southern Ghana: a critique of land policy under neo-liberalisation', Uppsala: Nordiska Afrikainstitutet.

Amin, A. and N. Thrift (2002) *Cities: Reimagining the Urban*, Cambridge: Polity Press.

Amnesty International (2011) '"When we sleep, we don't sleep". Living under threat of forced eviction in Ghana', Housing is a Human Right, www.amnesty.org/download/Documents/24000/afr2800320011en.pdf, accessed 4 August 2018.

Amoako, C. (2016) 'Brutal presence or convenient absence: the role of the state in the politics of flooding in informal Accra, Ghana', *Geoforum*, 77: 5–16.

Anamzoya, A. S. and S. Tonah (2012) 'Chieftaincy succession dispute in Nanum, northern Ghana: interrogating the narratives of the contestants', *Ghana Journal of Geography*, 4: 83–101.

Ansell, C. and J. Torfing (eds) (2016) *Handbook on Theories of Governance*, Edward Elgar.

Appadurai, A. (1996) *Modernity at Large: Cultural Dimensions of Globalization*, Minneapolis, MN: University of Minneapolis Press.

—— (2000) 'Spectral housing and urban cleansing: notes on millennial Mumbai', *Public Culture*, 12(3): 627–51.

Arimah, B. C. (2010) 'Slums as expressions of social exclusion: explaining the prevalence of slums in African countries', United Nations Human Settlements Programme (UN-Habitat), www.oecd.org/development/perspectivesonglobaldevelopment/46837274.pdf, accessed 4 August 2018.

Aryeetey, E. and C. Udry (2010) 'Creating property rights: land banks in Ghana', *American Economic Review Papers and Proceedings*.

Austin, D. (1964) *Politics in Ghana 1946–1960*, Oxford: Oxford University Press.

Awuah, K. G. B. and F. N. Hammond (2013) 'Prognosis of land title formalization in urban Ghana: the myth and reality of awareness and relevance', *African Studies Quarterly*, 14(1/2): 55–75.

Awumbila, M. and E. Ardayfio-Schandorf (2008) 'Gendered poverty, migration and livelihood strategies of female porters in Accra, Ghana', *Norsk Geografisk Tidsskrift (Norwegian Journal of Geography)*, 62(3): 171–9.

Awumbila, M., G. Owusu and J. K. Teye (2014) 'Can rural–urban migration into slums reduce poverty? Evidence from Ghana', Migrating Out of Poverty, Working Paper 13.

Ayee, J. (1997) 'The adjustment of central bodies to decentralization: the case of the Ghanaian bureaucracy', *African Studies Review*, 40(2): 37–57.

—— (2013) 'The developmental state experiment in Africa: the experiences of Ghana and South Africa', *The Round Table: the Commonwealth Journal of International Affairs*, 103(3): 1–22.

Ayee, J., A. K. D. Frempong, R. Asante and K. Boafo-Arthur (2001) 'Local power struggles, conflicts and conflict resolution: the causes, dynamics and policy implications of land-related conflicts in the greater Accra and eastern regions of Ghana', Research Report no. 3, Dakar: CODESRIA.

Ayee, J., T. Søreide, G. P. Shukla and T. Minh Le (2011) 'Political economy of the mining sector in Ghana', Public Sector Reform and Capacity Building Unit, World Bank.

Bailey, G. (2014/15) 'Accumulation by dispossession: a critical assessment', *International Socialist Review*, 95.

Baptista, I. (2013) 'Practices of exception in urban governance: reconfiguring power inside the state', *Urban Studies*, 50(1): 39–50.

Barnett, C. and S. Parnell (2016) 'Ideas, implementation and indicators: epistemologies of the post-2015 urban agenda', *Environment and Urbanization*, 28(1): 87–98.

Barry, M. and E. K. Danso (2014) 'Tenure security, land registration and customary tenure in a peri-urban Accra community', *Land Use Policy*, 39: 358–65.

Barry, M., J. F. Dewar, I. Whittal and F. Muzondo (2007) 'Land conflicts in informal settlements: Wallacedene in Cape Town, South Africa', *Urban Forum*, 18: 171–89.

Beall, J., T. Goodfellow and D. Rodgers (2011) *Cities, Conflicts and State Fragility*, London: London School of Economics and Political Science.

Beckett, S. (1955) *Molly – A Novel*, New York: Grove Press.

Benda-Beckmann, K. von (1981) 'Forum shopping and shopping forums: dispute processing in a Minangkabau village in West Sumatra', *Journal of Legal Pluralism*, 19: 117–62.

Bening, R. B. (1999) *Ghana: Regional Boundaries and National Integration*, Accra: Ghana Universities Press.

Benjamin, S. (2008) 'Occupancy urbanism: radicalizing politics and economy beyond policy and programs', *International Journal of Urban and Regional Research*, 32(3): 719–29.

Bentsi-Enchill, K. (1964) *Ghana Land Law: An Exposition, Analysis and Critique*, London: Sweet and Maxwell.

Berry, S. (2002) 'Debating the land question in Africa', *Comparative Studies in Society and History*, 44(4): 638–68.

Bevir, M. (2013) *Governance: A Very Short Introduction*, Oxford: Oxford University Press.

Bierschenk, T. and J. P. Olivier de Sardan (2003) 'Powers in the village: rural Benin between democratisation and decentralisation', *Africa. Journal of the International African Institute*, 73(2): 45–173.

Biswal, T. (1992) *Ghana: Political and Constitutional Developments*, New Delhi: Northern Book Centre.

Blundo, G. and J. P. Olivier de Sardan (eds) (2006) *Everyday Corruption and the State. Citizens and Public Officials in Africa*, London: Zed Books.

Boamah, E. F. and M. Walker (2016) 'Legal pluralism, land tenure and the production of "Nomotropic urban spaces" in post-colonial Accra, Ghana', *Geography Research Forum*, 36: 86–109.

Boone, C. (2003) 'Decentralisation as political strategy in West Africa', *Comparative Political Studies*, 36: 355–80.

Boone, C. and D. Kwame Duku (2012) 'Ethnic land rights in western Ghana: landlord–stranger relations in the democratic era',

Development and Change, 43(3): 671– 93.

Bourdieu, P. (1977) *Outline of a Theory of Practice*, Cambridge: Cambridge University Press.

Braimah, J. A., H. H. Tomlinson and O. Amkwatia (1997) 'History and traditions of the Gonja', African Occasional Papers no. 6, University of Calgary Press.

Brown, A. (2015) 'Claiming the streets: property rights and legal empowerment in the urban informal economy', *World Development*, 76: 238–48.

Brown, A., C. Msoka and I. Dankoco (2015) 'A refugee in my own country: evictions or property rights in the urban informal economy?', *Urban Studies*, 52(12): 2234–49.

Brukum, N. J. K. (1998) 'The socio-economic underdevelopment of northern Ghana under British colonial rule', *Transactions of the Historical Society of Ghana*, New Series no. 2, pp. 117–31.

Bryceson, D. and D. Potts (eds) (2006) *African Urban Economies: Viability, Vitality or Vitiation*, Palgrave Macmillan.

Bryman, A. (2008) *Social Research Methods*, 3rd edn, Oxford: Oxford University Press.

Campbell, J. M. (2015) *Conjuring Property: Speculation and Environmental Futures in the Brazilian Amazon*, Seattle and London: University of Washington Press.

Cammett, M. and L. M. MacLean (2013) *The Politics of Non-State Social Welfare*, Cornell, NY: Cornell University Press.

Campion, B. B. and E. Acheampong (2014) 'The chieftaincy institution in Ghana: causers and arbitrators of conflicts in industrial jatropha investments', *Sustainability*, 6: 6332–50.

Carmody, P. and F. Owusu (2016) 'Neoliberalism, urbanization and change in Africa: the political economy of heterotopias', *Journal of African Development*, 18(18): 61–73.

Chazan, N. (1983) An Anatomy of Ghanaian politics: Managing Political Recession 1969–1982, Boulder, CO: Westview Press.

Chenwi, L. (2013) 'Unpacking "progressive realisation", its relation to resources, minimum core and reasonableness, and some methodological considerations for assessing compliance', *De Jure*, 46(3): 742–69.

Chernoff, J. M. (2003) Hustling Is Not Stealing: Stories of an African Bar Girl, Chicago, IL: University of Chicago Press.

Codjoe, S. N. A. (2004) 'Population and land use/cover dynamics in the Volta river basin of Ghana, 1960–2010', Ecology and Development Series no. 15, The Netherlands: Cuvillier Verlag Gottingen.

Cohen, B. (2006) 'Urbanization in developing countries: current trends, future projections, and key challenges for sustainability', *Technology in Society*, 28(1): 63–80.

Cooke, E., S. Hague and A. McKay (2016) 'The Ghana poverty and inequality report: using the 6th Ghana Living Standards Survey'.

Crawford, G. (2004) 'Democratic decentralisation in Ghana: issues and prospects', POLIS Working Paper no. 9, School of Politics and International Studies, University of Leeds.

DANIDA (Royal Danish Ministry for Foreign Affairs) (1995) 'Ghana; En politisk og økonomisk oversigt', Copenhagen: DANIDA.

Darko, E. and L. Atazona (2013) 'Literature review of the impact of climate change on economic development in northern Ghana: opportunities and activities', Overseas Development Institute.

Das, V. (2011) 'State, citizenship, and the urban poor', *Citizenship Studies*, 15(3/4): 319–33.

Davis, M. (2006) *Planet of Slums*, London: Verso.

De Boeck, F. and M.-F. Plissart (2014) *Kinshasa: Tales of the Invisible City*, Leuven University Press.

De Soto, H. (2000) *The Mystery of Capital: Why Capitalism Triumphs in the West and Fails Everywhere Else*, New York: Basic Books.

De Souza, F. (2001) 'The future of informal settlements: lessons in the legalization of disputed urban land in Recife, Brazil', *Geoforum*, 32: 483–92.

Deininger, K. (2003) 'World Bank land policies for growth and poverty reduction', Washington, DC: World Bank.

Demsetz, H. (1967) 'Toward a theory of property rights', *American Economic Review*, 57: 347–59.

Demissie, F. (ed.) (2007) *Postcolonial African Cities: Imperial Legacies and Postcolonial Predicaments*, London and New York: Routledge.

Department of State (1996) 'Country report on human rights: Ghana', Washington, DC: Department of State.

Diao, X., F. Cossar, N. Houssou and S. Kolavalli (2014) 'Mechanization in Ghana:

emerging demand, and the search for alternative supply models', *Food Policy*, 48: 68–181.

Dickson, K. B. (1968) 'Background to the problem of economic development in northern Ghana', *Annals of the Association of American Geographers*, 58(4): 686–96.

Diener, S., S. Semiyaga, C. B. Niwagaba, A. M. Muspratt, J. B. Gning, M. Mbéguéré, J. E. Ennine, C. Zurbrugga and L. Strandea (2014) 'A value proposition: resource recovery from faecal sludge – can it be the driver for improved sanitation?', *Resources, Conservation, and Recycling*, 88: 32–8.

Dietz, T., K. van der Geest and F. Obeng (2013) 'Local perceptions of development and change in northern Ghana', in J. Yaro (ed.), *Rural Development in Northern Ghana*, New York: Nova Science Publishers, pp. 17–36.

Du Plessis, J. (2005) 'The growing problem of forced eviction and the crucial importance of community-based, locally appropriate alternatives', *Environment and Urbanization*, 17: 123–34.

Earle, L. (2016) 'Urban crises and the new urban agenda', *Environment and Urbanization*, 28(1): 77–86.

Evans, P. B., D. Rueschemeyer and T. Skocpol (eds) (1983) *Bringing the State Back In*, Boston, MA: Harvard University Press.

Farouk, B. R. and M. Owusu (2012) '"If in doubt, count": the role of community-driven enumerations in blocking eviction in Old Fadama, Accra', *Environment and Urbanization*, 24(1): 47–57.

Ferguson, J. (1999) *Expectation of Modernity: Myths and Meanings of Urban Life on the Zambian Copperbelt*, Berkeley: University of California Press.

Fernandes, E. and A. Varley (eds) (1998) *Illegal Cities: Law and Urban Change in Developing Countries*, London: Zed Books.

Ferrazzi, G. (2006) 'Ghana Local Government Act 1993; a comparative analysis in the context of the review of the Act', Local Government and Poverty Reduction Programme (LGPRSP), Accra.

Fitzpatrick, D. (2006) 'Evolution and chaos in property rights systems: the third world tragedy of contested access', *Yale Law Journal*, 115(5): 996–1048.

Flyvbjerg, B. (2004) 'Five misunderstandings about case-study research', in C. Seale, G. Gobo, J. F. Gubrium and D. Silverman (eds), *Qualitative Research Practice*, London and Thousand Oaks, CA: Sage, pp. 420–34.

Foucault, M. (1991) 'Governmentality', in G. Burchell, C. Gordon and P. Miller (eds), *The Foucault Effect: Studies in Governmentality*, Chicago, IL: University of Chicago Press.

Fourchard, L. (2011) 'Between world history and state formation: new perspectives on African cities', *Journal of African History*, (52): 223–48.

Freund, B. (2007) *The African City: A History*, Cambridge: Cambridge University Press.

Fridy, K. S. (2007) 'The elephant, umbrella, and quarrelling cocks: disaggregating partisanship in Ghana's fourth republic',

African Affairs, 106(423): 281–305.

Fukuyama, F. (2013) 'What is governance?', *Governance: An International Journal of Policy, Administration, and Institutions*, 26(3): 347–68.

Geschiere, P., B. Meyer and P. Pels (eds) (2008) *Readings in Modernity in Africa*, Oxford: James Currey.

Gilbert, A. (2007) 'The return of slum: does language matter?', *International Journal of Urban and Regional Research*, 31: 697–713.

—— (2009) 'Extreme thinking about slums and slum dwellers: a critique', *SAIS Review*, XIX(1): 35–8.

Gillespie, T. (2013) 'Struggles over urban space in Accra, Ghana', PhD thesis, University of Leeds.

—— (2016) 'Accumulation by urban dispossession: struggles over urban space in Accra, Ghana', *Transactions of the Institute of British Geographers*, 42: 66–77.

Gleeson, B. and N. Low (2000) 'Revaluing planning: rolling back neo-liberalism in Australia', *Progress in Planning*, 53(2): 83–164.

Grant, R. (2006) 'Out of place? Global citizens in local spaces: a study of the informal settlements in the Korle Lagoon environs in Accra, Ghana', *Urban Forum* 17(1):1–24.

—— (2009) *Globalizing City: The Urban and Economic Transformation of Accra, Ghana*, New York: Syracuse University Press.

Greenhouse, C. J. (2012) 'The "state idea" in theory and practice', *Reviews in Anthropology*, 41(3): 154–72.

GRG (Government of the Republic of Ghana) (1992) *The Constitution for the Republic of Ghana*.

—— (2011) *Land Administration Project, Phase Two. Project Implementation Main Manual*, Accra: Ministry of Lands and Natural Resources.

—— (2012a) *Ghana National Urban Policy Action Plan*, Accra: Ministry of Local Government and Rural Development.

—— (2012b) *Yam Sector Development Strategy*, Ghana.

—— (2015) *Ghana National Spatial Development Framework (2015–2035). Executive Summary*.

—— (2016) *Land Use and Spatial Planning Act. Act 925*.

—— (2017) *Land Bill*, Accra: Ministry of Lands and Natural Resources.

Grischow, J. and G. H. McKnight (2003) 'Rhyming development: practising post-development in colonial Ghana and Uganda', *Journal of Historical Sociology*, 16(4): 517–49.

GSS (Ghana Statistical Service) (2003) 'Ghana child labour survey 2001', Accra: Ghana Statistical Service.

—— (2013) '2010 Population and housing census: national analytical report', Ghana Statistical Service.

—— (2014a) 'Ghana living standards survey round 6 (GLSS 6): Child labour report', Ghana Statistical Service.

—— (2014b) '2010 Population and housing census: District analytical report, Accra Metropolitan', Ghana Statistical Service.

Guyer, J. I. (2009) 'On possibility: a response to "How is anthropology going?'", *Anthropological Theory*, 9(4): 355–70.

Habyarimana, J., H. Macartan, D. N. Posner and J. M. Weinstein (2009) *Coethnicity: Diversity and the Dilemmas of Collective Action: Diversity and the Dilemmas of Collective Action*, Russell Sage Foundation.

Hagmann, T. and D. Péclard (2010) 'Negotiating statehood: dynamics of power and domination in Africa', *Development and Change*, 41(4): 539–62.

Hansen, K. T. and M. Vaa (eds) (2004) *Reconsidering Informality: Perspectives from Urban Africa*, Nordiska Afrikainstitutet.

Hansen, T. B. and O. Verkaaik (2009) 'Introduction – urban charisma on everyday mythologies in the city', *Critique of Anthropology*, 29(1): 5–26.

Hardt, M. and A. Negri (2001) *Empire*, Boston, MA: Harvard University Press.

Hart, K. (1973) 'Informal income opportunities and urban employment in Ghana', *Journal of Modern African Studies*, 11(1): 61–89.

Harvey, D. (2003) *The New Imperialism*, Oxford: Oxford University Press.

—— (2007) *A Brief History of Neoliberalism*, Oxford: Oxford University Press.

—— (2008) 'The right to the city', *New Left Review*, 53: 23–40.

Heller, P. (2009) 'Democratic deepening in India and South Africa', *Journal of Asian and African Studies*, 44(1): 123–49.

Helmke, G. and S. Levitsky (2004) 'Informal institutions and comparative politics: a research agenda', *Perspectives on Politics*, 2(4): 725–40.

Herbst, J. (2000) *States and Power in Africa*, Princeton, NJ: Princeton University Press.

Hoffman, D. (2017) *Monrovia Modern: Urban Form and Political Imagination in Liberia*, Durham, NC: Duke University Press.

Honneth, A. (1995) *The Struggle for Recognition. The Moral Grammar of Social Conflicts*, Cambridge: Polity Press.

Horvath, A., B. Thomassen and H. Wydra (2015) *Breaking Boundaries: Varieties of liminality*, Oxford and New York: Berghahn Books.

Housing the Masses (2010) 'Final report to People's Dialogue on human settlements on community-led enumeration of Old Fadama community, Accra, Ghana', sdinet.org/publication/ghana-final-report-to-peoples-dialogue-on-human-settlements-on-community-led-enumeration-of-old-fadama-accra/, accessed 4 August 2018.

Huchzermeyer, M. (2011) *Cities with Slums: From Informal Settlement Eradication to a Right to the City in Africa*, South Africa: UCT Press.

Iliffe, J. (1995) *Africans: The History of a Continent*, Cambridge: Cambridge University Press.

Isin, E. F. and G. M. Nielsen (eds) (2008) *Acts of Citizenship*, Chicago, IL: University of Chicago Press.

Isin, E. F. and B. S. Turner (eds) (2002) *Handbook of Citizenship Studies*, London: Sage.

Jacobs, J. M. (1996) *Edge of Empire: Postcolonialism and the City*, London: Routledge.

Jönsson, J. (2007) 'The overwhelming minority: traditional leadership and ethnic conflict in Ghana's northern region', CRISE Working Paper no. 30, University of Oxford.

Kaika, M. (2017) '"Don't call me resilient again!": The New Urban Agenda as immunology ... or ... what happens when communities refuse to be vaccinated with "smart cities" and indicators', *Environment and Urbanization*, 29(1): 89–102.

Kaplan, R. (1994) 'The coming anarchy', *Atlantic Monthly*, 273: 44–75.

Kay, G. B. (ed.) (1972) *The Political Economy of Colonialism in Ghana: A Collection of Documents and Statistics 1900–1960*, Cambridge: Cambridge University Press.

Keenan, S. (2015) *Subversive Property: Law and the Production of Spaces of Belonging*, London: Routledge.

Kleemann, J., J. N. Inkoom, M. Thiel, S. Shankar, S. Lautenbach and C. Fürst (2017) 'Peri-urban land use patterns and its relation to land use planning in Ghana, West Africa'. *Landscape and Urban Planning*, 165: 280–94.

Kludze, A. K. P. (1998) 'Chieftaincy jurisdiction and the muddle of constitutional interpretation in Ghana', *Journal of African Law*, 42(1).

Konadu-Agyemang, K. (2000) 'The best of times and the worst of times: structural adjustment programs and uneven development in Africa: the case of Ghana', *Professional Geographer*, 52(3): 469–83.

Koster, M. and M. Nuijten (2016) 'Coproducing urban space: rethinking the formal/informal dichotomy', *Singapore Journal of Tropical Geography*, 37: 282–94.

Kwankye, S. O., J. K. Anarfi, C. A. Tagoe and A. Castaldo (2009) Independent north–south child migration in Ghana: the decision making process', Working Paper T–29, Development Research Centre on Migration, Globalization and Poverty, London: DfID.

Ladouceur, P. A. (1979) *Chiefs and Politicians: The Politics of Regionalism in Northern Ghana*, London: Longman.

Landau, L. B. (2014) 'Conviviality, rights, and conflict in Africa's urban estuaries', *Politics & Society*, 42(3): 359–80.

Langer, A. and U. Ukiwo (2007) 'Ethnicity, religion and the state in Ghana and Nigeria: perceptions from the street', Centre for Research on Inequality, Human Security and Ethnicity, University of Oxford.

Langevang, T. (2008) '"We are managing!": uncertain paths to respectable adulthoods in Accra, Ghana', *Geoforum*, 39(6): 2039–47.

Larbi, W. O. (2011) 'Ghana's Land Administration Project: accomplishments, impacts, and the way ahead', Paper presented at the World Bank Conference on Land and Poverty Reduction, Washington, DC, 18–20 April.

Lentz, C. (1995) 'Unity for development: youth associations in north-western Ghana', *Africa*, 65(3): 395–429.

Locatelli, F. and P. Nugent (eds) (2009) *African Cities. Competing Claims on Urban Spaces*, Leiden: Brill.

Lombard, M. (2013) 'Struggling, suffering, hoping, waiting: perceptions of temporality in two informal neighbourhoods in Mexico', *Environment and Planning D: Society and Space*, 31: 813–29.

Lombard, M. and C. Rakodi (2016) 'Urban land conflict in the global south: towards an analytical framework', *Urban Studies*, 53(13): 2683–99.

Long, N. (2001) *Development Sociology: Actor Perspectives*, London: Routledge.

Longi Felix, Y. T. and C. K. Mbowura (2014) 'The Konkomba yam market: a study of a migrant community in an urban setting', *International Journal of Humanities and Social Science*, 4(6[1]): 276–84.

Lund, C. (2003) 'Bawku is still volatile. Ethno-political conflict and state recognition in northern Ghana', *Journal of Modern African Studies*, 41(4): 587–610.

—— (2006) 'Twilight institutions; public authority and local politics in Africa', *Development and Change*, 37(4): 685–705.

—— (2008) *Local Politics and the Dynamics of Property in Africa*, Cambridge and New York: Cambridge University Press.

—— (2011) 'Property and citizenship: conceptually connecting land rights and belonging in Africa', *Africa Spectrum*, 46(3): 71–5.

—— (2014) 'Of what is this a case? Analytical movements in qualitative social science research', *Human Organization*, 73(3): 224–34.

Lund, C. and C. Boone (2013) 'Introduction: Land politics in Africa – constituting authority over territory, property and persons', *Africa*, 83(1): 1–13.

Lynch, K. (2005) *Rural–urban Interaction in the Developing World*, London: Routledge.

MacGaffey, W. (2009) 'The blacksmiths of Tamale: the dynamics of space and time in a Ghanaian industry', *Africa*, 79(2): 169–85.

Maclean, L. M. (2004) 'Mediating ethnic conflict at the grassroots: the role of local associational life in shaping political values in Côte d'Ivoire and Ghana', *Journal of Modern African Studies*, 42(4): 589–617.

Mandich, G. and V. Cuzzocrea (2015) '"Domesticating" the city: family practices in public space', *Space and Culture*, 1–13.

Mann, M. (1993) *The Sources of Social Power*, New York: Cambridge University Press.

Manor, J. (1999) 'Directions in development; the political economy of democratic decentralization', Washington, DC: World Bank.

Marshall, T. H. (1950) *Citizenship and Social Class, and Other Essays*, Cambridge: Cambridge University Press.

Mason, A. C. (2005) 'Constructing authority alternatives on the periphery: vignettes from Colombia', *International Political Science Review*, 26(1): 37–54.

McFarlane, C. and J. Silver (2017) 'The political city: "seeing sanitation" and making the urban political in Cape Town', *Antipode*, 49(1): 125–48.

Mcgranahan, G., D. Schensul and G. Singh (2016) 'Inclusive urbanization: can the 2030

Agenda be delivered without it?',
Environment and Urbanization,
28(1): 13–34.

Merrifield, A. (2013) *The Politics
of the Encounter: Urban Theory
and Protest under Planetary
Urbanization*, Athens: University
of Georgia Press.

Migdal, J., A. Kohli and V.
Shue (1994) *State Power and
Social Forces: Domination and
Transformation in the Third
World*, Cambridge: Cambridge
University Press.

Mitchell, T. (2002) *Rule of Experts:
Egypt, Techno-Politics, and
Modernity*, London: University of
California Press.

Mitra, S., J. Mulligan, J. Schilling,
J. Harper, J. Vivekananda and
L. Krause (2017) 'Developing
risk or resilience? Effects of
slum upgrading on the social
contract and social cohesion in
Kibera, Nairobi', *Environment and
Urbanization*, 29(1): 103–22.

Mohanty, M. (2006) 'Urban
squatters, informal sector and
livelihood strategies of the poor in
Fiji Islands', *Development Bulletin*,
70: 65–8.

Moore, S. F. (1973) 'Law and social
change: the semi-autonomous
field as an appropriate subject of
study', *Law and Society Review*,
7(4): 719–46.

Munro, W. A. (2001) 'The political
consequences of local electoral
systems: democratic change
and the politics of differential
citizenship in South Africa',
Comparative Politics, 33: 295–313.

Myers, G. (2011) *African Cities:
Alternative Visions of Urban Theory
and Practice*, London and New
York: Zed Books.

—— (2017) *Garbage, Governance*

*and Sustainable Development in
Urban Africa*, London: Routledge.

Nielsen, M. (2011) 'Inverse
governmentality: the
paradoxical production of peri-
urban planning in Maputo,
Mozambique', *Critique of
Anthropology*, 3(4): 329–58.

Nkurunziza, E. (2008)
'Understanding informal urban
land access processes from a legal
pluralist perspective: the case
of Kampala, Uganda', *Habitat
International*, 32: 109–20.

Obeng, C. K. (2016) 'Effect of
location incentives on regional
distribution of foreign direct
investment in Ghana', Munich
Personal RePEc Archive, mpra.
ub.uni-muenchen.de/70131/1/
MPRA_paper_70131.pdf,
accessed 4 August 2018.

Obeng-Odoom, F. (2011) 'The
informal sector in Ghana under
siege', *Journal of Developing
Societies*, 27: 355–92.

—— (2014) 'Urban land policies
in Ghana: a case of the emperor's
new clothes?', *Review of Black
Political Economy*, 41: 119–43.

Oberhauser, A. M. and M. A. Yeboah
(2011) 'Heavy burdens: gendered
livelihood strategies of porters in
Accra, Ghana', *Singapore Journal
of Tropical Geography*, 32(1):
22–37.

Obrist, B., V. Arit and E. Macamo
(eds) (2013) *Living the City:
Processes of Invention and
Intervention*, Münster and New
York: LIT Verlag.

Oteng-Ababio, M., A. A. Owusu,
G. Owuse and C. Wrigley-
Asante (2017) 'Geographies of
crime and collective efficacy in
urban Ghana', *Territory, Politics,
Governance*, 5(4): 459–77.

Otto, J. M. (2009) 'Rule of law promotion, land tenure and poverty alleviation: questioning the assumptions of Hernando de Soto', *Hague Journal on the Rule of Law*, 1: 173–95.

Overseas Development Institute (2005) *Revised Report for DFID Ghana*, Accra: Centre for Policy Analysis.

Owusu, G. (2005) 'Small towns in Ghana: justifications for their promotion under Ghana's decentralisation programme', *African Studies Quarterly*, 8(2): 48–69.

—— (2008) 'Indigenes' and migrants' access to land in peri-urban areas of Accra, Ghana', *International Development Planning Review*, 30(2): 177–98.

—— (2009) 'Internal boundaries and district administration: a challenge to decentralisation and district development in Ghana', *Geografiska Annaler: Series B, Human Geography*, 91(1): 57–71.

—— (2010) 'Social effects of poor sanitation and waste management on poor urban communities: a neighborhood-specific study of Sabon Zongo, Accra', *J. Urbanism: Int. Res. Plac. Urban Sustain.*, 3(2): 145–60.

Owusu, G., S. Agyei-Mensah and R. Lund (2008) 'Slums of hope and slums of despair: mobility and livelihoods in Nina, Accra', *Norsk Geografisk Tidsskrift*, 62: 180–90.

Owusu, M. (2013) 'Community-managed reconstruction after the 2012 fire in Old Fadama, Ghana', *Environment and Urbanization*, 25: 243–8.

Oxfam (2016) 'The weak link: the role of local institutions in accountable natural resource management: Ghana', Oxfam America.

Paller, J. W. (2012) 'Political accountability in Ghanaian slums: evidence from the grassroots', Briefing paper, Ghana Center for Democratic Development (CDD-Ghana).

—— (2014) 'Informal institutions and personal rule in urban Ghana', *African Studies Review*, 57(3):123–42.

—— (2015) 'Informal networks and access to power to obtain housing in urban slums in Ghana', *Africa Today*, 62(1): 31–55.

Patel, K. (2013) 'The value of secure tenure: ethnographic accounts of how tenure security is understood and realised by residents of low-income settlements in Durban, South Africa', *Urban Forum*, 24: 269–87.

Peck, J. and A. Tickell (2002) 'Neoliberalizing space', *Antipode*, 34: 380–404.

Pellow, D. (2002) *Landlords and Lodgers: Socio-Spatial Organization in an Accra Community*, Westport, CT: Praeger.

Peters, P. (2004) 'Inequality and social conflict over land in Africa', *Journal of Agrarian Change*, 4(3): 269–314.

Pierre, J. (1999) 'Models of urban governance. The institutional dimension of urban politics', *Urban Affairs Review*, 34(3): 372–96.

Pieterse, E. (2008) *City Futures: Confronting the Crisis of Urban Development*, London: Zed Books.

—— (2010) 'Cityness and African urban development', Research Working Paper 42, African Centre for Cities, Cape Town/ United Nations University–

World Institute for Development Economics,.

Pinson, G. and C. Morel Journel (2016) 'The neoliberal city – theory, evidence, debates, territory, politics', *Governance*, 4(2): 137–53.

Plange, N. K. (1984) 'The colonial state in northern Ghana: the political economy of pacification', *Review of African Political Economy*, 31: 29–43.

Porter, G., K. Hampshire, A. Abana, A. Tanle, K. Esia-Donkoh, R. O. Amoako-Sakyi, S. Agblorti and S. A. Owusu (2011) 'Mobility, education and livelihood trajectories for young people in rural Ghana: a gender perspective', *Children's Geographies*, 9(3/4): 395–410.

Post, A. E., V. Bronsoler and L. Salman (2017) 'Hybrid regimes for local public goods provision: a framework for analysis', *Perspectives on Politics*, 15(4): 952–66.

Potts, D. (2012) 'Challenging the myths of urban dynamics in sub-Saharan Africa: the evidence from Nigeria', *World Development*, 40(7): 1382–93.

Quayson, A. (2014) *Oxford Street, Accra: City Life and the Itineraries of Transnationalism*, Durham, NC, and London: Duke University Press.

Rakodi, C. (2006) 'Social agency and state authority in land delivery processes in African cities; compliance, conflict and cooperation', *International Development Planning Review*, 28(2): 263–85.

Ribot, J. and N. L. Peluso (2003) 'A theory of access', *Rural Sociology*, 68(2): 153–81.

Robinson, J. (2006) *Ordinary Cities: Between Modernity and Development*, Questioning Cities Series, London and New York: Routledge.

Rose, C. (1998) 'Canons of property talk, or, Blackstone's anxiety', *Yale Law Journal*, 108(3): 601–32.

Rose, N. and P. Miller (1992) 'Political power beyond the state: problematics of government', *British Journal of Sociology*, 43(2): 173–205.

Roy, A. (2005) 'Urban informality: towards an epistemology of planning', *Journal of the American Planning Association*, 71(1): 147–58.

—— (2009) 'Civic governmentality: the politics of inclusion in Beirut and Mumbai', *Antipode*, 41(1): 159–79.

Sager, T. (2011) 'Neo-liberal urban planning policies: a literature survey 1990–2010', *Progress in Planning*, 76: 147–99.

Saglio-Yatzimirsky, M. C. (2013) *Dharavi: From Mega-Slum to Urban Paradigm*, Routledge India.

Sandbrook, R. (2000) *Closing the Circle: Democratization and Development in Africa*, London: Zed Books.

Santos, B. de Souza (2006) 'The heterogeneous state and legal pluralism in Mozambique', *Law and Society Review*, 40(1): 39–75.

Sarantakos, S. (1994) *Social Research*, London: Sage.

Schindler, S. (2017) 'Reflections on the New Urban Agenda: the New Urban Agenda in an era of unprecedented global challenges', *International Development Planning Review*, 15: 349–54.

Scott, J. (1997) *Seeing Like a State*, New Haven, CT, and London: Yale University Press.

Shabane, I., M. Nkambwe and R. Chanda (2011) 'Landuse, policy, and squatter settlements: the case of peri-urban areas in Botswana', *Applied Geography*, 31(2): 677–86.

Shachar, A. and R. Hirschl (2007) 'Citizenship as inherited property', *Political Theory*, 35(3): 253–87.

Shaw, T. (2013) 'The integration of multiple layers of land ownership, property titles and rights of the Ashanti people in Ghana', *Urban Forum*, 24: 155–72

Shepherd, A. and E. Gyimah-Boadi (2004) 'Bridging the north south divide?', Background paper, 2005 World Development Report, siteresources.worldbank.org/INTWDR2006/, accessed 4 August 2018.

Sikor, T. and C. Lund (2009) 'Access and property: a question of power and authority', *Development and Change*, 40(1): 1–22.

Simon, D., H. Arfvidsson, G. Anand, A. Bazaz, G. Fenna, K. Foster, G. Jain, S. Hansson, L. M. Evans, N. Moodley, C. Nyambuga, M. Oloko, D. C. Ombara, Z. Pater, B. Perry, N. Primo, A. Revi, B. van Niekerk, A. Wharton and C. Wright (2015) 'Developing and testing the Urban Sustainable Development Goal's targets and indicators – a five-city study', *Environment and Urbanization*, 28(1): 49–63.

Simone, A. M. (2004) *For the City Yet to Come: Changing African Life in Four Cities*, Durham, NC, and London: Duke University Press.

Simone, A. M. and A. Abouhani (eds) (2005) *Urban Africa: Changing Contours of Survival in the City*, London: Zed Books.

Songsore, J. (2009) 'The urban transition in Ghana: urbanization, national development and poverty reduction', London: IIED.

Songsore, J., P. Amponsah, O. Alhassan, M. Kala, S. K. Avle and M. A. Chama (2014) 'Environmental health and disaster risks, livelihoods and ecology within the Korle-Lagoon complex in Accra, Ghana', Ghana Universities Press.

Spichiger, R. and P. Stacey (2014) 'Ghana's land reform and gender equality', Working Paper 01, Danish Institute for International Studies.

Stacey, P. (2012) 'Struggles for the attainment of public authority in the Gold Coast and Ghana: competing logics of state formation and local politics in East Gonja 1930–2010', PhD dissertation, International Development Studies, Roskilde University, Denmark.

—— (2014) '"The chiefs, elders, and people have for many years suffered untold hardships": protests by coalitions of the excluded in British Northern Togoland, UN Trusteeship Territory, 1950–57', *Journal of African History*, 55(3): 423–44.

—— (2015) 'Political structure and the limits of recognition and representation in Ghana', *Development and Change*, 46(1): 25–47.

—— (2016) 'Rethinking the making and unmaking of traditional and statutory institutions in post-Nkrumah Ghana', *African Studies Review*, 59(2): 209–30.

—— (2018) 'Urban development and emerging relations of informal property and authority in Accra', *Africa*, 88(1): 63–80.

Stacey, P. and C. Lund (2016) 'In a state of slum: governance in an informal urban settlement in Ghana', *Journal of Modern African Studies*, 54(4): 591–615.

Standing, G. (2011) *The Precariat: The New Dangerous Class*, London: Bloomsbury Academic.

Staniland, M. (1975) *The Lions of Dagbon: Political Change in Northern Ghana*, Cambridge: Cambridge University Press.

Stevenson, L. (2007) Review of 'Anthropology in the margins of the state', by Veena Das and Deborah Poole (eds), Santa Fe: School of American Research Press, 2004, *PoLAR: Political and Legal Anthropology Review*, 30(1): 140–44.

Storper, M. and A. J. Scott (2016) 'Current debates in urban theory: a critical assessment', *Urban Studies*, 53(6): 1114–36.

Strauss, M. and S. Liebenberg (2014) 'Contested spaces: housing rights and evictions law in post-apartheid South Africa', *Planning Theory*, 13(4): 428–48.

Sundar, N. (2014) 'Mimetic sovereignties, precarious citizenship: state effects in a looking-glass world', *Journal of Peasant Studies*, 41(4): 469–90.

Sutton, I. (1989) 'Colonial agricultural policy: the non-development of the Northern Territories of the Gold Coast', *International Journal of African Historical Studies*, 22(4): 637–69.

Swanson M. W. (1977) 'The sanitation syndrome: bubonic plague and urban native policy in the Cape Colony, 1900–1909', *Journal of African History*, 18(3): 387–410.

Tanabe, S. (ed.) (2008) *Imagining Communities in Thailand: Ethnographic Approaches*, Thailand: Mekong Press.

Thomas, R. G. (1973) 'Forced labour in British West Africa: the case of the Northern Territories of the Gold Coast 1906–1927', *Journal of African History*, 14(1): 79–103.

Thorsen, D. (2010) 'The neoliberal challenge: what is neoliberalism?', *Contemporary Readings in Law and Social Justice*, 2: 188–214.

—— (2017) 'Reconfiguring migration: an introduction', *Africa*, 87(2): 300–303.

Tilly, C. (2005) *Identities, Boundaries and Social Ties*, Boulder, CO, and London: Paradigm Publishers.

Tonah, S. (2012) 'The politicisation of a chieftaincy conflict: the case of Dagbon, northern Ghana', *Nordic Journal of African Studies*, 21(1): 1–20.

Toulmin, C. (2008) 'Securing land and property rights in sub-Saharan Africa: the role of local institutions', *Land Use Policy*, 26: 10–19.

Trefon, T. (2011) 'Urban–rural straddling: conceptualizing the peri-urban in Central Africa', *Journal of Developing Societies*, 27: 421–43.

Treisman, D. (2007) *The Architecture of Government; Rethinking Political Decentralisation*, Boston, MA: Cambridge University Press.

Turner, J. F. C. (1972) 'Housing as a verb', in J. F. C. Turner and R. Fichter (eds), *Freedom to Build: Dweller Control of the Housing Process*, New York: Collier-Macmillan.

UN (United Nations) (1997) 'Glossary of environment statistics. Studies in methods',

Series F, no. 67, New York: United Nations

—— (2015) *Transforming Our World: The 2030 Agenda for Sustainable Development*, New York: United Nations.

UN-Habitat (2003a) *The Challenge of Slums: Global report on human settlements*, London: Earthscan.

—— (2003b) 'Slums of the world: the face of urban poverty in the new millennium?', Working paper, New York: UN-Habitat.

—— (2010) 'The state of African cities 2010: governance, inequality and urban land markets', New York: UN-Habitat.

—— (2011) 'Participatory slum upgrading and prevention, Millennium City of Accra, Ghana', UN-Habitat.

Uphoff, N. (1989) 'Distinguishing power, authority and legitimacy: taking Max Weber at his word by using resources-exchange analysis', *Polity*, 22(2): 295–322.

Van der Geest, K. (2011) 'North–south migration in Ghana: what role for the environment?', *International Migration*, 40(S1): 70–93.

Walters, W. (2004) 'Some critical notes on "governance"', *Studies in Political Economy*, 73(1): 27– 46.

WaterAid (2009) 'A study on land tenure in urban areas report (Ghana)'.

Watson, V. (2009) 'The planned city sweeps the poor away …: urban planning and 21st century urbanization', *Progress in Planning*, 72: 151–93.

Watts, M. (2003) 'Development and governmentality', *Singapore Journal of Tropical Geography*, 24(1): 6–34.

World Bank (2015) 'Rising through cities in Ghana: Ghana urbanization review', Overview Report, Washington, DC: World Bank.

Yeboah, M. A. and K. Appiah-Yeboah (2009) 'An examination of the cultural and socio-economic profiles of porters in Accra, Ghana', *Nordic Journal of African Studies*, 18(1): 1–21.

Index

Note: Page numbers in italic indicate images; page numbers followed by *n* indicate an endnote with relevant number.

www.ingramcontent.com/pod-product-compliance
Lightning Source LLC
Chambersburg PA
CBHW050430280326
41932CB00013BA/2053